Medieval Welsh Poems

BY THE SAME AUTHOR

Poetry
The Significance of Flesh: Poems, 1950–1983
Here & There: Poems, 1984–1993
Ordinary Time

Translations
The Odes and Epodes of Horace
Medieval Welsh Lyrics
The Earliest Welsh Poems
Twentieth Century Welsh Poems
Living a Life: Selected Poems by Gwyn Thomas
The Plays of Saunders Lewis (4 vols.)
Bobi Jones: Selected Poems
The World of Kate Roberts
Saunders Lewis: Selected Poems
Where There's Love: Welsh Folk Poems of Love and Marriage
The Light in the Gloom: Poems and Prose by Alun Llywelyn-Williams

Non-Fiction
Pendragon: Arthur and His Britain
Other Words: Essays on Poetry and Translation

Short Stories (as P.G. Thomas)
The Retired Life

Novel (with Gertrude Clancy)
Death Is a Pilgrim: A Canterbury Tale

MEDIEVAL WELSH POEMS

Joseph P. Clancy

FOUR COURTS PRESS

Set in 10.5 on 12.5 point Bembo for
FOUR COURTS PRESS LTD
7 Malpas Street, Dublin 8, Ireland
e-mail: info@four-courts-press.ie
and in North America
FOUR COURTS PRESS
c/o ISBS, 920 N.E. 58th Avenue, Suite 300, Portland, OR 97213

A catalogue record for this title
is available from the British Library

ISBN 1–85182–696–3 hbk
ISBN 1–85182–783–8 pbk

SPECIAL ACKNOWLEDGMENT

Published with the financial support of the Welsh Books Council.

Printed in Great Britain
by MPG Books, Bodmin, Cornwall

CONTENTS

5

CONTENTS

II. THE POETS OF THE PRINCES (*c.*1100–*c.*1285)

CONTENTS

III. THE POETS OF THE GENTRY (c.1285–c.1525)

7

CONTENTS

CONTENTS

CONTENTS

CONTENTS

INTRODUCTION

This anthology of Welsh poems from *c.*575 to *c.*1525 is based on my two previous collections, *Medieval Welsh Lyrics* (1965) and *The Earliest Welsh Poems* (1970), both long out of print. I have omitted some poems from those anthologies, added others, and extensively revised my earlier translations in the light of the many recent scholarly editions of the original texts that make such revision not only possible but necessary.

As with the earlier books, my aim is to provide for the general reader the most substantial collection of medieval Welsh verse yet rendered into English, in translations that will support the claim that this poetry is one of the finest literary achievements of the Middle Ages.

Poetry at its best outlives its original occasion, and many of these poems make an immediate impact. Others, however, can be adequately comprehended and fully enjoyed only when the reader knows and to some extent imaginatively re-creates their original world. I have clarified particular circumstances and references through notes and a glossary, but the bulk of this introduction will be devoted to helping readers over what may be a barrier to an appreciation of the poems, the problem of what C.S. Lewis called 'unshared backgrounds', both historical and literary.

The very earliest poems in Welsh that have survived, those by Taliesin and Aneirin, take us back into a world almost as alien to a modern Briton as to an American. They were composed by, for, and about *Gwŷr y Gogledd*, the Men of the North, in the later sixth century. They reflect the pressures of warfare among the various Celtic kingdoms in the west and the north of the island of Britain, of warfare against the Picts, who held the northern area of modern Scotland, and of warfare against the Anglo-Saxons, who had occupied not only the entire southeast of Britain but also the two eastern regions north of the Humber known as Deira and Bernicia. Much is still unclear about the history of this period, but we can see, in part if not always reliably from the poetry, its basic outlines. There was continued British resistance to Anglo-Saxon expansion in the north throughout the later sixth century, with Urien, king of Rheged, playing a dominant role, but this resistance was weakened by frequent struggles among the Celtic leaders, in one of which Urien was killed. What sounds very much like a last-ditch attempt to stop the invaders was made by Mynnyddog, king of Gododdin, who sent a picked force of mounted warriors south from Edinburgh to the crossroads fortress at Catraeth, Catterick in modern Yorkshire, an expedition that ended in the deaths of almost all its men. There is no general agreement about the importance of this battle, but

Kenneth Jackson's view of it is worth consideration: 'The result of the victory at Catterick was that Aethelfrith the king of Bernicia greatly strengthened his position, and was able to make himself king of united Northumbria, that is Bernicia and Deira. It was no doubt in his time that the Anglian settlers began to spread widely into the Pennines and northward into Lothian.'[1] Despite further attempts at holding or driving back the invaders, the outcome has been stated succinctly by William Rees: 'The late sixth and early seventh century saw the isolation of the Welsh from the rest of the Celtic peoples, and hence-forth they were to have a separate development and a separate history.'[2]

But there was continuity as well as separation. What survives of the earliest poetry was brought to Wales, presumably orally by the bards, during the seventh and eighth centuries and later recorded by scribes. Not only in the eighth and ninth but in the twelfth and thirteenth centuries Welsh poets looked back to the sixth-century poetry of the North, and particularly that of Taliesin, as establishing their central tradition. This is, no doubt, partly 'mythic': it is probable that Taliesin and Aneirin saw themselves, and their fellow-poets whose work has not survived, as continuing a very ancient Celtic tradition rather than establishing a new one. But the survival of their works alone did, in the eyes of their successors, give them the status of founders, as it gave to their poetry, so responsive to the events of the period in which it was composed, the qualities of heroic legend.

It was therefore appropriate for Saunders Lewis to call the Welsh poetic tradition 'Taliesinic'. It is in Taliesin that we find the first, and some of the finest, examples of the generalized eulogy, the celebration of a particular victory, the petition for reconciliation with an offended patron, and the eulogy for a leader, types of poem that bards for the next thousand years considered central to their poetic function. For this is social, ceremonial, and aristocratic poetry, panegyric poetry, and its task, as Saunders Lewis defined it, is 'the portrayal of an ideal which is the bond of unity of tribe or society or nation.'[3]

It is less the Christian warrior-ethic of these poems that may put off the modern reader – in one form or another that ethic is still with us, even if many Christians and non-Christians cannot accept it, and it is at least possible to view it sympathetically in its historical context – than the celebration of particular individuals as incarnations of that ethic, the tradition of public eulogy itself and its idealizing conventions. This is by no means only a modern reaction: earlier in the sixth century the monk Gildas had denounced Maelgwn, ruler of Gwynedd (d. 549), because 'your excited ears hear not the praises of God, not the melodious music of the church, but empty praises of yourself from the mouths of criminals who grate on the hearing like raving

1 *Angles and Britons* (Cardiff, 1963), p. 70.   2 *An Historical Atlas of Wales* (London, 1959), p. 17.
3 'The Essence of Welsh Literature', in *Presenting Saunders Lewis*, edited by Alun R. Jones and Gwyn Thomas (Cardiff, 1973), p. 156.

hucksters – mouths stuffed with lies and liable to bedew bystanders with their foaming phlegm.'[4] We are more likely to react negatively to eulogy on sceptical rather than religious grounds. I cannot think offhand of any modern poems in English that are unqualified, uncomplicated eulogies: W.B. Yeats' 'Easter 1916' is a fair example of the modern poet's need to deal with complexity rather than straightforwardly eulogize.

Are there ways around this problem for us, steeped as we are in a poetry that has been for several centuries private, individualist, and democratic? If our poets are understandably wary of eulogizing public figures, we can still recognize the emotions involved in the general response to such events as the assassination of President John F. Kennedy or the sudden accidental death of Princess Diana. And however much we may find it debased by political conventions and party conferences, eulogy remains with us as appropriate for such occasions as the conferring of honorary degrees, the recognition of institutional service, and of course funerals, though it seldom takes the form of poetry. It is worth noting that eulogies and elegies, for public as well as private individuals, still make up a considerable proportion of the work of many Welsh-language poets, very aware that this is their central tradition.

Certainly we have not struck courage, benevolence, and leadership from the list of qualities worth admiration, and this should enable us to accept and enjoy the medieval Welsh poems that celebrate these within their own hierarchical society. And there is more to the best of these eulogies, in the sixth and later centuries, than simple praise: A.O.H. Jarman has stressed in Taliesin's poems 'their implicit emphasis on the king's understanding of the social implications of his position and his sense of responsibility for the well-being of the community which he rules'.[5]

Apart from the eulogistic tradition, the reader should find few problems with the poems of Taliesin himself. The two battle poems and the elegy for Owain ab Urien have the 'progessive' structure – in action or in thought and feeling – that we take as the norm for poetry, and the eulogies to Urien and his court will not seem far removed from such a structure because of their brevity. It is with *The Gododdin*, the long poem by Taliesin's contemporary Aneirin, that the reader confronts the major peculiarity of medieval Welsh poetic construction.

First of all, the Welsh bard differs strikingly from Anglo-Saxon and Middle-English as well as other medieval European poets in leaving narrative to (prose) story-tellers. Even when dealing with such events as victory or defeat in battle, he composes a 'lyric' – by which I mean simply the use of language to express the thoughts and feelings of a single speaker in a single situation (though one

---

4 Quoted from M. Winterbottom's translation by Ifor Williams, 'Gildas, Maelgwn and the Bards', in *Welsh Society and Nationhood*, edited by R.R. Davies et al. (Cardiff, 1984), p. 22. 5 *A Guide to Welsh Literature I*, edited by A.O.H. Jarman and Gwilym Rees Hughes (Cardiff, 1992), p. 58.

should keep in mind that throughout the medieval period the poems were delivered with harp accompaniment, that *canu*, to sing, is the usual word for poetic composition, and that *bardd*, poet, derives from a word meaning 'praise-singer'). The poet normally assumes that his audience knows the basic story and concentrates on celebration or lamentation combined with compressed allusions to characters and actions, something true even of Taliesin's 'narrative' poems.

Second, and most important: while some of these lyrics 'progress' in expected fashion from a beginning through a middle to an end, the usual lyric employs what I call 'radial' structure, circling about, repeating, and elaborating the central theme. It is all 'middle', we might say, with apparently interchangeable structural units, and this departs entirely from the 'progressive' structure we tend to regard as the only proper mode. It would be foolish to deny that until one becomes accustomed to this the reader may sometimes find it wearying, and even some Welsh critics agree with Rachel Bromwich that 'the early poetry is as a whole remarkable for the perfection of small units of expression rather than for sustained design'.[6] Gwyn Williams argued, however, that 'the absence of a centred design, of an architectural quality', is not a weakness 'but results from a specific view of composition', and he related this to 'stone circles or the contour-following rings of the forts' and 'the inter-woven inventions preserved in early Celtic manuscripts and on stone crosses'.[7] I agree with Williams that this poetry is based on a structural principle unfamiliar to us but possessing its own validity, that it deserves to be approached without prejudice and judged by its results. That this is indeed the central medieval Welsh structural tradition is evident not only in the works of the *Cynfeirdd* (early poets) but of their successors the *Gogynfeirdd* (rather early poets, usually called in English 'The Poets of the Princes') and the *Beirdd yr Uchelwyr* (The Poets of the Gentry). As I have remarked, we encounter it with full force and, it must be admitted, initially bewildering effect in *The Gododdin*.

The Gododdin deals with the catastrophic defeat of the British raid on Catraeth referred to earlier. Seldom has there been a better opportunity for narrative (and several modern novelists have taken advantage of it); seldom has a poet more deliberately refused the opportunity. Instead, Aneirin as himself a participant circles about the battle itself, alluding to particular incidents and interweaving celebrations of the heroism of the war-band and of individual warriors and laments for their loss with bitter reflections on the folly of the raid itself and the feasting that preceded it. *The Gododdin*, then, cannot be read as a narrative poem, an 'epic', but neither, I believe, should it be read as simply a collection of elegies. Granted the severe textual problems, which not only render some sections impossible to understand clearly but leave one uncertain

---

6 'The Character of the Early Welsh Tradition', in *Studies in Early British History*, edited by Nora K. Chadwick (Cambridge, 1954), p. 90.   7 *The Burning Tree* (London, 1956), p. 15.

whether there is an opening stanza and certainly without a concluding one, the poem has still a powerful cumulative effect that is missing when one reads only a few excerpts. That is why I have attempted to translate the 'total' poem, and in both of the surviving and sometimes differing texts. (For further comment, see the Notes.) I should also warn readers that they might do well to accustom themselves to the shorter poems before trying *The Gododdin*, magnificent though it often is.

It has been thought until recently that the groups of short works now generally called 'saga poems' were what survived from prose stories by individual authors who employed verse for monologue and dialogue at moments of high emotion. It seems more likely, though, that various poets either assumed their audiences' knowledge of the stories or provided brief prose summaries by way of introducing their own treatments of the material, and that a scribe later collected and assembled these. In any case, what we have are poems from different moments in the stories, and we are left to reconstruct the narratives behind them from clues given by the poems themselves. Of the three most important groups of saga poems, as far as can be judged from what is extant, the first, here entitled 'The Fall of Rheged', may according to Thomas Owen Clancy be 'a product of the last phase of Welsh literature among the northern British'.[8] It deals with the death of Urien, the ruler praised by Taliesin, and the subsequent downfall of his kingdom. Despite the uncertainties remarked in the Notes and the fragmentary nature of several poems, I have thought it worthwhile to translate in sequence all the material that survives, but the reader may wish to look first at the three most substantial and moving poems: #2, usually entitled 'The Head of Urien' when printed on its own; #3, 'The Corpse of Urien'; and #11, 'The Hearth of Rheged', which was probably composed a century or more after the other poems and can be seen, Thomas Clancy suggests, 'as a contemplation of a vanished heroic past'.

The Rheged poems are found in manuscript between two poems from a different 'saga', that of Llywarch Hen. Whatever the historical basis may have been, Llywarch was linked to the fall of Rheged by presenting him as a surviving cousin of Urien who journeyed from Rheged to Powys in northeastern Wales, where he continued, with the aid of his sons, to fight the invading English. The third group of saga poems also centres on Powys, and deals with the seventh-century prince Cynddylan, defeated and killed by the English in the region of present-day Shrewsbury, and with his sister Heledd: it is she who speaks, after her brother's death and the downfall of the kingdom, in all of these poems.

These saga poems differ markedly from the work of Taliesin and Aneirin. Whereas the earlier poems were deeply concerned with current events and

8 *The Triumph Tree: Scotland's Earliest Poetry* AD 550–1350 (Edinburgh, 1998), p. 152.

composed in the poet's own voice, these are dramatic re-creations that look back, with longing and anguish, to the heroic defeats of earlier centuries. The verse-form, too, differs notably from the forms employed in Taliesin's poems and *The Gododdin*: the saga poets use three-line stanzas and incremental repetition, with the refrain opening each stanza. Too little survives of the early literature for us to be certain this was a new literary development, but these intense, sombre poems must have had an immediate resonance for a ninth-century audience at a time when the Anglo-Saxons of Mercia were thrusting deep into North Wales. Jenny Rowland has commented pointedly that 'even when the saga tale is closer to pseudo-history, the stories themselves are plausible, not fabulous ... The presentation of semi-legendary lore about historical characters suggests the englynion [stanzaic] sagas are the works of higher rather than popular bards.'[9]

From the seventh through the eleventh centuries only this saga poetry and a scattering of other poems survive. It is certain that the 'Taliesinic' tradition continued, but the eulogistic poetry of these times has generally perished. Thomas Parry observes that 'there were famous kings ruling over Wales in the course of this long period, like Rhodri the Great, king of Gwynedd, who reigned from 844 till 878, and Hywel the Good, Rhodri's grandson, who began his reign as King of Dyfed, and ended his life in 949 or 950 as King of all Wales ... And yet we do not possess today a single line of eulogy addressed to either of these renowned kings.'[10]

Parry states one reason for the loss of so much of this poetry: 'this is the period, in the whole history of Wales, about which we can find the least information of any kind – the most troubled and destructive period in the whole course of the ages.' There was, in addition to frequent internal conflicts as well as struggles with the Anglo-Saxons, the new menace of Danish raiders between 800 and 1000: in the looting and burning of monasteries as well as fortresses it is likely that many manuscripts perished, and in any case the oral tradition that preserved poems by Taliesin and Aneirin failed to preserve much of the work of their successors. It is possible, of course, that the poems were not considered worth preserving; that they existed, and that court poets were highly honoured, is evident from the prominent place given to bards in the laws of Hywel the Good.[11] It is possible, too, that Parry paints too black a picture of the age: Nora Chadwick sees the ninth and tenth centuries as marked by 'the gradual absorption of the Welsh ruling dynasties by the royal house of Gwynedd in the north, and the gradual approximation to a Wales united under a single ruling family'.[12] There was not only unification but, in

---

9 *Early Welsh Saga Poetry* (Cambridge, 1990), pp 172–3. **10** *A History of Welsh Literature*, translated by H. Idris Bell (Oxford, 1955), pp 8–9. **11** See D. Jenkins, *The Law of Hywel Dda: law texts from Medieval Wales* (Llandysul, 1986). **12** 'The Welsh Dynasties in the Dark Ages', in *Wales through the Ages I*, edited by A. J. Roderick (Llandybie, 1959), p. 57.

South Wales, co-operation with English rulers, though the tenth-century poem *The Prophecy of Britain* expresses a passionate rejection of those who followed this policy. The unity Chadwick refers to was shattered in the century before 1066, in part by the feuds of the Welsh princes, but for the reader of Welsh poetry its temporary existence is important less for its own age than for the centuries after the Norman Conquest of England, when Gwynedd was widely accepted as the domain of the rightful ruler of Wales and the earlier unity was longed for by some of the Poets of the Princes and achieved, however briefly, by two of their rulers.

For convenience I have grouped poems from these centuries under the heading of 'A Miscellany of Poems'. Some comments on individual works will be found in the Notes, but a few remarks may be useful here. 'Lament for Cynddylan' continues the eulogistic tradition: it was presumably composed immediately after the death of the prince who would be mourned, two centuries later, in the Heledd saga, and the poems show the differences between poetry for a particular occasion and that composed as dramatic re-creation. 'In Praise of Tenby', also in the eulogistic tradition, gives us more of a picture of aristocratic society in its relaxed and joyful moments, and more delight in the natural setting of the fortress, than we find in other early poems. The poem I have entitled 'Song for a Small Boy', with its female speaker if not necessarily poet, is usually called a 'cradle song' and considered as not only charming in itself but suggestive of a lost body of poems reflecting the more informal aspects of life. Andrew Breeze has stated, however, that 'it bears the marks of professional bardic poetry', and suggests that it has 'tragic' implications.[13] 'Geraint ab Erbin' is a vigorous poem from what may have been a group of saga poems centred on Arthur; the poem I have called 'In Memoriam' is, with its surprising ending, very much a backwards look at the heroic past.

The response to nature that is regarded as typically Celtic, close observation implying or expressing delight in weather, sky, sea, plants, and animals as fellow-creatures, simply because they exist, is not found in the earliest poems, but it is present in a number of the later works of this period. It is most evident in the sole surviving riddle poem; more often, the experience of the natural world is blended with other experiences, often tragic, as in some of the saga poems and 'The Leper of Aber Cuawg' (which may also have originated in a lost saga). It is closest to existing independently in such a lyric as 'Mountain Snow', but even here it blends with 'gnomic sayings', utterances about man or nature that have universal significance. There are textual problems enough to make anyone hesitate to generalize, but I hazard a guess that three kinds of lyric, classifying by subject-matter only, may once have existed independently, the heroic or tragic monologue or dialogue, the nature poem, and the gnomic

---

13 *Medieval Welsh Literature* (Dublin, 1997), p. 20.

poem, and that two and sometimes all three are blended in the two poems just cited, in Llywarch Hen's 'Complaint in Old Age', and in 'Winter and Warfare'.

Christianity, first brought to the island during the Roman occupation of Britain that ended in 410 and vigorously preached in the sixth century by Saint David and others, is present in Welsh poetry as a vital force in people's lives from the beginnings. It is assumed as a 'shared background' in most of the poems, but Taliesin composes a thoroughly Christian elegy for Owain ab Urien, and the brevity of Aneirin's references to confession, communion, and eternal life should not lead us to think that religion was a matter of indifference to the Welsh or their poets. Religious references occur chiefly in mournful contexts, but this is true of Anglo-Saxon poetry also, and the poetry of the *Cynfeirdd*, naturally enough under the historical circumstances, is not often joyful. It is possible that much poetry in which religious experience was central existed but was destroyed or never recorded. A few such poems are extant, and I have included three, entitling them 'Mourning in Maytime', 'Prelude to a Pilgrimage', and 'Benediction'.

A large body of prophetic verse exists from the centuries immediately before and after the Norman Conquest, including poems in which legends of Taliesin and Myrddin combine with prophecies of the defeat of the English, probably as the result of poems becoming mixed and altered in the process of oral transmission. Despite the interest of portions of such poems, I prefer not to use excerpts, and I did not wish to translate any of these poems in its entirety. I have instead included what is generally recognized as the finest of the prophetic poems, *The Prophecy of Britain*: it reflects the concept of a united Wales that had become possible by the tenth century (and that would echo in other prophetic poems thereafter), and even its cry for a union of Celtic peoples seems nowadays less impossibly visionary than it once did.

For Wales, the Norman Conquest was not a matter of '1066 and all that'. The Welsh fought against the invaders, with varying degrees of success and with much quarreling among their own leaders, for the next two centuries. By 1100, John Davies observes, 'Welsh control had successfully been restored over the greater part of Wales',[14] and in the following years the boundary between the territory of the Norman Marcher Lords in the east and southeast and the realms of the Welsh princes was basically established.

'Wales by the end of the twelfth century,' R.R. Davies states, 'was a country of two peoples, Welsh and Anglo-Norman ... The relationship was in part one of deep hatred and mutual fear ... The protracted nature of the Norman conquest of Wales and its uneven and spasmodic character meant that resentment was refuelled in each generation from a new stock of memories and atrocities.'[15] To the bards of the twelfth and thirteenth centuries the battle

---

14 *A History of Wales* (London, 1993), p. 108. **15** *The Age of Conquest: Wales 1063–1415* (Oxford,

against the invaders often seemed much the same struggle that had been going on since the time of Taliesin, and they drew on the earlier poetry in celebrating the rulers of their times. 'There was much pride in the Welsh way of life,' comments D. Myrddin Lloyd, 'and in the rights and privileges deriving from the native legal system and the pattern of society. A renewed confidence and pride had followed the rolling back of the Anglo-Norman tide. The precarious liberty thus gained had to be strenuously defended, and it needed no great insight to be agonizingly aware of how much depended on the qualities of the rulers – not only valour, but also coolness and sagacity. Panegyric had always been the prevailing mode of Celtic verse, but it is not hard to understand that then, of all times, the "contemplation of rulers" should have acquired the significance it did, and that it should give such power and reality to so much of the court poetry.'[16]

There were, however, new and complicating factors that often make the poetry a quite inadequate mirror of the political realities of the age. The Welsh poetic tradition enabled the court bards to respond to the individual military achievements of their princes; it did not equip them to cope with far more complex situations than had existed in Taliesin's age. 'In reality,' as Lloyd acknowledges, 'Welsh fought Welsh as often as they fought the English, marriages and military accommodations with Norman lords and the English royal line were common ... but on all this the poets were to maintain an eloquent silence'.[17]

Rather than attempt a summary of Welsh history during the tangled centuries from the death of Gruffudd ap Llywelyn, Prince of Gwynedd and King of Wales, in 1063, to the end of Welsh independence with the death of Llywelyn ap Gruffudd in 1282, I have supplied reasonably detailed annotation to the eulogies of leading rulers of the age, trusting that this would provide a sufficient background for the poems. What is clear in general is that the inability of many Welsh princes to conceive of their country with its own language, laws, and customs as a single political entity prevented them from moving into the feudal structure needed to counter the Anglo-Norman structure that was eventually imposed upon them. Glyn Roberts has argued, however, that this does not explain adequately the Welsh failure to achieve the political unity England had attained by the beginning of the eleventh century, and suggests that 'a more valid, though partial, explanation of Welsh disunity is geography; the central upland and highland mass ... certainly gave local particularism a physical basis. But, quite simply, the main reason for disunity in Wales was the close proximity of England.'[18]

There is a marked contrast between the preservation of a large body of court poetry from the twelfth and thirteenth centuries and the failure to

1987), p. 100.   **16** 'The Poets of the Princes', in *Guide I*, p. 157.   **17** *Guide I*, p. 161.   **18** 'Wales on the Eve of the Norman Conquest', in *Wales through the Ages I*, pp 77–8.

preserve most of the work that preceded it, such a contrast that literary historians have tended to give Gruffudd ap Cynan (1055-1137) credit for a revival
of poetry during his reign. 'Tradition maintains,' writes Thomas Parry, 'that
Gruffudd brought musicians and poets with him from Ireland [where he had
spent some time in exile] to his court in Gwynedd, and that he was responsible for some reform in both arts.'[19] However this may be, Welsh independence
during this period and the patronage, and sometimes participation, of the
princes made possible what Parry praises as 'a body of artistic achievement
which is a miracle of beauty and strength ... the poetry of those who are
called the Poets of the Princes, or the Gogynfeirdd.'[20]

Daniel Huws has called attention to the fact that it was one anonymous
individual's decision, soon after 1282, to create what is known as *The
Hendregadredd Manuscript* which is responsible for preserving these poems as a
'monument to the extinguished independent rule of Wales. He set about
collecting the poetry of the court poets associated with the Welsh rulers of the
previous two centuries...When scholars speak of the 'Poets of the Princes' they
tacitly acknowledge the chapter of Welsh literary history defined by this
anonymous complier.'[21] His purposes and taste, shared by his close contemporaries who added other poems, are also responsible, one should note, for limit-
ing our knowledge of the poetry of these centuries – Myrddin Lloyd, after
explaining that there were different 'grades' of poets and that it is only work
by the highest of these that has been preserved, expresses the sentiments of
many readers when he exclaims: 'Would that the work of lower orders had
survived.'[22]

Although there are striking stylistic differences between *Cynfeirdd* and
Gogynfeirdd poetry, the employment of 'radial structure' continued, and the
eulogistic tradition flourished. Even more than with the *Cynfeirdd*, the modern
reader must recognize that for the medieval Welsh bard his role was not explo-
ration but celebration, not the sensitive revelation of self at a single historical
moment but the enactment of permanently valid ritual, and approach this
poetry by attempting to understand its conventions and to cultivate a taste for
ritual well performed. Some expansion of the experiential range of the poetry
is evident. Devotional poems by the bards appear in far greater numbers
(though, as must be noted so often, the disappearance of so much earlier
poetry may mean that this signifies continuity rather than change), and these
act as a powerful counterpoint to the praises of heroic prowess, reflecting the
medieval tension between the demands, and attractions, of the transient earthly
life and the Christian vision of divine love, redemption, and eternal happiness.
In Wales as elsewhere at this time, however, the bards also began composing
secular love poems as well. Most of these, with Hywel ab Owain Gwynedd's a

19 Parry, p. 45. **20** Parry, p. 44. **21** *Medieval Welsh Manuscripts* (Cardiff, 2000), p. 76.
22 *Guide I*, p. 158.

notable exception, are adaptations of the eulogistic tradition to the praise of noblewomen, but they show the entrance of continental courtly-love conventions into Welsh poetry. Though nature for the *Gogynfeirdd* is not the central experience it had been for some of the earlier poets and would be for Dafydd ap Gwilym and his fourteenth-century contemporaries, in Gwalchmai's 'Exultation' as in poems by Hywel ab Owain Gwynedd and others it is nonetheless an essential part of the total poem.

I have chosen poems by Cynddelw Brydydd Mawr (fl. 1155–1200), whose high opinion of his own work has generally been endorsed by modern critics, to present a cross-section of the types of poem composed by the *Gogynfeirdd*. The eulogy and its close relations, the elegy and the petition for reconciliation, are represented by his poems for Madawg ap Maredudd, Owain Gwynedd, and the Lord Rhys: the differences in emphasis and tone among these poems are worth observing, lest one be tempted to think all eulogies are much the same. There is one brief love lyric, of the kind more often found in later centuries (and which, along with a mock-elegy for a rooster not included here, leads one to suspect that there were more of such 'frivolous' poems by the court poets than were recorded), and a longer and more formal love poem; there is, exceptionally for the period, a personal elegy, for the poet's son; and there is a devotional lyric of a kind popular in the age, the death-bed poem.

My selection of other poems for this as for the earlier and later periods is designed to provide readers with a sampling of the best and most representative poetry that survives from that time, and to suggest as fully as possible within the limits of an anthology thematic variety and variations on a theme. I must add that the length of some of the best *Gogynfeirdd* poems has restricted the number that could be included.

While there are exceptions, the style of the *Cynfeirdd* is marked in general by a tendency to terseness, to brief assertions and descriptions with few metaphors and similes within the single unit of verse, and to an amplification of the theme by means of a series of stanzas that frequently use repetition of initial or terminal lines. The result is a curious combination of simplicity and succinctness with reiteration and, at times, prolixity. The *Gogynfeirdd*, while they retain some of the stylistic features of their predecessors, develop a style that elaborates and deliberately courts obscurity by the constant use of syntactic breaks in the flow of the sentence, apposition, and a multiplicity of metaphors. Ceri W. Lewis calls this poetry 'unquestionably the most difficult corpus of verse to have survived in Welsh', in which 'we can detect a conscious effort ... to make their craft an esoteric art,'[23] and Daniel Huws says of its 'dense, mannered style' that it 'could be majestic at its best, as in the work of Cynddelw, and ponderous and impenetrable at its worst'.[24] Some other char-

---

23 'The Court Poets: Their Function, Status, and Craft', in *Guide I*, p.145. **24** Huws, p. 85.

acteristics of the style were described, despairingly, by an earlier translator, H. Idris Bell:

> The style is exclamatory rather than predicative; such minor but useful parts of speech as articles, prepositions, pronouns, and the copula are freely dispensed with, and even the finite verb is used sparingly, its place being taken by the verb-noun. Constant use is made of compound words, both nouns and adjectives, which can often be represented in another language only by a complete clause. When, finally, we add the effect of such verbal devices as *cynghanedd*, rhyme, assonance, and alliteration, it will be seen how hopeless is the translator's task.[25]

Lest the reader conclude from this that trying to read these poems in translation is equally hopeless, I should add that one's difficulties are with the 'surface' – Myrddin Lloyd remarks that 'it is a feature of Celtic art that ornament often covers the whole surface, usually in interlacing patterns', and that 'this aesthetic is very evident in Gogynfeirdd poetry'.[26] Unlike some modern poetry, there is seldom any doubt about the basic thoughts and feelings in the poem. I must confess, however, that in selecting poems I have tended towards those whose subject-matter is most likely to engage a modern reader and overcome the problems of translation.

All ages, one may say, are times of transition, but some ages more than others. The end of the thirteenth century and the first part of the fourteenth was such an age, for Welsh society in general and Welsh poets in particular. Ceri W. Lewis states that 'the complete collapse of the independent Welsh principality ... created a crisis of major proportions for that highly trained professional class of bards that had made heroic praise of the defending Welsh princes the prime function of its poetic activity. For, to all appearances, that activity had finally lost its *raison d'être.*'[27]

In the light of this, it seems remarkable that Wales was to produce its greatest poetry after 1282 and its conquest by Edward I. But while Edward built the great castles at Conwy, Caernarfon, Cricieth, and Harlech to keep the rebellious North firmly under English control, divided the country into shires and imposed on it the English administrative structure, and established trading-towns peopled with English colonists, he otherwise, as Arthur Bryant stated, 'left Wales much as he found it ... He left [the Welsh] the most precious thing of all – their language and, with a few exceptions, their Welsh officers and

---

25 *The Development of Welsh Poetry* (Oxford, 1936), p.42.   26 *Guide I*, p. 159.   27 'The Content of the Poetry and the Crisis in the Bardic Tradition', in *A Guide to Welsh Literature II*, edited by A.O.H. Jarman, Gwilym Rees Hughes, and Dafydd Johnston (Cardiff, 1997), p. 81.

chieftains to fill the English legal and administrative posts ... He left them, in other words, not a Welsh State ... but the wherewithal of Welsh nationhood.'[28]

In the centuries after the Edwardian Conquest Welsh soldiers served in the English armies against Scotland and France, Welsh leaders built their manor houses after the latest English styles, and many Welshmen were drawn into the commercial life of the towns. John Davies comments, however, that 'when the princes enjoyed power, the allegiance of the Welsh was fractured, but the Conquest and the adversity which followed served to strengthen their self-awareness. That awareness was expressed in a series of anti-English revolts, but it was also expressed in delight in the achievements of those Welshmen who served the English crown and in pride in the Welsh connections of the king himself. This ambiguity in the attitude of the Welsh towards England, the complex interweaving of sympathy and antipathy which developed in the centuries after the Conquest, would be characteristic of many Welsh patriots to the present day.'[29]

The most significant of the anti-English revolts referred to by Davies was that of Owain Glyndŵr, from 1400 to 1410, which A.D. Carr calls 'at once a national rising, a social protest, a feudal conspiracy, and a civil war. It is one of the most important events in the history of Wales, not so much for what it achieved as for what it represents; in the words of Gwyn A. Williams, "modern Wales begins in 1410".'[30] The hostility towards the English that led to Owain's rising and brief rule as Prince of Wales would later bring many Welshmen to support Henry VII, grandson of Owen Tudor of Anglesey, against Richard III. Ironically, it was Henry VIII, son of 'the Welsh king', who struck the severest blow to Welsh cultural independence: after the Act of Union in 1536, English was made the sole official language of Wales. That date may be taken as symbolic – what Thomas Parry refers to as 'the curse which was brought by the laws and the general policy of the Tudors'[31] consisted in drawing away from Wales many of those who had become the poets' patrons after 1282, the *uchelwyr*.

The term *uchelwyr* is variously translated as 'nobility' or 'gentry', and I have followed a standard reference book[32] in using the latter for this anthology, but Welsh historians tend to find neither term really satisfactory. Carr defines them as 'free landed proprietors of good stock whose standing and influence in their localities stemmed from their position at the centre of a network of kinsmen and dependants and from the ties of blood and obligation.' Their importance for Welsh literature, he notes, is that 'they were at once the patrons and nour-ishers of the native literary tradition and the class from which the poets them-selves came'.[33]

---

28 *The Age of Chivalry* (New York, 1964), p. 92. **29** John Davies, p. 163. **30** 'The Historical Background, 1282-1550', in *Guide II*, pp 11–12. **31** Parry, p. 162. **32** Meic Stephens ed., *The New Companion to the Literature of Wales* (Cardiff, 1998), p.591. **33** *Guide II*, pp 2–3; p. 21.

It was the new dominance of the gentry which is responsible for both continuity and change in the poetry of the fourteenth and later centuries. Eulogy continued, and it is often emphasized that its patrons were frequently lettered men capable of appreciating bardic art, but the emphasis in general shifts from the praise of military prowess and leadership to generosity and hospitality, as one can see in the poems by Iolo Goch, Gruffudd Llwyd, and their successors. A.T.E. Matonis, examining the elegies from this period, finds that 'the loss of force, of credibility, of creative energy in the bulk of the panegyric addressed to the *uchelwyr* dramatizes the loss of the national, political significance of men of the highest rank in post-Conquest Wales,' and she speaks of 'the hollowness of much post-Conquest panegyric. The *uchelwyr* were not hegemonous princes on whose shoulders the fate of a nation depended. There could be nothing calamitous for Powys, or Gwynedd, or Deheubarth, as a consequence of their individual deaths.'[34] That her strictures do not apply to the best eulogies and elegies, however, is evident from such poems as Iolo Goch's praise of Sir Hywel and Owain Glyndŵr, Dafydd Bach's celebration of Christmas revels at a nobleman's court, and Guto'r Glyn's mourning for Siôn ap Madog.

That this tradition was subject to abuse can be seen in Gruffudd Llwyd's 'In Defense of Praise' and Siôn Cent's 'The Bards', the latter a scathing attack on eulogistic poets for hyperbole and excessive love of the world and its goods, and both the attack and the defense are based on religious grounds. It is hardly surprising to find many devotional lyrics in this period, and as in English devotional poetry of the same age, the poet usually speaks less as an individual than as the voice of the Christian community in praising the Trinity, Jesus Christ, the Blessed Virgin and the saints, confessing mankind's sinfulness and praying for forgiveness, as in Gruffudd Gryg's 'Christ the King' and Huw Cae Llwyd's 'The Cross'. A more individual note may be heard in the work of Siôn Cent: in his whole-hearted dedication to poems of moral meditation and religious praise he is unque among these poets, but even so, the meditations on mortality and sin are in a very traditional medieval vein quite similar to English poetry of the same period. Llywelyn Goch, on the other hand, numbers among other sins in his 'Confession' adulterous love for the woman, Lleucu Llwyd, to whom he had sung a deeply moving elegy; Ieuan Brydydd Hir speaks as himself a pilgrim to St Winifrede's Well, and Guto'r Glyn composes within a very personal setting in the devotional poems of his old age, though the conventions of eulogy to a patron and pious celebration are still present.

For elevated panegyric and devotional poetry the bards continued to use at times verse-forms developed by the *Gogynfeirdd*, represented in this collection by, among others, Gruffudd ap Maredudd's elegy for Gwenhwyfar, Dafydd Nanmor's praise of Rhys ap Maredudd, and Gutun Owain's 'A Winter Haven'.

---

34 'The *Marwnadau* of the *Cywyddwyr*', in *Studia Celtica* (1983/4), p. 168; pp 161–2.

Literary historians have tended, indeed, to divide the poetry of the fourteenth century between 'the later *Gogynfeirdd*' and poets using a new verse-form, the couplet known as the *cywydd deuair hirion* But I agree with Dafydd Johnston that this is an artificial and misleading division, since 'not only were these poets composing at the same time, but also the same poet sometimes composed in both styles',[35] and I have followed his practice in arranging the poems in roughly chronological order.

The *cywydd* as a verse-form was an innovation in fourteenth-century Wales, and its introduction was a response by the highest grade of bards to the need for expanding subjects and themes to suit the tastes of their new patrons, to entertain as well as eulogize.[36] It was developed by a remarkable generation of poets after about 1335: the surviving texts give the impression of an explosion of creative energy, though which of them was responsible for what is far from clear. Putting it much too simply, a fairly plain pre-existing form of couplet was enriched by bringing into it stylistic features of *Gogynfeirdd* poetry, including compound nouns and adjectives and the systematic sound-patterning known as *cynghanedd*. Dafydd ap Gwilym is usually credited with being the pioneer in using the form for love poems (compare the earlier poems by Iorwerth Fychan and Gruffudd ap Dafydd[37]), and Iolo Goch with developing it as a medium for panegyric by bringing into it the essentials of earlier praise-poetry. Although Dafydd ap Gwilym also eulogized patrons in this form, Eurys Rowlands has claimed that 'Iolo Goch set a new pattern, a pattern which was necessary for the remaining centuries of bardism'.[38] Whatever the truth of this, through the next two centuries and beyond the *cywydd* was the dominant verse-form, and the selections in this anthology show how adaptable it was for expressing a wide variety of experiences, from thanks for a patron's gift to lamenting his or her death, from sombre brooding on the decay of the flesh to visions of heavenly glory, from the genial pleasures of a court to the grimness of battle to sheep-dealing and seafaring, from exuberant delight in bird and beast to vexation with the weather, from praise of a mistress' eyebrow to joyful love-making, complaints of frustration, and bawdy knockabout farce.

Two features of these poems call for particular comment. We can find the familiar modes of logical or associative structure in some poems, and in a few there is even a narrative rather than a lyric base. But what I have been calling 'radial structure' is frequent, and it reaches its extreme in poems made up

---

35 *Blodeugerdd Barddas o'r Bedwaredd Ganrif ar Ddeg* (Swansea, 1989), p. 15. 36 For an excellent study of the relationship between fourteenth-century poetry and what precedes it, see Huw M. Edwards' *Dafydd ap Gwilym: Influences and Analogues* (Oxford, 1996). 37 What is apparent in both of these poets, for all their use of older verse-forms, is the general shift in love lyric from using the lover's complaint as a basis for eulogy to using eulogy as the basis for the lover's complaint. See Helen Fulton's *Dafydd ap Gwilym and the European Context* (Cardiff, 1989). 38 'Iolo Goch', in *Celtic Studies*, edited by James Carney and David Greene (London, 1968), p. 138.

almost entirely of descriptive and metaphoric imagery, for praising a gift as in Tudur Aled's 'The Stallion', for a *llatai*, a love-messenger, as in Dafydd ap Gwilym's poems to a skylark and to the wind, for an object of affection, as in Llywelyn ab y Moel's praise of his woodland hideout, or of detestation, as in Iolo Goch's 'The Ship'. The whole point of these poems is the series of images; there is, for the most part, no sense that one couplet must be where it is in the poem, no experience of moving through a sequence of thoughts and feelings each of which flows naturally from the other. It is no wonder that different texts of the same poem will sometimes have a quite different sequence of couplets. What these poems, and others that use this structure partially rather than throughout, suggest as the foundation for their aesthetic is that the stance of celebration (or its opposite, denunciation) gives the poet a singular kind of perspective, one in which a process in time, the basis not only for narrative but for most other kinds of lyric poetry, is unimportant, in which all aspects of the central celebrated thing matter equally and are ideally to be perceived simultaneously. We might say that these poets, like their predecessors, use 'spatial' rather than 'temporal' form.

The second characteristic to be noted is the frequent use of *sangiad*, a break or syntactic side-step in the flow of the sentence. To illustrate, here is the finale of Dafydd ap Gwilym's poem on his failure with the girls of Llanbadarn:

> O dra disgwyl, dysgiad certh,
> Drach 'y nghefn, drych anghyfnerth,
> Neur dderyw ym, gerddrym gâr,
> Bengamu heb un gymar.

In the first three lines the forward movement of the sentence is concentrated in the first half of each line, the second half providing a kind of parenthetical commentary:

> From too much looking, stern lesson,
> Backwards, sight of weakness,
> It happened to me, strong song's friend,
> To bow my head without one companion.

This is a fairly simple example of a constantly used device. The opening lines of Iolo Goch's poem to the ploughman provide a much more complex one:

> Pan ddangoso, rhyw dro rhydd,
> Pobl y byd, peibl lu bedydd,
> Garbron Duw, cun eiddun oedd,
> Gwiw iaith ddrud, eu gweithredoedd,

> Ar ben Mynydd, lle bydd barn,
> I gyd, Olifer gadarn,
> Llawen fydd, chwedl diledlaes,
> Llafurwr, tramwywr maes.

Literally, the sequence of lines and phrases is this:

> When show, a time of freedom,
> The world's people, lively throng of the baptized,
> In dear God's presence, desire it was,
> Bold proper language, their deeds,
> On top of Mount, where will be judgment,
> All, mighty Olivet,
> Cheerful will be, joyful story,
> The ploughman, traverser of a field.

In no line does the sentence flow uninterruptedly, and there are particularly drastic breaks between closely related words, 'deeds' and 'all', 'Mount' and 'Olivet', a device known as *trychiad*.

Thomas Parry explained *sangiad* as originating within the oral tradition from the need for 'metrical phrases, elements put into the poem not for the sake of meaning but for that of the metre ... it must be remembered about Welsh poetry that it attaches as much honour to metre as to thought'.[39] But the effects of *sangiad*, at least in the best poems, are more than merely metrical. One does find, frequently enough, that the *sangiadau* are riddling or almost meaningless, but they often produce a peculiar effect of multiplicity, of continuous parenthetical reflection simultaneous with the development of the main theme. This is certainly true for Dafydd ap Gwilym's lines quoted above, and one can note as well the effectiveness of *sangiadau* in heightening the farcical confusion of Dafydd's 'In a Tavern'. In general, the cywydd-poets use the device to heighten the style and to slow down the movement of what, given a seven-syllable line, might otherwise be too rapid a flow: it provides a necessary weight and dignity, as in the passage quoted from Iolo Goch.

However alien this device may seem initially, I find it is easy to become accustomed to it, especially if one tries speaking the poems (which were, after all, composed for oral delivery), with pauses in the voice for the *sangiadau*. It may be some consolation to readers who find themselves bewildered at their first encounter with certain passages that their experience is likely to mirror that of modern Welsh readers of the original texts. And let me assure possibly discouraged readers that the frequency of *sangiadau* varies from poet to poet and poem to poem, that most of the lyrics present no serious difficulties, and

---

39 Parry, p. 146.

that in any case obscurities caused by the device are of the surface not the depths, complexities of expression rather than of thought or feeling, and that inability to see relevance or even meaning in a particular phrase will often be shared by the Welsh reader and the translator and seldom mars the enjoyment of the poem as a whole.

Gwyn Thomas has said of Dafydd ap Gwilym that he 'claims a place all to himself in the history of our poetry, and that not because he stands apart from the tradition but because his personality and his genius are like a bright splash of paint in the middle of it.'[40] Whatever the actualities of his life, the person in Dafydd's poems has a fullness not found in any other medieval Welsh poet, and the Morfudd poems ('seven score and seven *cywyddau*', he himself said, of which almost forty have survived) treat a long-lasting love affair with a range of experience and complexity of emotion beyond any other love poems of the period. 'No other Welsh poet,' says John Rowlands, 'can vary the tone of his voice as much as Dafydd',[41] and particularly notable is the humour he often brings to his dealings with Morfudd and other women: if he can sing sweetly and tenderly, he can also denounce in comic frenzy the obstacles to love's fulfilment, and find in himself the chief figure of fun.

It is in Dafydd, too, that we find the fullest response to nature among these poets, and as with his contemporaries and successors, nature usually appears as a background in love poems. 'Background', though, is not really the proper word: the lady may not be exactly an afterthought, but love for her allows the poet to dwell on the beauties of the grove to which he invites her or the creature he sends her as a messenger of love.

Dafydd ap Gwilym composed eulogies to patrons and devotional poems, some in other verse-forms than the *cywydd*, but I have preferred to select works that illustrate something of his range in poems of love and nature. I have tried with his contemporaries, Iolo Goch and Gruffudd Gryg, to present a cross-section characteristic of a bard's body of work. With Guto'r Glyn in the following century I have again tried to suggest the variety and individual voice of this bard, and to show how his poems reflect both continuity and change in the development of the medieval lyric.

'When recovery from the effects of the war of Glyndŵr began,' writes Eurys Rowlands, 'there began also the most flourishing century in the history of Welsh poetry,'[42] a period in which, Thomas Parry declared, 'the poetry [was] decorative and polished in expression, and the authors as great as any who have ever written in the language.'[43] I have included a number of bards from this period, as from the later fourteenth century (for which I must confess a preference), but I have excluded prophetic poetry as having by and large chiefly historical interest,[44] and there are fewer eulogies and elegies for patrons than

---

40 *Y Traddodiad Barddol* (Cardiff, 1976), p. 149.   **41** Alun Llwyd ed., *50 o Gywyddau Dafydd ap Gwilym* (Swansea, 1980), p. 23.   **42** *Celtic Studies*, p. 135.   **43** Parry, p. 161.   **44** See R. Wallis

would show this body of poetry in its true proportions. I have tried, where more than one poem from a bard is included, to suggest something of his range, but the number of poems chosen should not be taken as a fair guide to a particular bard's achievement, and not every good poet of the time is represented.

Readers have the right to be indifferent to a translator's problems, the constant diplomatic negotiations and compromises required for poetic translation, and to care only about the final product. But they also have the right to know how closely the translations re-create the original poems, and so I must say something of my dealings with style and versification.

I have tried to suggest the styles of the originals, including the constant use of stock words and phrases characteristic of oral poetry. But I have for the most part avoided, because of personal discomfort and the taste of our time, the use of archaic diction, even where this is a trait of the Welsh poem. I have, however, used the colloquial style that is a feature of our own poetry quite sparingly, only where the original seemed to permit it, and have attempted an elevated style where this was demanded by the nature of the work. I have above all tried, as much as linguistic differences allow, to mirror the movement within the lines of sentence, clause, and phrase in the Welsh, to capture the flow of the original poem, though distortion of this has often been a practical necessity.

The nature of the Welsh language, which expresses the indefinite article by omitting the definite and can express a genitive relationship by word-order alone, together with the use of compound words, allows more to be contained in a line, especially a short line, than is always possible in the English equivalent, and I have had to omit adjectives sometimes and whole phrases on a few occasions, consoling myself with the fact that these were present mainly for melodic purposes rather than as essential to the meaning. I have in general retained as much as possible the stylistic peculiarites noted earlier, particularly the use of *sangiad*: while there is the risk of obscuring still further a difficult poem, I do not believe that simplifying difficulties is a proper task for the translator.

One feature of style I have been unable to reproduce adequately is the compounding of nouns and adjectives, constant in the *Gogynfeirdd* and their fourteenth-century successors, less frequent in the later bards. The opening line of a poem by Dafydd ap Gwilym, *Y don bengrychlon grochlais,* can be rendered with English compounds as 'Curly-topped loud-crying wave', but his address to a seagull as *esgudfalch edn bysgodfwyd* (swift-proud bird fish-fed) creates more of a problem: 'fish-feeding' will do, but can one compound in

Evans' 'Prophetic Poetry' in *Guide II*, pp 256-74, for the importance of this poetry in relation to Owain Glyndŵr's rising and the way the poems found 'their fulfilment in the [Tudor] victory at Bosworth Field in August 1485'.

English, as these poets regularly do in Welsh, such adjectives as 'swift-proud'? In general I have compounded where I could do so comfortably, and occasionally compounded where the Welsh does not in an attempt to make up in slight measure for the many times I have had to destroy a compound in translation. One source of pleasure in the Welsh is certainly lost, and one major stylistic change during these centuries is obscured for the reader, but I see no help for it.

Loss of the original music is inevitable in all translation, and poetic translators must do their best to create an acceptable equivalent. More is lost in translating medieval Welsh poetry than perhaps in any other language. For the *Gogynfeirdd* in particular, but often for later poets as well, sound was at least as important as sense, and the bard frequently strives less for originality of diction and image than for the weaving of polished and complex melodies out of traditional themes and language. 'Indeed,' Thomas Parry comments, 'there is often but little meaning in the verse; hundreds of the lines are not much more than eulogistic sounds.'[45] At their best, though, beautiful sounds – English translation, which cannot replicate the music of the originals, leaves the reader with a quite inadequate notion even of those poems with more substantial content.

Some of the reasons for considering the melodic qualities of the *Gogynfeirdd* impossible to reproduce or to match in English can be briefly noted. It was their practice to compose lyrics of sometimes a hundred lines or more using a single terminal rhyme for the entire poem or for each long section, e.g., one poem by Cynddelw, of 132 lines, consists of six long monorhymed passages. Had a translator the technical facility to duplicate this, the effect would still, I believe, be too alien for the English ear to bear, and would certainly require excessive distortion of other elements in the poem. And then there are the patterns of secondary rhymes in certain of the metres, and the use of *cynghanedd* in the individual lines.

The opening stanza of Gruffudd ap Maredudd's elegy for Gwenhwyfar, composed at a time when the metre and music of Welsh poetry had evolved into very strict forms, will provide a brief illustration:

> Haul Wynedd, neud bedd, nid byw unbennes
> Heb ennill ei chyfryw;
> Henw gorhoffter a dderyw,
> Hoen lloer, hun oer heno yw.

The verse form is one of the most frequently used, *englyn unodl union*, a monorhymed quatrain employing, as is standard practice, syllabic metre (10, 6, 7, 7). The main rhyme is the diphthong *yw* (pronounced 'ee-oo'); Welsh verse

---

45 Parry, p. 48.

not only permits but sometimes requires rhyming on unaccented syllables, as in the second and third lines. The first line contains the tripartite form of *cynghanedd* known as *cynghanedd sain*: parts 1 and 2 rhyme (Wynedd – bedd), part 3 is linked with part 2 by the strict consonantal repetition known as *cynghanedd groes* (**n**id bedd – **n**id **b**yw). The syllables after the main rhyme in line 1 are alliteratively linked with the opening syllables of line 2 (un**benn**es – Heb e**nn**ill). Line 3 employs *cynghanedd lusg*, in which the penultimate syllable rhymes with a preceding syllable (gorho**ffter** – dd**eryw**). Line 4 uses *cynghanedd sain* again (lloer – oer; **h**un oer – **h**eno).

The impossibility of an English translator duplicating this or producing an equivalent is, I trust, apparent. The *Cynfeirdd* are less strict in their sound-patterns, as are the earlier *Gogynfeirdd*, but the use of *cynghanedd* in every line became a requirement in the *cywydd* well as other verse-forms, as a look at the earlier quotations from Dafydd ap Gwilym and Iolo Goch will show. I see no point in explaining further, here or in the Notes, the various original verse-forms I cannot reproduce: readers who wish to learn more about these should consult the appendix on 'Welsh Versification' in Gwyn Williams' *An Introduction to Welsh Poetry* (London, 1953) or, for a more detailed discussion of the later poetry, Eurys Rowlands' chapter on '*Cynghanedd*, Metre, Prosody' in Jarman and Hughes' *Guide II*, cited in previous notes.

In all their verse the Welsh poets used terminal rhyme. I have dispensed with this in order to retain more of the sense and particularly the movement of the originals, but have kept though often loosely their syllabic metrical base. In the case of the *cywydd*, I have used unrhymed couplets with one stressed and one unstressed final syllable to produce one effect of the *cywydd* patterns (see again the quotations from Dafydd ap Gwilym and Iolo Goch): it should be possible for the reader to detect the tendency of the bards to shift from the freer use of run-on lines and couplets in the fourteenth century to the tightly epigrammatic and self-contained couplets of the fifteenth, a development similar to that in the English pentameter couplet from Jonson and Donne to Dryden and Pope. And I have made frequent but unsystematized use of alliteration, assonance, and internal rhyme, especially for the later poetry. In short, I have tried to convey the 'feel' of the original poems, and to make where needed as rich a melody as my command of English permits, while still striving for reasonably close translation.

I have generally used the Welsh names and spellings for persons and places, and have therefore provided a concise guide to the pronunciation of Welsh. The texts on which I have based the translations are cited in the Notes. Titles, division into sections, and punctuation sometimes follow editorial practice in the texts, sometimes are based on my own preference. Allusions are normally explained in the Glossary, but where a poem required extensive historical comments I have supplied these in the Notes.

In my earlier collections I acknowledged my indebtedness to the late Sir Thomas Parry and Professor Thomas Jones, and to Professor D. J. Bowen, and am happy to repeat it here. For the present volume I am grateful, as so often in recent years, to Professor R. M. Jones for his generous encouragement and advice, and to my wife, as ever, for her patience and support.

My son Thomas, who was born the year my first book of Welsh translations was published, is presently a lecturer in Celtic at the University of Glasgow, and urged me to undertake these revisions, not only encouraged and advised but provided a much-needed jump-start by commissioning the revised translations of Taliesin, Aneirin, 'The Fall of Rheged', and 'Song for a Small Boy' for his anthology *The Triumph Tree*. It is only fitting, then, that the book be dedicated to him.

Aberystwyth, Ceredigion
The Feast of St David
1 March 2003

THE PRONUNCIATION OF WELSH

The Welsh alphabet uses 28 letters: a, b, c, ch, d, dd, e, f, ff, g, ng, h, i, l, ll, m, n, o, p, ph, r, rh, s, t, th, u, w, y.

In general, the consonants represent the same sound-values as in English spelling, with these exceptions:

c   always the sound in 'cat', never the sound in 'cease'.

ch   as in 'loch' or 'chutzpa'.

dd   the sound of 'th' in 'breathe'; Welsh uses its 'th' only for the sound in 'breath'.

f   as in 'of'.

ff   as in 'off'.

g   always the sound in 'give', never the sound in 'germ'.

ll   there is no equivalent sound in English; the usual advice is to pronounce 'tl' rapidly as if it were a single sound, or to put the tip of the tongue on the roof of the mouth and hiss.

ph   as in 'physic'.

r   the sound is always trilled.

rh   the trilled 'r' followed by aspiration.

s   always the sound in 'sea', never the sound in 'does'. 'Si' is used for the sound represented in English by 'sh'; English 'shop' becomes Welsh 'siop'.

Welsh letters stand always for pure vowel-sounds, never as in English spelling for diphthongs. The vowels can be long or short; a circumflex accent is sometimes used to distinguish the long vowel.

a   the vowel-sounds in as in 'father' and (American) 'hot'.

e   the vowel-sounds in 'pale' and 'pet'.

i   the vowel-sounds in 'green' and 'grin'. The letter is also used for the consonantal sound represented in English spelling by 'y'; English 'yard' becomes Welsh 'iard'.

o   the vowel-sounds in 'roll' and (British) 'hot'.

u   pronounced like the Welsh 'i'. Never used as in English spelling for such sounds as 'oo' and 'uh'.

w   the vowel sounds in 'tool' and 'took'. English 'fool' becomes Welsh 'ffŵl'. The letter is also used consonantally as in English 'dwelling', e.g., Gwen.

y   in most monosyllables and in final syllables pronounced like the Welsh 'i'. In other syllables it stands for the vowel-sound in 'up', and this is also its sound in a few monosyllables like 'y' and 'yr'.

The following diphthongs are used in Welsh; the chief vowel comes first:

ae, ai, au:	the diphthong sound in 'write'.
ei, eu, ey	'uh-ee'.
aw	the diphthong sound in 'prowl'.
ew	the short Welsh 'e' followed by 'oo'.
iw, yw	'ee-oo'.
wy	'oo-ee'
oe, oi, ou	the diphthong sound in 'oil'.

The accent in Welsh is placed, with few exceptions, on the next to last syllable: Mórfudd, Llanbádarn.

I. THE EARLY POETS
*c.575–c.*1100

TALIESIN

THE BATTLE OF GWEN YSTRAD

Catraeth's men set out at daybreak
Round a battle-winning lord, cattle-raider.
Urien he, renowned chieftain,
Constrains rulers and cuts them down,
Eager for war, true leader of Christendom.
Prydain's men, they came in war-bands:
Gwen Ystrad your base, battle-honer.
Neither field nor forest shielded,
Land's protector, your foe when he came.
Like waves roaring harsh over land
I saw savage men in war-bands.
And after morning's fray, torn flesh.
I saw hordes of invaders dead;
Joyous, wrathful, the shout one heard.
Defending Gwen Ystrad one saw
A thin rampart and lone weary men.
At the ford I saw men stained with blood
Down arms before a grey-haired lord.
They wish peace, for they found the way barred,
Hands crossed, on the strand, cheeks pallid.
Their lords marvel at Idon's lavish wine;
Waves wash the tails of their horses.
I saw pillaging men disheartened,
And blood spattered on garments,
And quick groupings, ranks closed, for battle.
Battle's cloak, he'd no mind to flee,
Rheged's lord, I marvel, when challenged.
I saw splendid men around Urien
When he fought his foes at Llech Wen.
Routing foes in fury delights him.
Carry, warriors, shields at the ready;
Battle's the lot of those who serve Urien.

    And until I die, old,
    By death's strict demand,
    I shall not be joyful
    Unless I praise Urien.

IN PRAISE OF URIEN

Urien of Yrechwydd,   most bountiful of Christians,
Much you bestow   on the men of this land.
As you gather in,   so you give away.
Joyful Christendom's poets   as long as you live.
Greater is the joy   to have such a hero,
Greater is the glory   of Urien and his offspring,
Since he is chieftain,   ruler supreme,
Wayfarers' refuge,   powerful champion.

Lloegr-men know him   as they will report:
Death's what they get   and pain a-plenty,
Their dwellings ablaze   and their garments seized,
And heavy losses   and grievous hardship,
Getting no deliverance   from Urien of Rheged.

Rheged's defender,   renowned lord, land's anchor,
I delight in you   from all that's reported:
Savage your spear-thrust   when battle is sounded.
When you charge into battle   you wreak a slaughter,
Houses fired before daybreak   by Yrechwydd's lord.

Most fair, Yrechwydd,   and most bountiful its men.
No safeguard for Angles: round the bravest ruler,
The bravest offspring.   You yourself are best:
Was not nor will be   ever your equal.
When one beholds him   great is the terror.
Ever joy around him,   round a spirited monarch,
Around him rejoicing   and abundant riches,
Golden king of the north,   high lord of monarchs.

And until I die, old,
By death's strict demand,
I shall not be joyful
Unless I praise Urien.

THE COURT OF URIEN

My place of ease,   with Rheged's men:
Respect and welcome   and mead in plenty,
Plenty of mead   for celebration,

And splendid lands   for me in abundance,
Great possessions   and gold and wealth,
Wealth and gold,   and high honour,
High honour   and fulfilled desire,
Desire fulfilled   to do me good.

He slays, he hangs,   supplies, provides,
Provides, supplies,   in the lead, he slays.
He gives great honour   to the world's poets.
The world for certain   submits to you.
At your will,   God, for your sake,
Has made lords groan   fearing destruction.
Rouser of battle,   defender of the land,
Land's defender,   battle's rouser,
Constant around you   hooves stamping,
Stamping of hooves   and drinking of beer.
Beer for the drinking   and a splendid dwelling,
And a splendid garment   was handed to me.

Llwyfenydd's people   all entreat you
With a single voice,   the great and the small.
Taliesin's praise-song   will entertain them.
You are the best   whose qualities ever
I have heard of,   and I will praise
All that you do.

And until I die, old,
By death's strict demand,
I shall not be joyful
Unless I praise Urien.

THE WAR-BAND'S RETURN

Throughout one year   one steady outflow:
Wine, bragget, mead,   valour's reward.
A host of singers,   a throng around spits,
Torques round their heads,   their places honoured.
Each went on campaign   eager for combat,
His steed beneath him,   making for Manaw
And greater gain,   profit in plenty,
Eight score, the same colour,   of calves and cattle,
Milch cows and oxen,   and each of them comely.

I could not be joyful   were Urien slain,
Much loved before he left   for spears' clashing contention,
With white hair soaked   and a bier his fate,
With cheek bloodstained,   besmeared with blood.
Proud steadfast man,   his wife made widow,
My true sovereign,   my true reliance,
My lot, my bulwark, my chief,   before savage strife.

Go, fellow, to the door,   see what's causing commotion.
Is it earth shaking?   Is it sea rushing in?
The chant grows louder   from marching men:
Be there foe on hill,   Urien will shake him;
Be there foe in dale,   Urien will strike him;
Be there foe on mountain,   Urien conquers him;
Be there foe on hillside,   Urien shatters him;
Be there foe in ditch,   Urien smites him.
Foe on path, foe on peak,   foe at every bend,
Not one sneeze or two   will shield him from death.

There would be no famine: herds of cattle surround him.
Battle-keen conqueror,   well-armed, weapons gleaming,
Like death his spear   mows down his foes.

   And until I die, old,
   By death's strict demand,
   I shall not be joyful
   Unless I praise Urien.

THE BATTLE OF ARGOED LLWYFAIN

   There was a great battle, Saturday morning,
   From the time the sun rose till it set.
   Fflamddwyn came on, in four war-bands.
   Goddau and Rheged were mustering,
   Summoned men, from Argoed to Arfynydd:
   They were given not one day's delay.
   Fflamddwyn shouted, big at boasting:
   'Have my hostages come? Are they ready?'
   Answered Owain, bane of the East:
   'They've not come, are not here, are not ready,
   And a cub of Coel's line must be pressed
   Hard before he'd render one hostage.'

Shouted Urien, lord of Yrechwydd:
'If a meeting for peace-talk's to come,
Let our shield-wall rise on the mountain,
And let our faces lift over the rim,
And let our spears, men, be raised high,
And let us make for Fflamddwyn amidst his war-bands,
And let us slay him and his comrades.'
    Before Argoed Llwyfain
    There was many a dead man.
        Crows grew crimsoned from warriors.
And the war-band charged with its chieftain:
For a year I'll shape song to their triumph.

    And until I die, old,
    By death's strict demand,
    I shall not be joyful
    Unless I praise Urien.

PETITION FOR RECONCILIATION

A ruler most valiant   I'll not abandon:
It is Urien I seek,   to him will I sing.
When my warrant comes   I will find a welcome
In the best of regions   beneath the best of rulers.

No great matter to me,   those princes I see:
I'll not go to them;   with them I'll not be:
I'll make for the north   to mighty monarchs:
Though for high stakes   I should lay a wager,
No need to boast,   Urien will not spurn me.

Llwyfenydd's land,   mine are their riches,
Mine is their good will,   mine their generosity,
Mine are their garments   and their luxuries,
Mead from drinking-horns,   and no end of good things
From the best of kings,   most generous I've heard of.

Kings of every tribe,   all to you are bound.
Before you, they complain,   one must give way.
Though once I was willing   to mock an old man,
None better I loved   before I knew him.
Now it is I see   how much I possess:

43

Save to God on high   I will not surrender him.
Your regal sons,   most generous of men,
They will make their spears sing   in enemy lands.

And until I die, old,
By death's strict demand,
I shall not be joyful
Unless I praise Urien.

LAMENT FOR OWAIN AB URIEN

Soul of Owain ab Urien,
    May his Lord attend to its needs.
Rheged's lord, a green burden hides him,
    It was no light thing to praise him.
Locked below, a famed song-praised man,
    Dawn's wing-tips his whetted spears,
For there is found no equal
    To splendid Llwyfenydd's lord,
Reaper of foes, grasper,
    Of father and grandfather's make.
When Owain cut down Fflamddwyn,
    No more to it than sleeping:
Asleep is Lloegr's broad war-band
    With light upon their eyes.
And those who fled but little,
    They were bolder than was need:
Owain punished them fiercely
    Like a wolf savaging sheep.
Splendid man, clad in pied war-gear,
    He'd grant steeds to suppliants:
Though he'd store up like a miser,
    It was shared, for his soul's sake.
Soul of Owain ab Urien,
    May his Lord attend to its needs.

ANEIRIN

THE GODODDIN (*Text A*)

1   Man's mettle, youth's years,
    Courage for combat:
    Swift thick-maned stallions
    Beneath a fine stripling's thighs,
    Broad lightweight shield
    On a trim charger's crupper,
    Gleaming blue blades,
    Gold-bordered garments.
    Never will there be
    Bitterness between us:
    I do better by you,
    In song to praise you.
    The bloodsoaked field
    Before the marriage-feast,
    Foodstuff for crows
    Before the burial.
    A dear comrade, Owain;
    Wrong, his cover of crows.
    Sad wonder to me, in what land
    Marro's one son was slain.

2   Betorqued, to the fore wherever he'd charge,
    Shy of breath before a maid, he'd earn his mead.
    Rent the front of his shield, when he heard the war-cry,
        He'd spare none he pursued.
    He'd not turn from a fight till blood flowed;
    Like rushes he mowed men who'd not flee.
    The Gododdin tell, in the court's great hall,
    How before Madawg's tent when he'd return
    There would come but one man in a hundred.

3   Betorqued, a warrior, enemy's net,
    Eagle's rush at river-mouths when roused.
    His pledge was a purpose kept;
    He bettered his intent: he was not turned back.
    They fled before Gododdin's war-host,
    Bold the pressure on Manawyd's land.
    Neither mail-coat nor shield gave protection:

45

None could, on mead he was nourished,
Be kept from Cadfannan's stroke.

4 Betorqued, to the fore, a wolf in his fury,
The gold-collared warrior won beads of amber.
Gwefrfawr was worth much, for wine from a horn
He drove back the attack, blood on cheek.
Though Gwynedd and the northlands should come
    Through Ysgyrran's son's war-plan,
    Shattered shields.

5 Betorqued, to the fore, well-armed in combat,
Till his death a fearless man in a fray:
Champion charging at the head of war-hosts,
Five times fifty would fall before his blades.
There fall, of Deifr's and Brennych's men,
A hundred score to perdition in a single hour.
Meat for wolves, before the marriage-feast,
Tid-bit for crows, before the altar.
Before the burial, the bloodsoaked field.
For mead in the hall, among the hosts,
While there's a singer Hyfaidd Hir will be praised.

6 Men went to Gododdin, laughing and chaffing,
Savage in battle, lances aligned.
A brief year in peace they stay quiet.
Bodgad's son, his hand-craft wrought slaughter.
Though they go to churches for shriving,
The old and the young, the bold and the meek,
True is the tale, death confronted them.

7 Men went to Gododdin, laughter-loving.
Assailants in a war-host, keen for combat,
They would slaughter with swords, in short order.
A pillar in combat, bountiful Rheithfyw.

8 Men went to Catraeth, in high spirits their war-band.
Pale mead their portion, it was poison.
Three hundred under orders to fight.
And after celebration, silence.
Though they go to churches for shriving,
True is the tale, death confronted them.

9 Men went to Catraeth, mead-nourished war-host,
   Strong, vigorous – wrong should I not praise them –
   With great dark-socketed crimson blades.
   Close-ranked, stubborn, the warhounds fought.
   Of Brennych's war-band I'd have thought it a burden :
   Should I leave one in human form alive.
   I lost a comrade, I was steadfast,
   Ready man in combat, hard for me to leave him.
   The hero sought no father-in-law's dowry,
   Cian's young son from Maen Gwyngwn.

10 Men went to Catraeth at dawn:
   Their fears had been left behind.
   Three hundred clashed with ten thousand.
   He stains spears ruddy with blood,
   Most valiant bulwark in battle,
   Before Mynyddawg Mwynfawr's war-band.

11 Men went to Catraeth at dawn:
   Their mettle shortened their lives.
   They drank mead, yellow, sweet, ensnaring;
   Many a singer for a year was merry.
   Crimson their swords, let their blades stay uncleansed,
       Lime-white shields and four-sided spearpoints,
   Before Mynyddawg Mwynfawr's war-band.

12 A man went to Catraeth at daybreak:
   He made mockeries of war-hosts.
   They made certain biers were needed.
   With the most merciless blades in Christendom
   He fashioned, sooner than mention truce,
   A bloodbath and death for one who faced him.
   When he moved to the fore of Gododdin's war-host
   Brave Neirthiad did what he boldly planned.

13 A man went to Catraeth at daybreak.
   He guzzled mead-suppers at midnight.
   Woeful, fellow-warrior's lament,
   His campaign, hot-blooded killer.
       There hurried to Catraeth
       No great man with aims
           So expansive over mead;

None from Eidyn's fortress
   Would so completely
      Break up enemy ranks.
Tudfwlch Hir, from his land and homesteads,
Would slay Saxons at least once a week.
His valour will stay long-lasting,
Kept in mind by his splendid comrades.
When Tudfwlch came, people's sustainer,
Spearmen's post was a killing ground, Cilydd's son.

14 A man went to Catraeth at dawn,
Lordly face like a shield-wall.
Sharply they'd attack, they'd gather spoils,
Loud as thunder the crash of shields.
Ardent man, prudent man, singular man,
He'd rip and he'd pierce with spear-points.
Deep in blood he would strike with blades,
Hard-pressed, steel weapons on heads.
In the hall the hewer bowed humbly.
Facing Erthgi, war-hosts would groan.

15 It is told, of the region of Catraeth,
Men fall, long was the grief for them.
Through thick, through thin, they fought for the land,
The sons of Godebawg, a loyal people.
Long biers bore men drenched in blood.
Wretched was the lot, fate's strict demand,
Allotted to Tudfwlch and Cyfwlch Hir.
Though by candle's light we drank bright mead,
Though good was its taste, it was long detested.

16 First out of Eidyn's bright fort, he inspired
Faithful warriors who'd follow him.
Blaen, on down pillows, would pass around
The drinking-horn in his opulent hall.
The first brew of bragget was his.
Blaen took delight in gold and purple;
First pick of sleek steeds raced beneath him:
At sound of battle his high heart earned them.
First to raise the war-cry, gainful return,
Bear in the path, ever slow to retreat.

17 Force in the front line,
 Sunlight on pasture.
 Lord, where can be found
 Ynys Brydain's heaven?
 Rough the ford before the warrior,
 Shield as a shelter.
 Splendid his drinking-horn
 In Eidyn's great hall,
 His grandeur a display.
 His mead made one drunk;
 He would drink strong wine.
 In combat, a reaper,
 He would drink sweet wine,
 Battle-bold of mind,
 Battle-leeks reaper.
 Battle's bright arm,
 They sang a battle-song.
 Battle-armoured,
 Battle-pinioned,
 His shield was sheared thin
 By warfare's spears.
 Comrades fell
 In warfare's strife:
 Unfaltering his fighting,
 Blameless he avenged them.
 His rage was appeased
 Before green turf covered
 The grave of Gwrwelling Fras.

18 They revere what is right.
 They stain three spear-shafts,
 Fifty, and five hundred.
 Three hounds with three hundred,
 Three horsemen of war
 From gold-smithied Eidyn,
 Three mail-clad war-bands,
 Three gold-torqued leaders,
 Three furious horsemen,
 Three peers in battle,
 Three leaping as one,
 They routed foes savagely.
 Three in hard fighting,
 They slew foes easily,

49

Gold in close combat,
Three rulers of men
Who came from the Britons,
Cynri and Cynon,
Cynrain of Aeron.
The wily tribes
Of Deifr would ask:
Has there come from the Britons
A man better than Cynon,
Foe-stabbing serpent?

19 I drank wine and mead in the hall.
　　　　Numerous his spears
　　　　In the clash of men:
　　　　　　He'd furnish food for eagles.
　　When Cydwal charged the battle-cry rose
　　With the green of dawn wherever he came.
　　He'd leave shields in splinters, shattered.
　　　　Stiff spears the splitter
　　　　Cut down in combat:
　　　　　　He'd break the front rank.
　　The son of Sywno, a wise man knew it,
　　　　Sold his life to purchase
　　　　A famous name.
　　　　　　He'd strike with sharpened blade.
　　He had cut down Athrwys and Affrai.
　　As pledged, he intended an onslaught:
　　　　He would make corpses
　　　　Of men brave in battle;
　　　　　　He'd attack in Gwynedd's front line.

20 I drank wine and mead in the hall.
　　Since I drank, I attacked the border, mournful fate.
　　Not harmless, a reckless heart:
　　When all would fall back, you'd attack.
　　Glory come to you, for you would not sin;
　　World-renowned was reckless Breichior.

21 Men went to Catraeth, they were far-famed:
　　Wine and mead from gold cups was their drink
　　For a year, according to noble custom,
　　Three men and three score and three hundred, gold-torqued.
　　Of those who went forth after lavish drink

But three won free through battle prowess:
Aeron's two war-hounds and Cynon came back,
And I, soaked in blood, for my praise-song's sake.

22   My kinsman in carousal, no concern was ours,
Save what came of the feast, steel-hard warlord.
At court he was not kept short of mead.
He'd lay layer upon layer, with steady strokes,
Staunch in conflict, staunch in distress.
The Gododdin do not tell, after battle,
That any was keener than Llifiau.

23   Weapons scattered,
Column shattered, standing his ground,
Great the havoc,
The hero turned back the Lloegr-men's swarm.
He planted shafts,
In the front line, in the spear-clash.
He laid men low,
Made wives widows, before his death.
Graid fab Hoywgi,
Confronting spears, formed a rampart.

24   Hero, shield held below his freckled brow,
    His stride a young stallion's.
There was battle-hill din, there was fire,
There were swift spears, there was sunlight,
There was crows' food, a crow's tid-bit.
And before he was left at the ford,
As the dew fell, graceful eagle,
Beside the wave's spray, near the slope,
The world's poets pronounce him great of heart.
His war-plans cost him what by rights was his;
Wiped out, his picked warriors by foemen.
And before his burial below Eleirch Fre
    There was valour in his breast,
His blood had washed over his war-gear.
Undaunted, Buddfan fab Bleiddfan.

25   Wrong to leave him unremembered, large his achievement:
He'd not leave a breach out of cowardice.
He did not leave his court, reward of song,
On New Year's Day, of his own will.

Though his land be desert, it was not for ploughing.
Too bitter the conflict, generous warlord,
Lord drenched in blood, after the wine-feast,
Gwenabwy fab Gwen, the battle of Catraeth.

26 It was true, as Cadlew declared:
No man's horses could overtake Marchlew.
He would plant spears in a conflict
From a leaping, wide-ranging steed.
Though not reared for burdens, for hardship,
Fierce his sword-stroke at his station.
He would plant ashen spears from his hand's clutch
    Atop his steaming trim roan.
The lord much-loved would share his lavish wine;
He would slash with furious bloodstained blade:
As a reaper hacks in turning weather,
So Marchlew made the blood gush forth.

27 Isag, much-esteemed man from the south,
Like the flow of the sea his ways,
    Congenial and generous,
    And well-mannered drinking mead.
Where his weapons delve, they call it quits,
Not wishy-washy, no shilly-shally.
His sword rang in the heads of mothers.
Warfare's wall, Gwyddnau's son was renowned.

28 Ceredig, cherished his fame,
He would seize, would preserve renown.
Pet cub, at peace before his death-day came,
    Supreme his courtesy.
May one who loved songs come, in due time,
To heaven's land, recognition's home.

29 Ceredig, beloved leader,
Ferocious champion in battle,
Battlefield's gold-fretted shield,
Spears broken to bits, splintered,
Sword-stroke furious, not feeble,
Like a man he'd hold the spearmen's post.
Before earth's grief, before suffering,
Firm in purpose he'd stand his ground.

May welcome be his among the host
With the Trinity, in total unity.

30 When Caradawg would charge into battle,
Like a wild boar, three war-hounds' slayer,
Bull of the war-host, hewer in combat,
He'd provide wolves food with his hand.
My witness is Ywain fab Eulad,
And Gwrien and Gwyn and Gwriad,
From Catraeth, from the carnage,
From Bryn Hyddwn, before they were taken.
After bright mead held in hand,
Not a one saw his father.

31 Men launched the assault, leapt forwards as one.
Short-lived, drunk above clarified mead,
Mynyddawg's war-band, renowned in battle:
For their feast of mead, their lives were payment,
Caradawg and Madawg, Pyll and Ieuan,
Gwgon and Gwion, Gwyn and Cynfan,
Steel-weaponed Peredur, Gwawrddur and Aeddan,
Attackers in a battle of shattered shields.
And though they were being slain, they slew.
None to their own regions returned.

32 Men launched the assault, nourished as one
For a year over mead, grand their design.
How sad their tale, insatiable longing,
Bitter their dwelling, no mother's son cherished them.
How long the grief for them and the yearning
For ardent men of wine-nourished lands.
Gwlgawd of Gododdin, for lively men
He provided renowned Mynyddawg's feast,
And its price, the battleground of Catraeth.

33 Men went to Catraeth in force, in full cry,
Swift steeds and dark-blue war-gear and shields,
Spear-shafts held high and spear-points sharp-edged,
And glittering mail-coats and swords.
He'd take the lead, he'd bore through war-hosts:
Five times fifty would fall before his blades.
Rhufon Hir, he'd give gold to the altar,
And rewards and rich gifts to the singer.

34 Never was built a hall so acclaimed,
   So great, so mighty for slaughter.
   You'd prove worthy of mead, firebrand Morien.
   He'd not say, Cynon, that he'd make no corpses,
   Armour-clad, loud-shouting spearman:
   His sword sounded atop the rampart.
   No more than a broad-based rock will budge
   Would he be budged, Gwid fab Peithan.

35 Never was built a hall so renowned.
   Save for Morien, heir of Caradawg,
   There came from combat, lordly his ways,
   No fiercer fighter than Fferog's son.
   Firm his hand, he'd inflame a runaway horseman,
   Bold warrior, refuge for a frightened war-band.
   Before the war-host of Gododdin his shield was shattered:
       Hard-pressed, he was steadfast.
   On the day of battle he was quick to act, bitter the recompense:
   Mynyddawg's man would prove worthy of mead-horns.

36 Never was built a hall so faultless.
   [...]
   Than kind-hearted Cynon, jewel-decked lord.
   Rightly he'd sit in the place of honour.
   Whoever he'd strike was not struck again.
   Sharp-pointed his spears,
   Shield in pieces, he'd bore through war-hosts,
   Speedy his steeds, front-runners.
   On the day of battle his blades were deadly
   When Cynon would charge in the green of dawn.

37 He attacked full force, at the forefront:
   He drove out the foe, he drew the line.
   Spear-thrusting lord, laughing in combat,
   He displays his valour, like Elffin,
   Far-famed Eithinyn, wall of war, bull of battle.

38 He attacked full force, at the forefront,
   For mead in the hall and drinks of wine.
   He planted his blades between two war-hosts,
   Superb horseman before the Gododdin,
   Far-famed Eithinyn, wall of war, bull of battle.

39 He attacked full force for eastern herds.
    The war band rose, shields shredded.
    Shield rent before Beli's bellowing cattle,
    Lord deep in blood, border's fleet defender,
    He sustains us, grey-haired, on a charger,
    Prancing steed, stubborn ox, gold-torqued warrior.
    The boar made a pact before the line, cunning man,
    Deserving of his due, a cry of resistance:
    'Let him that calls us to heaven protect us in battle.'
        He brandishes his war-spears.
    Cadfannan gained plunder, great his praise:
    No dispute that a war-band lay prostrate before him.

40 For the feast, most sad, disastrous,
    For settled, for desolate land,
    For the falling of hair from the head,
    Among warriors, an eagle, Gwyddien.
    Fiercely he defended them with his spear,
    A planner, a tiller, its owner.
    Morien defended
    Myrddin's praise-song, and placed the chieftain
    In earth, our strength, our support.
    Worth three men, for a maid's favour, Bradwen;
    Worth twelve, Gwenabwy fab Gwen.

41 For the feast, most sad, disastrous,
    Hard worked, the shields in the fighting,
    In the fury of swordstrokes on heads.
    In Lloegr, torn flesh before three hundred lords.
    Who would seize a wolf's mane without sword in hand
        Needs a bold heart under his cloak.
    From the clash of rage and destruction
    Bradwen perished, he did not escape.

42 Gold on fortress wall,
    Battle's onslaught
    [...]
    [...]
    [...]
    [...]
    The living will tell
    Of a leader's doings,
    Of [...]

The living will not say that in the hour of slaughter
Cynhafal would not lend his support.

43 When you were a far-famed warrior
Fighting for enemies' fertile land,
Of right we were called outstanding, noteworthy men.
He was a firm door, firm fort of refuge;
He was gracious to earnest suppliants;
He was fortress for a war-host that trusted him:
Call for Gwynfyd, and there he'd be.

    * * *

45 I'm no wearied lord.
I'll avenge no affront.
I'll laugh no laughter
Under crawlers' feet.
Outstretched my knee
In an earthen dwelling,
A chain of iron
Around my two knees.
Of mead from drinking-horn,
Of Catraeth's men,
I, not I, Aneirin,
(Taliesin knows it,
Skilled in word-craft),
Sang *The Gododdin*
Before next day dawned.

46 The north's valour, a man enacted it,
Kind-hearted, bountiful lord by nature.
Does not walk the earth, mother has not borne,
One so comely and strong, iron-clad.
By his bright sword's strength he saved me,
From earth's harsh prison he brought me,
From a place of death, from a hostile land,
Cenau fab Llywarch, bold, undaunted.

47 The court of Senyllt, its cups brimming with mead,
    Would not be disgraced.
He'd set his sword against wrong-doing;
He'd set his strides to warfare;
He'd bear bloodstained men in his arms

Before Deifr's and Brennych's war-host.
Constant in his hall, swift horses,
Bloodied spears, and dark-blue war-gear,
A long brown spear in his hand,
And rushing about in his wrath,
Smile giving way to frown,
Bad-tempered and good in turn.
No sight of his men's feet in flight,
Heilyn, raider of every border.

48 Standing stone in cleared ground
On Gododdin's border
[...]
[...]
[...]
[...]
Season of storm,
Storm season,
[...] before the war-host.
From Din Dywyd
Came to us, came upon us
[...]
They strike harshly; they harrow the war-band.
Grugyn's shield, before battle's bull, its front was shredded.

49 His foe trembles before his blade,
Savage eagle, laughing in battle.
Sharp his stag-horns around Bancarw;
Speckled fingers, they crush a head.
Varied in mood: tranquil, turbulent;
Varied in mood: thoughtful, mirthful.
Briskly Rhys charges, furiously,
Not like those whose assault will falter.
Whoever he overtakes will not escape.

50 Unluckily the shield was pierced
Of kind-hearted Cynwal;
Unluckily he set his thighs
On a trim long-legged grey.
Dark his brown spear-shaft,
Darker his saddle.
The hero in his hut
Chews on the leg

Of a buck, his cell's wealth.
May he suffer this seldom.

51   Good fortune, Addonwy, you'd vowed to me:
What Bradwen did, you'd do; you'd slash, you'd burn;
You would do no worse than Morien.
You held neither far wing nor front line:
Bold eye, unblinking,
You did not see the great surge of horsemen.
They cut down, they did not spare Saxons.

     * * *

54   Ready warriors rose for combat.
A strong land will be heard in pursuit.
A wave is beating, bright wayfarer,
Where the lively, the noblest are.
Of stockade, not a stick can you see.
A worthy lord brooks no provoking;
Morial will bear no reproach in pursuit,
Savage sword-blade ready for bloodshed.

55   Ready warriors rose for combat.
A strong land will be heard in pursuit.
He slaughtered with cudgel and blade
And ferocious hooves men in battle.

56   Warriors rose for combat, formed ranks:
With a single mind they assaulted.
Short their lives, long their kinsmen long for them.
Seven times their sum of Lloegr-men they slew.
Their fighting turned wives into widows;
Many a mother with tear-filled eyelids.

57   Never was built a hall so flawless.
[...]
So generous, lion's rage, wide-ranging,
As kind-hearted Cynon, lord most fair.
Refuge in combat, on the far wing,
Door, war-host's anchor, noblest of blessings.
Of those I have seen, and I see, in the world
Wielding weapons, the bravest in battle.
He would slash the foe with sharpest blade:

Like rushes they'd fall before his hand.
Son of Clydno, long-praised, I will sing to you, lord,
    Praise unstinted, unstilled.

58   After wine-feast and mead-feast
    They furnished slaughter.
       Manly youth, highly praised,
    He made a stand
    Before Buddugre's slope:
       Crows arose, cloud-climbing.
    Warriors falling
    Like a fresh swarm on him:
       Not a move towards fleeing.
    Far-sighted, swift-moving,
    From grey steeds a sword-edge,
       From the mound a sword-stroke.
    Foremost at a feast, sleepless;
    No sleeplessness today:
       Rheiddun's son, lord of warfare.

59   After wine-feast and mead-feast they left us,
    Mail-clad men, I know death's sadness.
    Before hair turned grey came their slaughter.
    Before Catraeth, brisk was their war-band.
    Of Mynyddawg's men, great the grief,
    Of three hundred, but one man returned.

60   After wine-feast and mead-feast they charged,
    Men renowned in battle, reckless of life.
    Bright ranks round the wine-bowl, they dined together;
    Wine and mead and bragget, they made them theirs.
    Of Mynyddawg's men, I am woeful,
    Too many I lost of my true kinsmen.
    Of three hundred champions who charged on Catraeth,
    Alas, save one man, none returned.

61   As he'd always be when they rose for battle,
       Like a bouncing ball,
    So he'd be until they returned.
    So did the Gododdin
    Take wine and mead in Eidyn,
       Unyielding in close combat.

And beneath Cadfannan a stud of red steeds,
Wild horseman, in the morning.

62   Anchor, Deifr-router,
Serpent with fearsome sting,
He'd trample dark-blue armour
   In the war-band's vanguard.
Terrifying bear,
Furious defender,
He'd trample spears
In the day of battle
   On a wall of alder.
Lord Neddig's heir,
Through rage he furnished
A feast for birds
   From battle's din.
Rightly are you called, for your loyal deeds,
Foremost leader, wall of a war-band,
Merin fab Madiain, blessed was your birth.

63   Song befitting a war-band is found:
Soldiers were embroiled around Catraeth;
Bloodstained garments, trod on, were trampled;
   Battle's branches were trampled.
   Mead payment in mead-horn,
     It was made good by corpses.
Cibno will not say, after battle's furor,
Though he took communion, that he had his due.

64   Song befitting a noble war-band:
Roar of fire and thunder and flood-tide.
Superb courage, strife-embroiled horseman,
Red reaper, he hungered for war.
Tireless fighter, he would hasten to battle
   In whatever land he might hear it.
With his shield on his shoulder he'd lift a spear
   Like a glass of sparkling wine.
Silver held his mead, gold was his due.
Wine-fed was Gwaednerth fab Llywri.

65   Song befitting glittering battle-bands:
And after it's risen, a river will flood.

He sated grey eagles' grasping beaks;
   He furnished food for scavengers
Of gold-torqued men who went to Catraeth
On Mynyddawg, ruler of men,'s campaign,
There came blameless from among Gododdin's Britons
   No man much better than Cynon.

66   Song befitting a well-trained war-band.
   World's cheerful small corner, he was spendthrift:
   He would have, world-wide, singers' acclaim
   For gold and great steeds and mead-drunk men.
   But when he came from battle they'd praise
   Cynddilig of Aeron, bloodstained men.

67   Song befitting glittering battle-bands:
   On Mynyddawg, ruler of men,'s campaign,
   With the steeds of Eudaf Hir, Gwanannon's affliction,
   Was one who wore purple, land of broken men.

68   Cowards could not bear the hall's clamour
   Like a roaring fire when kindled.
   Tuesday, they donned their dark war-gear;
   Wednesday, their shields were made ready;
   Thursday, certain their devastation;
   Friday, carcasses were carried off;
   Saturday, fluent their working as one;
   Sunday, their crimson blades were wielded;
   Monday, men seen hip deep in bloodshed.
   The Gododdin say that after hard labour
   Before Madawg's tent on their return
   There would come but one man in a hundred.

69   Up early in the morning,
   Fighting before the front line.
   A breach, a blazing breakthrough:
   Like a boar you charged uphill.
   He was mannerly, was stern,
   Was dark-hued war-hawks' blood-bath.

70   Up early, at dawning,
   For hot work before the border.
   In the lead, leading, pursuing,

Before a hundred he charged to the fore.
Fiercely you'd fashion a blood-bath
Like quaffing mead while laughing;
Easily you'd cut down corpses,
Fleet-footed man's bold sword-stroke.
    So eagerly was it
    He'd kill an enemy,
        Gwrhafal, in the war-host.

71   He fell into the depths, headlong.
The ready lord will not do as he designed.
Loss of honour, his slaying with spear.
Ywain's way was to mount the rampart,
Plying, before burial, the best spear,
Pursuing disaster, loss of songs.
Grey death, his gauntlet's office,
He dealt with his mailcoat-stripping hand.
    The lord will deal out reward
    From his earthen casket,
Chill, sad, the praise, pallid cheeks.
Shy when a maid would sit in judgment,
Owner of horses and war-gear and ice-bright shields,
Comrade in combat, mounting, falling.

72   Battle-leader, he led to war:
The land's war-band loved the bold reaper.
Greensward bloodsoaked around the fresh grave.
Armour covered his crimson garments,
Trampler on armour, armour-trampler.
Weariness came down like death.
Spears splintered as battle begins,
A clear path was the aim of his spear-thrust.

73   I sang a splendid song of your dwelling's ruin
    And the hall that once was there.
It merited sweet ensnaring mead,
The champion's assault at dawn,
Fine tribute to Lloegr-men's war-bands.
Too great penance while they're let live.
Gwynedd's man, his glory will be heard;
Gwanannon will be his grave.
Steadfast, Cadafwy of Gwynedd,
War-band's bull, fierce clash of rulers,

Before a bed of earth, before burial.
Gododdin's border will be his grave.

74   A war-host accustomed to battle,
A lord, war-band's harsh-handed leader.
He was wise and refined and proud;
He was not rude to fellow-drinkers.
White horses whinnied under his protection:
It did Pobddelw's land no good.
We are called the wing and the vanguard in battle;
In the clash of spears, spears equally matched.
Honed blades' defense, champion in the fray,
Forceful man, flaming steel against the foe.

75   His war-steeds bore bloodstained war-gear,
    A red herd at Catraeth.
Blaenwydd fosters a fearless war-host,
War-hound charging a hill on the day of battle,
And renown, bright fame, will be ours.
From Hedyn's hand, a planting of iron.

76   A lord of Gododdin will be praised in song;
A lordly patron will be lamented.
Before Eidyn, fierce flame, he will not return.
He set his picked men in the vanguard;
He set a stronghold at the front.
In full force he attacked a fierce foe.
Since he feasted, he bore great hardship.
Of Mynyddawg's war-band none escaped
Save one, blade-brandishing, dreadful.

77   With Moried's loss, there was no shield:
They bore, they exalted the champion.
He carried blue blades in his hand;
Weighty spears threatened threatener's head.
From a dapple-grey steed, arching its neck,
Heavy the carnage before his blades.
When he triumphed in combat, not one to flee,
He earned our praise, sweet ensnaring mead.

      * * *

79 Lucky victor, light-hearted, fearful folks' backbone,
    With his blue blade that forced back a foreign foe,
    Mighty stalwart, massive his hand,
    Stout-hearted, clever, they press him hard.
        His way, to attack
        Before nine champions,
        Between friend and foe,
            And hurl defiance.
    I love the victor, his was a seat of honour,
    Cynddilig of Aeron, praiseworthy lion.

80 I loved his front-line attack at Catraeth
    In return for mead in the hall and wine.
    I loved it that he did not scorn a spear
    Before he was slain, far from green Uffin.
    I loved the heir of renown, he furnished bloodshed;
    He laid on with his sword in fury.
    The valiant will not say before the Gododdin
    That renowned Ceidio's son was not a champion.

81 Grief to me, after the hard struggle,
    The bearing of death's agony in anguish,
    And worse, heavy grief to me, the sight
    Of our warriors falling headlong.
    And long the moaning and the mourning
    For the home soil's stalwart men,
    Rhufon and Gwgon, Gwion and Gwlyged,
    Boldest men at their posts, staunch under stress.
    May their souls be, after the battle,
    Made welcome in heaven's land, home of plenty.

82 He drove back the press across a pool of blood;
    He cut down, boldly, rows that would not retreat.
    Tafloyw, with a flourish, would toss off a glass of mead;
        Before monarchs he'd toss a war-host.
    His counsel was sought where many will not speak;
        Were he crude, he'd not have been heard.
    Before the charge of axe-strokes and sharp-edged swords,
        A feast is held, his voice is called for.

83 War-host's haven,
    His blade a haven,
    With the war-band's vanguard

On the front line
In the day of battle,
In the clash of weapons.
They were heedless
After being drunk
With drinking mead.
There was no escape from
Our joyous charge
On the destined day.
　　When the tale is told
The assault was broken
Of steeds and warriors,
　　Sworn men's fate.

84　When a crowd of cares
Comes on me, I brood on my fear.
Breath failing
As in running, at once I weep.
The dear one I mourn,
The dear one I'd loved, noble stag.
With Argoed's men,
Alas, he always took his place.
Well did he press
Against war-hosts, for rulers' good,
Against rough wood,
Against grief's flood, for the feasts.
He escorted us to a blazing fire
And to white fleece and sparkling wine.
Geraint from the south, the war-cry was raised,
Gleaming white, fair the look of his shield.
Gracious lord of the spear, praiseworthy lord,
The sea's benevolence, I know its nature,
I know Geraint: you were a bountiful prince.

85　Ungrudging his praise, his renown,
Unbudging anchor in combat,
Unconquerable eagle of wrathful men.
Bent on battle, Eiddef was comely,
His swift horses were foremost in conflict,
　　Cub fostered on wine from the cup.
Before a green grave, his cheek turning pale,
A reveller he was, above clear mead from the cup.

65

86 Ruin to all low ground, a flood:
   His fetter, the same fullness.
     Rent the front of his shield,
     Hating hindrance, enraged,
      Rhufoniawg's defender.
   They were called on again, each side of the Aled,
   In the battle of horses and bloodstained war-gear.
     Immovable war-host,
     Mighty men in battle,
     Red the parish ground
      When they are aroused.
   In hard fighting he'd slash with his blade;
   He'd bear a harsh warning of battle.
   He would furnish song for New Year's.
   There could come before the son of Erfai,
   There could come before the proud boar,
   Any lady and maiden and noble.
   And when he was son of a rightful ruler,
   Among the men of Gwynedd, Clyd the merciful's blood,
     Before earth covered his cheek,
     Bountiful, prudent, undaunted.
      After praise and favour, sad
   The grave of Garthwys Hir from Rhufoniog's land.

* * *

88 A loss has come to me, unlooked-for.
   There comes, there will come, none heavier.
   Was not nourished in hall one bolder than he
     Or more steadfast in battle.
   And at Rhyd Benclwyd, foremost his horses,
   Far-reaching his fame, riddled his shield.
   And before Gwair Hir was hid under turf
   He'd earn mead-horns, Fferfarch's only son.

THE GODODDIN (*Text B*)

* * *

3 Standing stone on cleared ground [...]
Fair play before Gododdin's border [...]
    He brought the luxury
    Of wine tents for the land's good.
    Season of storm,
    Foreign ships, foreign war-band,
    Treacherous war-band,
Splendid ranks, swift before a champion.
    From Din Dywyd
    It came upon us, came to us.
Grugyn's shield, facing battlefields its front was shredded.

4 Ruin to all low ground, a flood:
His like, the same fullness.
    Rent the front of his shield,
    Hating hindrance, reckless,
        Rhufoniawg's defender.
They were seen again, on each side of the Aled,
His war-steeds and his bloodstained war-gear.
    They must be steadfast,
    Greatly gifted,
   Valiant men
        When they are aroused.
In hard fighting he'd slash with his blade:
A hundred bore a bitter warning from battle.
    He would furnish song for New Year's.
There could come before the son of Urfai,
There could come before the proud boar
Any lady and maiden and noble.
And since he was son of a rightful king,
Lord of Gwynedd's men, of Cilydd the merciful's blood,
    Before earth covered his cheek,
    Bountiful, prudent, sought out for
    His gifts and fame, and sad
Is the grave of Gorthyn Hir from Rhufuniog's border.

5 For the feast, most sad, disastrous,
For settled, for desolate land,
Three boars primed for combat at cock-crow

[...] Morien with his spear,
[...]
Against pagans and Gaels and Picts.
Very dear, the stiff red corpse of Bradwen,
Right hand of Gwenabwy fab Gwen.

6 For the feast, most sad, disastrous,
Heavy, grievous, most desolate land,
The battle-leader,
The bearded warrior [...]
[...] beholding Eidyn and its land.
His gauntlet was raised
Against pagans and Gaels and Picts.
Who tugs a wolf's mane without spear in hand
    Needs a brave heart under his cloak.
I will sing so that Morien should not die,
Right hand of Gwenabwy fab Gwen.

7 Good fortune, Addonwy, you'd vowed to me:
What Bradwen did, you'd do; you'd slash, you'd burn.
You held neither far wing nor front line.
Bold eye [...]
I have not seen from sea to sea
A horseman who'd be worse than [...]

8 Three hundred, gold-torqued, launched the assault,
Defending the land: there was slaughter.
Although they were being slain, they slew,
And till the world's end, they'll be honoured.
And of all those who went, companions,
Alas, save one man, none escaped.

9 Three hundred, gold-torqued,
Aggressive, accomplished;
Three hundred proud men,
Of one mind, well-armed;
Three hundred fierce horses
Bore them into battle.
Three hounds and three hundred:
Alas, they did not come back.

10 Savage in battle, stubborn under stress,
There was no truce he'd make in combat.

In the day of wrath he would not shun strife:
A raging boar was Bleiddig mab Eli.
He guzzled wine from brimming glasses.
And on the day of conflict he'd perform a feat
On a white stallion before he died:
He'd leave crimsoned corpses behind him.

11 Hard-pressed before the ford, he'd stiffen his troops,
War-band's firm spear.
Splendid his assault, mind bent on glory.
Skilful charge
His joyous charge, I heard his war-cry.
He'd make men lie low
And wives widows, before his death.
The right of Bleiddgi's son:
Confronting spears, to form a rampart.

12 Splendid your conduct [...]
[...] spears from him [...] you'd put to flight.
When all would turn back, you'd attack.
Were it wine, the blood of all those you struck dead,
You'd have plenty for three years and four:
You'd make short work of it for your steward.
Heaven's home be yours, because you would not flee.
World-famed was unshakable Breichiawl.

13 When he'd raid in the borderland, great was his fame;
He would earn his wine, gold-torqued warrior.
He'd give gleaming array to the brave;
He'd defend a hundred men, lordly hero,
Noble by nature, foreign horseman,
Cian's only son, from beyond Bannawg.
The Gododdin will not say on the field of battle
There was anyone fiercer than Llif.

14 Anchor, Deifr-router,
Serpent with fearsome sting,
Unbudgeable rock
    In the war-host's front line,
Power in readiness,
Violence under stress,
Overpayment
    Of spears' pressure:
Rightly are you called, for your loyal deeds,

Foremost leader, wall of all your countrymen,
Tudfwlch, forceful in battle, barred fortress.

15 Anchor, Deifr-router,
Serpent with fearsome sting
In the war-host's front line.
Rightly are you called, for your loyal deeds,
Foremost leader, wall of every people,
Merin fab Madiain, blessed was your birth.

16 Anchor, Deifr-router,
Unbudgeable rock
In the war-host's front line.
Many were crimsoned,
Both horses and men,
Before the Gododdin.
Fleet the baying hounds,
The war-band's rising,
Full cover of mist,
Before Merin's stronghold.

17 Shield hammered hard, he'd yield to no one:
He nursed his thirst for honour.
Heedless of war-gear and horses in the van of battle,
They'd plant bloodied spears of holly.
When my comrade was struck, he'd strike others:
He would bear no affront.
Firm in guarding the ford, he was proud
When his was the prize portion in the hall.

18 True what Tudlew told you,
That no man's horses overtook Marchlew.
Though not reared for hurdles, for hardship,
Strong was his sword-stroke at his station.
He'd scatter ashen spears from his hand's clutch
Atop his steaming trim bay.

19 Heaven's haven, longed-for land's home:
Woe is ours from yearning and ceaseless sorrow.
When noblemen came from Din Eidyn, a band
Of picked men from each provident region,
In strife with Lloegr's mingled war-hosts,
Nine-score to one on each mail-clad man,

Piled-up horses and war-gear and silken garments,
Gwaednerth held his own in battle.

20 Of Mynyddawg's band, when they launched the assault,
Bright ranks round the wine-bowl, they'd dined together:
For Mynyddawg's feast, my mind is woeful,
Too many have I lost of my true kinsmen.
Of three hundred, gold-torqued, who charged on Catraeth,
Alas, save one man, they did not escape.

21 Gododdin's picked men on shaggy mounts,
Swan-white steeds, war-harness drawn tight,
And in the vanguard attacking the war-host,
Fighting for Eidyn's forests and mead.
    Through Mynyddawg's war-plan
    Shields went spinning,
    Blades descended
        On pallid cheeks.
They loved [...] attacking;
They bore no disgrace, men who would not flee.

22 I drank deeply of mead in my turn,
Wine-fed before Catraeth, at a single gulp.
When he slashed with his blades, unbudging in battle,
    He was no sorry sight.
He was no ugly spectre, providing protection,
Baneful shield-bearer, Madawg of Elfed.

23 When he came to a conflict
No thought of survival.
Aeron's avenger,
He would charge, gold-adorned,
Britons' defender.
High-spirited, Cynon's horses.

24 Standing stone on cleared ground, on cleared ground a hill
On Gododdin's border [...]
    Foreign ship, foreign war-band
    [...]
    [...] motley war-band
    From Din Dywyd
        Came upon us.
Grugyn's shield, before battle's bull its front was shredded.

25 Gold on fortress wall,
    Ardent assault,
    Sinful not to be roused for battle.
    One [...] Saxon
    Rewarded the birds.
    [...]
    [...]
    The living will tell
    Of a leader's doings,
    Of one like a lightning-bolt.
    The living will not say
    That on the day of slaughter
    Cynhafal did not lend his support.

26 Who'll become heir
    With Heinif gone?
    One above the throng,
    Of the noblest name,
    He slew a great host
    To gain renown.
    He slew, son of Nwython,
    Of gold-torqued warriors
    A hundred princes
    That he might be praised.
    He was better when he went
    With the men to Catraeth:
    Wine-nourished man,
    Generous-hearted,
    A man brisk in battle,
    Mail-coat router,
    He was rough, he was reckless,
    On his stallion's back.
    There armed for battle,
    Brisk his spear and his shield
    And his sword and his dagger,
    Than Heinif ab Nwython
    No better man.

27 From beyond Merin Iddew, valiant in battle,
    Thrice as fierce as a fierce lion,
    Bubon wrought with mighty wrath.

28 Natural – on a charger to defend Gododdin;
       In the vanguard, swift his grey steed;
    Natural – that he should be fleet as a stag;
    Natural – before Deifr's picked men he'd attack;
    Natural – what he said, Golystan's son, would be heard,
       Though his father was no high lord;
    Natural – on Mynyddawg's behalf, shattered shields ;
    Natural – a crimson spear before Eidyn's lord, Urfai.

29 Stewards could not bear the hall's clamour.
    From the war-band, an outburst of fighting
    Like a roaring fire when kindled.
    Tuesday, they donned their comely war-gear;
    Wednesday, their common cause was savage;
    Thursday, envoys were pledged;
    Friday, carcasses were calculated;
    Saturday, unhindered their working as one;
    Sunday, crimson blades were shared by all;
    Monday, men seen hip deep in bloodshed.
    The Gododdin say that after long hard labour
    Before Madawg's tent on their return
    [There would come but one man in a hundred.]

30 He attacked in full force for eastern herds.
    Like a lion, I honour him:
    At Gwanannon, for mead the greatest valour.
    And a lucky warrior, splendid leader,
    Renowned Eithinyn mab Boddw Adaf.

31 Superb men, they have left us.
    They were wine-fed and mead-fed.
       For Mynyddawg's banquet
       I am grief-stricken,
          For a stern warrior's loss.
       Like peals of thunder
       Shields would resound
          Before Eithinyn's onslaught.

32 Early rising, at dawning,
    When warriors attack in a war-host,
    In the lead, leading, pursuing,
    Before a hundred he charged in front.
    He was as greedy for corpses

As for quaffing mead or wine,
   So eagerly was it
   He'd strike an enemy,
Ithael, fierce in assault.

33 Early rising, in the morning,
In conflict with a chief before the border,
   He was a bitter fighter
   In the van of battle,
   A beloved friend
     Where he chose to be.
He was mannerly, he was stern;
He was a dark-garbed spear-lord.

34 His blades were seen in the war-band,
Contending with a stubborn foe.
Before his shield's clamour they'd cower:
They'd flee before Eidyn's hill, countless men.
Those his hand grasped would not leave him.
   There were candles for him, and chanting.
Stubborn, shield shredded, when hard pressed he'd press on;
   He'd not strike twice: he'd strike when struck.
Frequent after the feast was his gift to the enemy;
   Bitterly was he dealt with.
And before he was covered with clods of earth
Edar earned the right to drink his mead.

35 Boldest man in a fortress,
Splendid supporter,
Bright [...]
Fierce [...]
[...]
[...] his purpose.
The Gododdin will not say, in the day of slaughter,
That Cynhafal did not lend his support.

36 Crimsoned blades
Covering the ground,
   Hero ruddied in his rage,
Champion, slayer,
He would be joyful,
   Wolvish at his post, war-host's wolf.
War-band's herb-garden,

Champion slaying,
  Before he was blinded, no weakling.
Rightly are you called, for your loyal deeds,
Foremost helmsman, wall of all your countrymen,
Tudfwlch, forceful in battle, barred fortress.

37 He encountered a bitter foe,
  Wrathful slayer of a raider band.
He was not hid from sight and outlawed;
Erf was no bitter-sweet fellow-drinker.
Grey horses snorted under his protection;
It did Pobddelw's land no good.
He withdrew, battle's bull, not an acre,
Stubborn in purpose, true leader.

38 He thrust beyond three hundred of the boldest;
He would mow down centre and wing.
He was worthy, in the van of the most bountiful war-band;
He'd bestow horses from his herd in winter.
He would sate black crows on the fortress wall
  Though he was not Arthur.
He did mighty deeds in combat,
A rampart in the front line, Gwawrddur.

39 Song most fit for a skilful war-band.
And before the loss of Aeron's door-bolt
The beaks of grey eagles gave praise to his hand;
  Enraged he furnished food for scavengers.
For the sake of Mynyddawg, ruler of men,
He set his side against enemy spears.
Before Catraeth the gold-torqued were brisk:
They struck, they cut down those who stood firm.
They were far from their land, whelps of war.
Seldom in battle from among Gododdin's Britons
  Was there one much better than Cynon.

40 Song most fit for a war-band is found:
Soldiers were embroiled around Catraeth;
Bloodstained garments, trod on, were trampled;
  Battle's branches were trampled.
  Retribution for mead-payment,
    It was made good by corpses.
Cibno will not say, after battle's furor,
Though he took communion, that he had his due.

41 His hand provided food for birds.
I revere him, mighty war-lord,
Savage warrior and slasher.
>   He was garbed in gold
>   In the front line,
>   In war-lords' fierce contention.
>   Battle's speckled wine-steward,
>   Third Fearsome One,
>   War-cry's pursuer,
>   Ferocious bear in attack,
>   War-host's arouser,
>   Talk of the war-band,
>   Comely was Cibno mab Gwengad.

42 Song most fitting a well-trained war-band.
World's cheerful small corner, he was spendthri

THE FALL OF RHEGED

1 Unhwch would counsel, savage warrior,
Enraged in peace parleys:
Better slay than supplicate.

Unhwch would counsel, savage warrior,
He wreaks carnage in combat:
I will lead Llwyfenydd's war-bands.

Unhwch would counsel, savage warrior:
It was said at Drws Llech
Dunawd fab Pabo will not run.

Unhwch would counsel, savage warrior,
Bitter wrath, the sea's laughter,
Inciter, triumphant lord.

Urien of Rheged, ardent, eagle's grip,
Foe to Unhwch, bountiful, bold,
Fierce in war, victorious ruler.

Urien of Rheged, ardent, eagle's grip,
Foe to Unhwch, ample owner,
Sea's store, comely streams, men's table.

2 A head I bear at my side:
   He led the charge between war-bands;
   It was Cynfarch's proud son owned it.

   A head I bear at my side:
   Kind Urien's head, he ruled a host,
   And on his white breast, a black crow.

   A head I bear on my belt:
   Kind Urien's head, he ruled a court,
   And on his white breast, crows banquet.

   A head I bear in my hand:
   He was shepherd for Yrechwydd,
   Noble-hearted, expender of spears.

   A head I bear next my thigh:
   He was the land's shield, he was battle's wheel,
   He was war's pillar, foe's snare.

   A head I bear on my left side:
   Better his life than his grave.
   He was the old folks' bulwark.

   A head I bear from Penawg's slope:
   Far-roving his war-bands;
   Head of Urien, lavishly praised.

   A head I bear on my shield:
   It did not dishonour me.
   Woe's my hand, for slashing my lord.

   A head I bear on my arm:
   He furnished for Brennych's land,
   After battle, a burden of biers.

   A head I bear from beside a stake:
   Head of Urien, valiant lord,
   And though Doomsday come, no matter.

   A head I bear in my hand's hard grasp:
   Bountiful lord, he once ruled a land;
   Prydain's pillar-head, it was removed.

A head I nurse that nursed me:
I know it did me no good,
Woe's my hand, it wrought harshly.

A head I bear from beside a hill:
On his mouth the frothing
Blood: woe's Rheged from today.

It has twisted my arm; it has savaged my ribs;
My heart it has broken:
A head I nurse that nursed me.

3 His slender white body is buried today
Under earth and stone:
Woe's my hand, Owain's father slain.

His slender white body is buried today
Within earth and oak:
Woe's my hand, my cousin slain.

His slender white body is buried today;
Under stone it was left:
Woe's my hand, the fate that befell me.

His slender white body is buried today
Within earth and turf:
Woe's my hand, Cynfarch's son slain.

His slender white body is buried today
Under earth and gravel:
Woe's my hand, the fate that beset me.

His slender white body is buried today
Under earth and nettles:
Woe's my hand, the fate designed for me.

His slender white body is buried today
Under earth and grey stone:
Woe's my hand, the fate that was mine.

4 Hard to find till Doomsday, our gathering
Around drinking-horns, around dipper,
Lord's retinue, Rheged's war-band.

Hard to find till Doomsday, our welcoming
Around drinking-horns, around dish,
Lord's retinue, Rheged's men.

5 Efrddyl's cheerless tonight
With many another:
At Aber Lleu, Urien slain.

Efrddyl's sad for his tribulation tonight
And the fate that beset me:
At Aber Lleu, her brother slain.

6 Friday I saw the great
Sorrow of Christendom's war-hosts,
Like a swarm that lacks a queen.

Rhun Rhyfeddfawr, he gave me
A hundred troops and a hundred shields,
And one troop was by far the best.

Rhun, suppliant's lord, he gave me
A hundred homesteads and a hundred oxen,
And one homestead was better than any.

In life, Rhun, ruler of war,
He curbed those with wicked ways,
Shackles on the steeds of the wicked.

7 How well I know my affliction:
Lively everyone, every summer;
None know anything of me.

8 Dunawd was bent, slaughter's horseman,
On making corpses in Yrechwydd,
Facing the onslaught of Owain.

Unhwch was bent, region's lord,
On wreaking carnage in Yrechwydd,
Facing the onslaught of Pasgen.

Gwallawg was bent, strife's horseman,
On making carcasses in Yrechwydd,
Facing the onslaught of Elphin.

Bran fab Ymellyrn was bent
On banishing me, on burning my hearths,
Wolf who'd yelp at a gap.

Morgant was bent, he and his men,
On banishing me, on burning my land,
Shrew who'd scrape at a crag.

9 I saw when Elno was slain
A blade scourged the rampart
Of Pyll and his people's camp.

Again I saw, after the war-cry,
A shield on Urien's shoulder:
Second best there was Elno Hen.

10 Need has come on Yrechwydd
From a horseman's death under spears:
Will there ever be another Urien?

Bald is my lord, bold is his nature:
Warriors love not his hatred.
He poured out a ruler's riches.

Urien's passion is grievous to me,
Raider in every region,
In the wake of Llofan Llaw Ddifro.

Tranquil the breeze next the slope.
A rare thing, one worthy of praise.
Save for Urien, no leader matters.

11 Many a lively hound and vigorous hawk
Were fed on its floor
Before this place was ruins.

This hearth, with its blanket of grey,
More common, once, on its floor
Mead, and drunken men pleading.

This hearth, nettles hide it:
While its defender was living
[It saw many a suppliant.]

This hearth, borage hides it:
When Owain and Elphin lived
Its cauldron would stew plunder.

This hearth, grey lichen hides it:
More common, once, for its food,
A savage fearless sword-stroke.

This hearth, a layer of briers hides it:
Blazing wood was its due.
Rheged had the habit of giving.

This hearth, thorns hide it:
More common, once, for its warriors
The friendly favour of Owain.

This hearth, reeds hide it:
More common, once, were bright
Tapers, and true companions.

This hearth, dock leaves hide it:
More common, once, on its floor
Mead, and drunken men pleading.

This hearth, a hog roots in it:
More common, once, were men's
Revels, and mirth around mead-horns.

This hearth, a hen scratches it:
Hardship could not harm it
While Owain and Urien lived.

This pillar, and that one there,
More common, once, around them
War-band's revels, and path to reward.

POEMS FROM THE LLYWARCH HEN SAGA

INVITATION TO LLANFAWR

'Noble rider of the field,
Echel's sword, Urien's fame,
Can you give an old man lodging?

'Noble rider of the plain,
When God cared for my welfare,
I ate not acorns like swine.'

'Llywarch Hen, be not downcast.
Lodging, friend, you will have.
Dry your eyes. Hush. Do not weep.'

'I am old, I do not grasp you.
Give me counsel: where shall I seek?
Urien dead, I am in need.

'Is your counsel to seek out Brân,
Splendid, cordial, renowned,
All the sons of Urien dead?'

'Trust not Brân; trust not Dunawd.
Do not seek them in hardship.
Herdsman of calves, take Llanfawr's road.'

'A Llanfawr lies overseas
Where the ocean roars beside it.
Lord, I know not: is it that one?

'A Llanfawr lies beyond Bannawg
Where the Clwyd enters Clywedawg,
And I know not: is it that, lord?'

'Trace the length of the Dyfrdwy
From Meloch to Traweryn.
Herdsman of calves, they lead to Llanfawr.'

LAMENT FOR PYLL

When my son Pyll was slain, there were shattered shreds
    And hair matted with blood
    And floods on the banks of the Fraw.

One could put up a hall with planks of shields
    While he stood his ground
    That were shattered by Pyll's hand.

    My choice, among all my sons,
    When each attacked his foe,
    Fair Pyll, like flame through a flue.

Well it was he set thighs on his steed's saddle,
    Both near and afar:
    Fair Pyll, like flame through a chimney.

He was a noble warlord; he was slow to make peace;
    He was a fort on the border.
    Fair Pyll, he was a golden leader.

    When he'd stop before his tent
    On a spirited stallion
    Pyll's wife could boast of a man.

    Facing Pyll, the strong man's skull was crushed.
Scarce is a haven where one might hide:
    The weak man's left defenceless.

    Fair Pyll, far-reaching your fame,
I rejoice in you, that you came as my son,
    And acknowledge you gladly.

    The shield that I gave to Pyll,
    Before he slept it was riddled.
    Bitter, to leave it neglected.

Though a horde from England came to Wales,
    And many from far off,
    Pyll showed them what he was made of.

EXHORTATION TO MAENWYN

Maenwyn, when I was your age,
No foot would trample my mantle,
None would plough my land without bloodshed.

Maenwyn, when I was eager,
With youngsters to follow me,
No foe would break through my border.

Maenwyn, when I was aroused,
Following me my youngsters,
No foe was fond of my fury.

Maenwyn, when I was strong-limbed,
I was savage in slaughter.
I did man's work, though I was a lad.

Maenwyn, consider with care:
Need of counsel's neglected.
Let Maelgwn seek another stweard.

My choice, a warrior wearing
Armour, sharp as a thorn:
No vain effort, whetting Maen.

Blessed be the strange old woman
          Who called from her hut door,
     'Maenwyn, leave not your knife behind.'

LLYWARCH AND GWÊN

'Worn thin is my shield borne at my left side:
          Though I'm old, I can hold it.
     I'll stand guard at Rhodwydd Forlas.'

'Arm not after feast; be untroubled of mind.
          Keen the wind; bitterness harsh.
     My mother says I am your son.'

'Well do I know in my heart
We spring from the self-same stock.
You are wasting good time, Oh Gwên.'

'Keen my spear, bright in combat:
I am ready to guard the ford.
Though I come not back, God keep you.'

'If you win free, I shall see you.
If you are slain, I shall mourn you.
Forfeit not honour, hard-pressed.'

'I'll not forfeit your honour, contentious man,
    When warriors arm for the border.
I'll bear hardship before I give way.'

'Running, the wave on the strand.
Resolve will quickly break.
Fight pledged, it's flight for the glib.'

'I intend to do what I say.
Shatter will spears where I stand.
I'll not say I will not flee.'

'Soft the fens, hard the hillside.
From horse-hoof bank's edge crumbles.
A pledge unperformed is worthless.'

'Streams spread round a fort's rampart.
    As for me, I am ready:
Shield-face shattered, before I retreat.'

'The horn that Urien gave you,
Its gold band about its mouth,
Blow it, if need comes on you.'

'Though I dread the need, facing England's warriors,
    I'll not sully my worth.
I will not awaken maidens.'

'When I was that youngster's age
Who puts on his spurs of gold,
It was swiftly I'd rush the spear.'

85

'Surely what you say must be so,
   Alive, your witness slain.
No oldster was weak when young.'

LAMENT FOR GWÊN

Gwên at Llawen stood guard last night:
   Hard-pressed, he did not flee.
Sad the tale on the green mound.

Gwên at Llawen stood guard last night,
   The shield on his shoulder.
Since he was my son, he was bold.

Gwên at Llawen stood guard last night,
   His shield at the ready.
Since he was my son, no escape.

Gwên sturdy of thigh stood guard last night
   On the bank of Rhyd Forlas.
Since he was my son, he did not flee.

Gwên, defender, it grieves my heart:
   A great loss is your death.
Hateful, no friend, is your slayer.

Gwên, well I knew your nature.
Yours, eagle's rush in river-mouths.
Were I lucky, you'd have escaped.

A wave booms; it covers the ebb.
When warriors go into battle,
Gwên, woe's the dotard who mourns you.

A wave booms; it covers the tide.
When warriors launch the attack,
Gwên, woe's the dotard who's lost you.

My son was a man; he was rightfully bold;
   He was Urien's nephew.
At Rhyd Forlas Gwên was slain.

Four and twenty sons have been mine,
A golden-torqued princely band.
Gwên was the best of them.

Four and twenty sons were once mine,
A golden-torqued princely host.
Gwên was his father's best son.

Four and twenty sons were my own,
Golden-torqued princely noblemen.
Next to Gwên they were mere lads.

Four and twenty sons in Llywarch's household,
        Brave men, fierce in combat.
    Too great fame becomes a fault.

Four and twenty sons, bred of my body:
        Because of my tongue, they were slain.
    Small fame is best: they were lost.

COMPLAINT IN OLD AGE

Before I was crook-backed, I had word-craft:
        My exploits were honoured.
    Argoed's men feasted me always.

Before I was crook-backed, I was bold:
    I was welcomed in the mead-hall
    Of Powys, Wales' paradise.

Before I was crook-backed, I was brilliant:
    My spear was frontmost, first-piercer.
    I'm hunchbacked, heavy-hearted, wretched.

Wooden crook, it's harvest-time:
    Red the bracken; stalks yellow.
    I've done with what I'm fond of.

Wooden crook, it's winter-time:
    Men are loud over liquor.
    Ungreeted is my bedside.

Wooden crook, it's springtime:
Cuckoos russet, clear their complaint.
I'm unloved by any maiden.

Wooden crook, it's summer-time:
Furrow is russet, shoots furling.
I loathe the look of your beak.

Wooden crook, familiar stick,
Prop up one old and heartsick,
Llywarch, forever babbling.

Wooden crook, be compliant:
Prop me up even better.
Llywarch am I, long-winded.

Wooden crook, sturdy stick,
God allows me support. You'll be called
A trusty staff for getting about.

Old age makes a mock of me
From my hair to my teeth,
And the shaft the young ones loved.

Old age makes me a mock
From my hair to my teeth,
And the shaft the women loved.

Wind brisk; white the fringe of the trees.
Stag bold; hillside hard.
Frail the old man, rouses slowly.

This leaf, wind is tossing it about:
Ah, sorry its lot.
It is old; it was born this year.

What I've loved since a lad is my loathing,
Girl, stranger, untried steed.
For me they are not fitting.

Four things I've ever most hated
Combine forces all at once,
Cough and age, sickness and grief.

I'm old, I'm alone, I'm misshapen, cold,
    Whose bed once was honoured.
I'm wretched, I'm bent in three.

I'm old, bent in three, I'm fitful, witless.
    I'm simple, I'm boorish.
Those who loved me love me not.

No maids love me; no one comes to see me.
    I cannot call about.
Alas, death will not visit me.

  No sleep, no joy visit me
  Since Llawr and Gwên were slain.
  I'm a cross carcass, I'm old.

Sorry the lot allotted to Llywarch
    Since the night he was born:
Long labour, with no relief.

POEMS FROM THE HELEDD SAGA

LAMENT FOR CYNDDYLAN

Stand outside, maidens, and look on
    The land of Cynddylan.
    Pengwern's court is a blazing fire.
    Woe to the young who'll beg for a cloak.

One tree in a hedgerow under attack,
    It escapes but seldom.
    What God wills, let it be done.

Cynddylan, ice in winter his heart,
    Thrust a boar through its head.
    He paid dearly for the beer of Tren.

Cynddylan, a spring heath-fire his heart,
    His countrymen's blessing,
  Defended Tren, desolate town.

  Cynddylan, borderland's fair pillar,
  Battle's chain-clad, stubborn lord,
  Defended Tren, his father's town.

  Cynddylan, a greyhound's heart,
When he alighted in combat's fury,
  He would slaughter many.

  Cynddylan, a wild boar's heart,
When he alighted in battle's onslaught,
  Layer upon layer of corpses.

  Cynddylan, a falcon's heart,
  Bird of prey, fiercely ravening,
  Stubborn cub of Cyndrwyn.

Cynddylan, Culhwch warrior, lion,
    Pursuing wolf in attack,
  The boar comes not back to his father's town.

Cynddylan, while he was spared he'd depart,
    His heart just as joyful,
  To battle as to a beerfest.

Cynddylan of Powys, cloaked in purple,
    Guests' hostel, lordly life,
  For Cyndrwyn's cub there's keening.

  Cynddylan the fair, Cyndrwyn's son,
  Unworthy to wear a beard round his nose
  The man no better than a maiden.

  Cynddylan, you are a harrier:
  You mean not to wear grey hair.
  At Trebwll, shattered your shield.

  Cynddylan, block the hillside
  Where the English come today.
  Concern for one person's worthless.

Cynddylan, block the passage
Where the English come through Tren.
One tree isn't called a forest.

THE EAGLE OF PENGWERN

Eagle of Pengwern, grey-crested, tonight
    Uplifted its war-cry,
  Avid for Cynddylan's flesh.

Eagle of Pengwern, grey-crested, tonight
    Uplifted its shrieking,
  Avid for flesh I cherished.

Eagle of Pengwern, grey-crested, tonight
    Uplifted its talon,
  Avid for flesh I cherish.

Eagle of Pengwern, it will cry long tonight.
    It will feast on men's blood.
  Tren's called an ill-fated town.

Eagle of Pengwern, long it cries tonight.
    It banquets on men's blood.
  Tren was called a shining town.

BASCHURCH

Baschurch, his resting place tonight,
    His final confinement,
  Battle's prop, heart of Argoed's people.

Baschurch, it is ploughed land tonight.
    It was my tongue did it.
  It is ruddied; too much is my longing.

Baschurch, it is narrow tonight
    For the heir of Cyndrwyn,
  The soil of fair Cynddylan's small plot.

Baschurch, it is fallow ground tonight;
    Its clover is bloodied.
  It is ruddied; too full is my heart.

Baschurch, it lost its high honours
    After English warriors slew
  Cynddylan and Elfan of Powys.

Baschurch, it is in ruins tonight;
    Its warriors are no more.
  God knows this, and I here.

Baschurch, it is glowing embers tonight,
    And I am heart-struck.
  It is ruddied; too great is my grief.

THE HALL OF CYNDDYLAN

The hall of Cynddylan is dark tonight,
    No fire, no pallet.
  I'll keen now, then be quiet.

The hall of Cynddylan is dark tonight,
    No fire, no candle.
  Who save God will keep me tranquil?

The hall of Cynddylan is dark tonight,
    No fire, no gleaming.
  For your sake my heart's aching.

The hall of Cynddylan, dark is its roof,
    Gone the glad companions.
  Woe's one whose good comes by chance.

The hall of Cynddylan, your beauty's lacking,
    In the grave is your shield.
  While he lived, no gate was shattered.

The hall of Cynddylan's forlorn tonight,
    Gone is its owner.
  Ah death, why let me linger?

The hall of Cynddylan's comfortless tonight
    Atop the rock's fastness,
  No prince, no people, no prowess.

The hall of Cynddylan is dark tonight,
    No fire, no singing.
  Cheeks wear out with weeping.

The hall of Cynddylan is dark tonight,
    No fire, no household.
  Frequent my tears at nightfall.

The hall of Cynddylan, seeing it stabs me,
    No roofing, no fire.
  Dead my lord, myself living.

The hall of Cynddylan's laid waste tonight,
    Gone the staunch champions,
  Elfan, betorqued Cynddylan.

The hall of Cynddylan is cheerless tonight,
    Gone the deference paid me,
  No men, no women, to tend it.

The hall of Cynddylan is still tonight,
    Having lost its leader.
  God of mercy, what shall I do.

The hall of Cynddylan, dark is its roof,
    Since they were slain by the English,
  Cynddylan and Elfan of Powys.

The hall of Cynddylan is dark tonight,
    No sons of Cyndrwyn,
  Cynon and Gwiawn and Gwyn.

The hall of Cynddylan, it hurts me each hour:
    Gone the great commotion
  I once saw at your hearthside.

SISTERS

Time was, when they were gracious,
·Cyndrwyn's daughters were loved,
Heledd, Gwladus, and Gwenddwyn.

I was pleased with having sisters.
I have utterly lost them all,
Ffreuer, Meddwyl, and Meddlan.

I had other sisters as well.
I lost all of them together,
Gwledyr, Meisir, and Ceinfryd.

BROTHERS

My brothers were slain at one stroke,
Cynan, Cynddylan, Cynwraith,
Defending Tren, desolate town.

Princes did not trample on Cynddylan's nest:
He never gave way a foot.
His mother nurtured no weakling.

Brothers I had, not lacking,
Who grew like hazel branches.
One by one, they've all gone.

Brothers I had God has taken from me.
My cursed fortune caused it.
They did not win fame by falsehood.

FFREUER

Blest is Ffreuer: how hurtful it is tonight,
With the household lost.
Through my tongue's evil fate they were slain.

Blest is Ffreuer: how sad it is tonight,
After Elfan's death,
And Cyndrwyn's eagle, Cynddylan.

It's not Ffreuer's death grieves me tonight:
    For my slain brothers
  I'll wake, I'll weep, come morning.

It's not Ffreuer's death causes me pain
    From twilight till dead of night.
  I'll wake, I'll weep, at dawnlight.

It's not Ffreuer's death that haunts me tonight,
    And makes my cheeks sallow,
  And my tears red by my bedside.

  Fair Ffreuer, brothers reared you:
  They sprang from no base stock,
  Men who'd not nurture cowardice.

  Fair Ffreuer, brothers were yours:
  When they heard a mighty war-host,
  Their faith did not desert them.

  Myself and Ffreuer and Meddlan,
  Though war may rage in each region,
  We care not, our side won't be slain.

THE WHITE TOWN

  White town on the wooded hill-breast,
  Its stock-in-trade always was this,
  Blood on the face of its grass.

  White town in its countryside,
  Its stock-in-trade, the green graves,
  The blood underneath men's feet.

  White town within its valley,
Festive the birds in battle's butchery:
    Its people have perished.

  White town between Tren and Trodwyd,
More common were torn shields coming from combat
    Than oxen at mid-day rest.

White town between Tren and Trafal,
More common was blood on the face of its grass
Than ploughing of fallow.

HELEDD WANDERER

This mountain, although it's taller,
I'll not bear it to lead my cow.
It's light to some, my garment.

Before my blanket was the tough skin of a goat
    Hungry for holly,
  It made me drunk, the mead of Bryn.

Before my blanket was the tough skin of a goat,
    Young goat fond of holly,
  It made me drunk, the mead of Tren.

After my brothers, in the Hafren's country,
    On the banks of the Dwyryw,
  Alas, God, that I go on living.

After well-trained horses with red-hued trappings
    And golden plumes,
  Lean my leg, I have no mantle.

Edeirniawn's cattle, they'd not go astray,
    They'd go on no one's journey
  In Gorwynion's lifetime, shrewd man.

Edeirniawn's cattle, they'd not go astray,
    With none would they journey,
  In Gorwynion's lifetime, wise man.

Were Gyrthmwl a woman, she'd be weak today,
    Loud would be her outcry:
  She is whole, her men demolished.

The turf of Ercal on fearless men
    Of the line of Morial,
  After it cares for them, crushes them.

Thin the breeze, sorrow thick.
The furrows remain, not those who made them.
Sad, those who were, are no more.

Wandering Heledd I'm called.
Oh God, to whom are given
My brothers' steeds and their lands?

I have fixed my eyes on fallow land
　　From Gorwynion's Mound.
Long the sun's road: longer my memories.

I have gazed from Dinlleu Gwrygon
　　On Ffreuer's country.
Yearning, for my slain brothers.

A MISCELLANY OF POEMS

SONG FOR A SMALL BOY

Specked, specked, Dinogad's coat,
I fashioned it of pelts of stoat.
Twit, twit, a twittering,
I sang, and so eight slaves would sing.
When your daddy went off to hunt,
Spear on his shoulder, club in his hand,
He'd call the hounds so swift of foot:
'Giff, Gaff – seek 'im, seek 'im; fetch, fetch.'
He'd strike fish from a coracle
As a lion strikes a small animal.
When to the mountain your daddy would go,
He'd bring back a stag, a boar, a roe,
A speckled mountain grouse,
A fish from Derwennydd Falls.
Of those your daddy reached with his lance,
Whether a boar or a fox or a lynx,
None could escape unless it had wings.

LAMENT FOR CYNDDYLAN

Fearsome invincible princes' warfare,
Rhiau and Rhirid and Rhiosedd,
And noble Rhigyfarch, ardent leader.
I shall mourn till I enter my oaken grave
Cynddylan's death in all his splendour.

Splendour of sword-play, did I think of
Going to Menai, though I had no ford?
I love him that greets me from Cemais' land,
Dogfeiling's prince, scourge of Cadell's line.
I shall mourn till I enter my humble oak
Cynddylan's death, deep-piercing loss.

Splendour of sword-play, to consider
Going to Menai, though I could not swim.
I love him that greets me from Aberffraw,
Dogfeiling's prince, dread of Cadell's line.
I shall mourn till I enter my silent oak
Cynddylan's death, and his warbands'.

Splendour of sword-play, restorative wine,
I am left with smile gone, old, grieving.
I lost when he fought for Pennawg's wealth
A brave man, unyielding, unsparing.
He attacked, past Tren, the arrogant land.
I shall mourn till I enter steadfast earth
Cynddylan's death, dear to fame.

Splendour of sword-play, how good the fortune
That Cynddylan had, lord of warfare.
Seven hundred picked men in his war-host,
When Pyd's son wished, how ready he was.
No bridal took place, he died unwed.
God knows the parish where he was buried.
I shall mourn till I enter the grave's acre
Cynddylan's death, nobility's fame.

Splendour of sword-play, how well I know it,
Every fish and beast will be finest.
To violence I've lost, men most valiant,
Rhiau and Rhirid and Rhiadaf

And noble Rhigyfarch, lord of all borders.
They drove their spoils from Taf's meadows;
Captives complained; cattle lowed, bellowed.
I shall mourn till I enter the narrowest plot
Cynddylan's death, famed on all borders.

Splendour of sword-play, do you see this?
My heart is burning like a firebrand.
I praised their men's and their women's riches:
    They could not refuse me.
Brothers were mine, it was better when they lived,
Strong-fisted cubs, steadfast stronghold.
At Caer Lwytgoed they accomplished it,
Blood beneath crows, and a fresh attack.
They shattered fine shields, Cynddrwyn's sons.
I shall mourn till I enter earth's rest
Cynddylan's death, most famed of lords.

Splendour of sword-play, great the plunder
At Caer Lwytgoed, Morial seized it,
Fifteen hundred cattle at battle's end,
Fourscore horses, and trappings as well.
The wretched archbishop in his four-edged cloak,
No book-grasping monks protected him.
Of those who fell on the fine prince's field
Came not clear from his fray brother to sister.
They came clear with their wounds streaming.
I shall mourn till I enter the sorry plot
Cynddylan's death, of all nobles most famed.

Splendour of sword-play, how pleasant I thought it
When I went through the Pwll and the Alun.
Fresh rushes beneath my feet till bedtime,
Feather pillows beneath my buttocks.
And though I go there, to my own region,
Not one friend remains; birds forbid them.

IN PRAISE OF TENBY

I beg God's grace, guardian of the parish,
Lord of heaven and earth, profoundly wise.

A splendid fort stands atop the flood:
Mirthful at New Year's is a bright headland.
And whenever the ocean booms its boast,
Bards are wont to carouse over mead-cups.
Swiftly the wave surges towards it:
They leave the grey-green sea to the Picts.
And may I, Oh God, for my prayer's sake,
When I keep my pledge, be at peace with you.

A splendid fort stands on the wide water,
A sturdy stronghold, sea-encircled.
Ask, Britain, for whom this is fitting:
Head of ab Erbin's house, may it be yours!
There were troops, there was song in the stockade,
And a cloud-high eagle tracking pale faces:
Before a high lord, before a foe-router,
Far-famed and fierce, they formed ranks.

A splendid fort stands on the ninth wave:
Splendid its people taking their ease.
Their fine life is not based on disdain,
It is not their way to be hard of heart.
I will tell no lie of my welcome:
Better Dyfed's serf than Deudraeth's yeomen.
The host of its free men, keeping a feast,
Comprise, in each pairing, the best in the land.

A splendid fort stands where a crowd creates
Pleasure and praise, and birds are loud.
Merry its melodies on New Year's Eve
For a bountiful lord, bold and brave.
Before he entered the oaken church,
He gave me wine and mead from a crystal cup.

A splendid fort stands on the sea-coast,
Splendidly is granted to each his portion.
I know in Dinbych, seagull gleaming,
The comrades of Bleiddudd, lord of the court.
Mine was the custom on New Year's Eve
Of a place by a prince brilliant in battle,
And a purple cloak, and a banquet's pleasures,
So that I am the tongue of Britain's bards.

A splendid fort stands that is roused by songs:
What honours I wished for were mine.
(I will not say 'rights'; I must keep decorum:
Who learns not this earns no New Year's gift!)
British writings the foremost concern
In that place where waves make their uproar:
May the cell I would frequent long remain.

A splendid fort stands, rising high,
Superb its pleasures, its praise far-famed.
Splendid its bounds, stronghold of heroes,
Withstanding the spray, long are its wings.
Harsh sea-birds assault the crest of the rock.
May wrath be banished beyond the hills,
And Bleiddudd's be the greatest blessing,
His memory kept in mind over ale.

The Lord of harmonious heaven bless them:
May Owain's great-grandson be one with his men.

THE LEPER OF ABER CUAWG

To linger on a hill's my heart's longing;
     Still it does not stir me.
   Brief my journey; bleak my homestead.

   Wind keen, bare the cattle-track.
   As trees don fair summer hues,
   I am feverish today.

I'm not agile; no men I maintain.
     I cannot get about.
   While the cuckoo will, let it sing.

   A loud cuckoo sings at dawn,
A clear song in the dales of Cuawg.
   Better's spendthrift than miser.

In Aber Cuawg cuckoos are singing
     On blossoming branches;
   Loud cuckoo, let it sing long.

In Aber Cuawg cuckoos are singing
    On blossoming branches;
  Woe's the leper who endlessly hears them.

In Aber Cuawg, singing are cuckoos;
    Sadness comes to my heart:
  One who heard them will not hear them too.

I listened to a cuckoo on the ivy-tree:
    My garments are looser;
  Grief for what I loved is greater.

On the height above the mighty oak
I listened to birds' voices.
Cuckoo loud; what they love, all remember.

Singer of endless song, cry full of longing,
    Flitting, hawk in flight,
  Clear-voiced cuckoo in Aber Cuawg.

Bird clamorous; valleys wet.
Bright is the moon; midnight cold.
Sad my mind, grieved by sickness.

Hilltop white; valleys wet; midnight long.
    Every skilful man's admired.
  My reward, an old man's slumber.

Birds clamorous; shingle wet.
Leaves fall; downhearted the outcast.
I won't deny it, I am sick tonight.

Birds clamorous; strand wet.
Bright the heavens; wide-reaching the wave.
Withered the heart with yearning.

Birds clamorous; strand wet.
Wave bright, wide-reaching motion.
What was loved in youth,
I'd love to have it once more.

Birds clamorous on Edrywy's height.
    Hounds' cry loud in the wild.
Birds clamorous again.

Start of summer, fair every shoot.
When warriors speed to the fray
I go not, disease will not let me.

Start of summer, fair the bankside.
When warriors speed to the field
I go not, disease pains me.

Hilltop pallid; ash-tree tips fragile.
From river-mouths spills the bright wave.
Far from my heart is laughter.

For me today is the end of a month
In the lodging that was left me.
Sad my mind; fever's on me.

Clear-sighted the onlooker.
The idle man's well-mannered.
Sad my mind; sickness wastes me.

Cattle in shed; bowl full of mead.
The fortunate wish no disturbance.
Understanding's bond, patience.

Cattle in shed; bowl full of ale.
Ways slippery; shower heavy.
Ford deep; heart ferments treachery.

Treachery ferments wrong-doing.
There'll be pain when it's purged,
The trading of much for little.

Prepared, a pit for the wicked.
When the Lord will judge, long day,
The false will be dark, the true bright.

Drinking-bowls upraised, skilful raider.
    Men cheerful over ale.
Stalks withered; cattle in shed.

I heard the heavy sounding wave,
Loud amid gravel and shingle.
Sad my mind, dejected tonight.

Oak-tops full-branched; ash bitter-tasting.
Cowparsnips sweet; wave laughing.
Cheek hides not the heart's distress.

Frequent the sighing that afflicts me,
As is now my custom.
God allows not good to the wretched.

Good's not allowed to the wretched,
Only sorrow and distress.
God won't undo what he's done.

A youth was leprous; he was a bold leader
In a king's court.
God be kind to the outcast.

Whatever's done in a house of aok
It is a wretch who reads it.
Man's hate here, God's hate on high.

WINTER AND WARFARE

Wind sharp, hill bare, hard to find shelter;
Ford turns foul, lake freezes.
A man could stand on one stalk.

Wave on wave covers the shoreline;
Shrill the shrieks from the peaks of the highlands;
One can scarce stand outside.

Cold the lake-bed from winter's blast;
Reeds withered, stalks broken;
Wind wrathful, woods stripped bare.

Cold the fishes' bed in the ice's shelter;
Stag lean, stalks bearded;
Evening brief, trees bent over.

Snow is falling, white its cover.
Soldiers go not campaigning.
Lakes cold, their colour sunless.

Snow is falling, hoar-frost white.
Idle a shield on an old man's shoulder.
Wind intense, it freezes grass.

Snow is falling upon the ice.
Wind sweeps through thick tree-tops.
Fine a shield on a brave man's shoulder.

Snow is falling, covers the valley.
Soldiers hasten to battle.
I go not, a wound will not let me.

Snow is falling on the slope.
Horse a prisoner; cattle lean.
Today is no summer day.

Snow is falling, white the mountainside.
    Ship's masts bare at sea.
A coward breeds many a scheme.

Gold rims around horns, horns around hosts.
Pathways cold, sky gleaming bright.
Twilight brief, tree-tops bowed down.

Bees in honeycombs; bird cries faint.
        Day bleak [...]
Hill-ridge white-mantled, dawn red.

Bees in shelter, cold lid on the ford;
        Frost freezes when it will.
Evade as one may, death will come.

Bees in captivity, green-hued the sea.
        Stalks withered, hillside hard.
Frigid, bitter, the world today.

Bees in refuge from winter's wetness.
        Stubble pale, hogweed hollow.
Evil trait in a man, cowardice.

Hunched stag seeks the coombe's sheltered end.
    Ice crumbles, countryside bare.
  The brave man survives many battles.

Bankside crumbles from a scrawny stag's hoof.
    High-pitched the screeching wind.
  One scarcely indeed stands outside.

* * *

Winter's first day, dark the top of the heather.
    Spuming the sea-wave.
  Day brief; let your counsel be done.

With shield's shelter and stallion's spirit
    And dauntless brave men,
  Fine the night for routing foes.

Strong the wind, trees stripped bare.
    Stalks withered, stag hardy.
  Faithful Pelis, what land is this?

Though the snow be high on Arfwl Melyn,
    Darkness would not give me grief.
  I could lead the host to Bryn Tyddwl.

Since you make for embankment and ford so readily
    As snow falls on the slope,
  Pelis, how came you so skilful?

Not a worry for me in Britain tonight
    Raiding Nuchein's lord's lands,
  On a white steed following Owain.

Before you bore arms and a shield,
    Defender of Cynwyd's host,
  Pelis, what region reared you?

The man God release from too strait a prison,
    A red-speared leader,
  Owain of Rheged reared me.

* * *

In the morning, at break of day,
When Mwng Mawr Drefydd was attacked,
Mechydd's steeds were not pampered.

Ale will not make me cheerful
Because of the news that was brought me:
Mechydd, branches now cover you.

Since the spearmen of Mwng slew Mechydd,
    Bold lad, I cannot credit it,
  Lord of heaven, you've caused me sadness.

Mechydd ap Llywarch, valiant nobleman,
    Cloak comely, swan-coloured,
  The first to tether his steed.

GERAINT AB ERBIN

Before Geraint, foe's affliction,
I saw white horses red-shanked,
And after battle, bitter grave.

Before Geraint, foe's pursuer,
I saw steeds red-shanked from strife,
And after battle, bitter brooding.

Before Geraint, foe's oppressor,
I saw white steeds, bloody their coats,
And after battle, bitter shelter.

At Llongborth I saw combat's fury,
And more biers than could be counted,
And men red before Geraint's rush.

At Longborth I saw slaughter,
Men contending, and bloodied heads,
Before great Geraint, his father's son.

At Longborth I saw spurs
And men who'd not flee from spears
And wine-drinking from bright glasses.

At Longborth I saw weapons,
Warriors, and blood flowing,
And after battle, bitter burial.

At Longborth I saw Arthur,
Brave soldiers, they'd hew with steel,
Emperor, combat's commander.

At Longborth Geraint was slain,
Brave soldiers from Dyfnaint's lands,
And before they were killed, they'd killed.

IN MEMORIAM

I have been where Gwenddolau was slain,
Son of Ceidio, pillar of songs,
When ravens were croaking for blood.

I have been where Brân was slain,
Son of Ywerydd, of widespread fame,
When carrion crows were croaking.

I have been where Llachau was slain,
Son of Arthur, wondrous in songs,
When ravens were croaking for blood.

I have been where Meurig was slain,
Son of Careian, of honoured fame,
When ravens were croaking for flesh.

I have been where Gwallawg was slain,
Son of a rightful line,
England's bane, son of Lleenawg.

I have been where Britain's warriors were slain,
From the east to the north.
I'm alive; they're in the grave.

I have been where Britain's warriors were slain,
From the east to the south.
I am alive; they are dead.

MOURNING IN MAYTIME

Fairest season, start of summer:
Birds clamorous, shoots fresh;
Plows in furrow, oxen yoked;
Sea green, countryside dappled.

When cuckoos sing on comely branches
    The greater is my sadness,
  Smoke harsh, sleeplessness plain,
  Since my kinsmen are dead and gone.

In hill, in dale, in the isles of the sea,
    In each way one may take,
  From Christ there's no isolation.

Our longing, our friend, our way was to go
    To the land of your exile.
Seven saints, and seven score, and seven hundred
    Have become one assembly:
With Christ they nurtured no fear.

    I beg a gift, may I not be denied,
    Peace, between God and me.
    May mine be the way to glory's portal:
    May I not, Christ, be sad in your assembly.

PRELUDE TO A PILGRIMAGE

    The very first word that I say
    When I rise in the morning:
    Christ's cross, be armour about me.

I clothe me today in my Lord's protection.
    I feel a single sneeze.
    It's not my god: I won't credit it.

    I will clothe myself splendidly.
    I'll not credit an omen, since it's false:
    The One who created me strengthens me.

My mind is bent on a journey,
Intending to take to sea.
A good purpose: may it be rewarded.

My mind is bent on counsel,
Intending to take to sea.
A good purpose: may the Lord be there.

A raven lifts its wing,
Intending to go far off.
A good purpose: may it be better.

A raven raises its wing
Intending to go to Rome.
A good purpose: may it be fine.

Saddle the white-muzzled chestnut,
Eager to run, rough-coated.
Heaven's Lord, God needs be with us.

Saddle the short-haired chestnut,
Smooth-paced in striving, steadily striding.
Where there's a nose, there'll be a sneeze.

Saddle the long-leaping chestnut,
Smooth-paced in striving, eagerly striding.
An unlucky sneeze stays not the brave.

Heavy earth's presence, brambles' leaves thick;
Bitter the horn of sweet mead.
Lord of heaven, speed my journey.

Ruler's Offspring, and triumphant Redeemer,
      And Peter, head of all peoples,
Saint Bridget, bless my voyage.

Intercession's sun, petition's Lord,
      Heavenly Christ, bounty's pillar,
May my action atone for my sin.

MOUNTAIN SNOW

Mountain snow, each region white;
Common the raven calling.
No good comes of too much slumber.

Mountain snow, deep dingle white;
Woods bend before wind's onslaught.
Many couples are in love
And never come together.

Mountain snow, wind tosses it;
Moonlight far-spread, dock-leaves pale.
Rare the rogue who claims no rights.

Mountain snow, stag nimble.
Common in Britain, bold warriors.
It takes time to know an outsider.

Mountain snow, stag in rut;
Ducks on the lake, sea white.
Slow the old, soon overtaken.

Mountain snow, stag roaming.
The heart laughs at what it loves.
Though a tale be told to me,
I know disgrace wherever it be.

Mountain snow, shingle white grit;
Fish in ford, shelter in cave.
Who acts harshly is hated.

Mountain snow, stag in flight.
Common for a lord, gleaming blade,
And mounting a saddle-bow,
And dismounting, anger well-armed.

Mountain snow, stag hunched up.
Many have muttered, truly,
This is not like a summer day.

Mountain snow, stag hunted;
Wind whistling over tower eaves.
Burdensome, Man, is sin.

Mountain snow, stag bounding;
Wind whistling over high white wall.
Common, stillness in beauty.

Mountain snow, stag in dale;
Wind whistling over rooftop.
Evil hides not, wherever it be.

Mountain snow, stag on sea-strand.
An old man misses his youth.
A foul face keeps a man down.

Mountain snow, stag in grove;
Raven dark-black, roebuck swift.
One free and well, strange he should moan.

Mountain snow, stag in rushes;
Marshes freezing, mead in cask.
Common for the injured to moan.

Mountain snow, tower's breast speckled;
Animals search for shelter.
Woe's the wife who has a bad husband.

Mountain snow, crag's breast speckled;
Reeds withered, herd shunning water.
Woe's the man who has a bad wife.

Mountain snow, stag in gully;
Bees are sleeping snugly.
Thief and long night are well-suited.

Mountain snow, liverwort in river.
Reluctant to take offence,
The sluggard won't soon avenge an insult.

Mountain snow, fish in lake;
Falcon proud, prince well-adorned.
One who has all does not moan.

Mountain snow, fir-top red.
Spear-thrusts fierce, frequent.
Ah, my brothers, the yearning.

Mountain snow, wolf swift-footed,
He prowls the edge of the wild.
Common, every hurt for the wretched.

Mountain snow, stag is not sluggish;
Rain is falling from the sky.
Sadness breeds total listlessness.

Mountain snow, deer fleet-footed;
Waves drench the edge of the beach.
The clever conceals his purpose.

Mountain snow, stag in glen;
Tranquil is summer, lake still.
Frost grey-bearded; the brave guard the border.

Mountain snow, wood's breast speckled.
Strong my arm and my shoulder.
May I not live to a hundred.

Mountain snow, reed-tips bare;
Branch tops bent, fish in the deeps.
No skill where learning's lacking.

Mountain snow, fish in ford;
Lean bowed stag seeks the snug coombe.
Yearning for the dead is useless.

Mountain snow, stag in woodland.
One well-off does not go on foot.
The coward breeds many wounds.

Mountain snow, stag on hillside;
Wind whistling over ash-tree tops.
Third foot for the old, his staff.

Mountain snow, stag swimming;
Ducks on lake, the lily white.
The rogue does not wish to listen.

Mountain snow, hens' feet red;
Water shallow where it babbles.
Disgrace grows greater with boasting.

Mountain snow, stag nimble.
Seldom the world concerns me.
Warning to the wretched is worthless.

Mountain snow, white its fleece.
Fine is a friend's dear face
Combined with frequent visits.

Mountain snow, housetops white.
If one's tongue should speak one's mind,
Not a soul would be neighbours.

Mountain snow, day has come.
Sick are the heavy-hearted; half-naked the needy.
Common, every harm to the foolish.

RIDDLE

Make out who this is: formed before the Flood,
Powerful creature,   fleshless, boneless,
Nerveless, bloodless,   headless and footless,
He's no older, no younger,   than when he began.
He is not put off   by terror or death;
He's never unneeded   by any creature:
Great God, so holy,   what was his origin?
Great are his wonders,   the One who made him.
He's in field, he's in wood,   handless and footless,
No sickness, no sorrow,   forever hurtless.
And he's the same age   as the five epochs;
He's older as well   than many times fifty;
And he is as broad   as the earth's surface;
And he was not born,   and he is not seen,
On sea and on land   he sees not, is unseen.
He's unreliable,   he'll not come when wanted;
On land and on sea,   he's indispensable;
He is unyielding,   he's beyond compare.
He's from the four corners,   he'll not be counselled;
He springs from a nook   above the sea-cliff;

He's roaring, he's hushed,   he has no manners;
He's savage, he's bold   when he goes cross-country;
He's hushed, he's roaring,   he is boisterous,
The loudest of shouts   on the face of the earth.
He's good, he's evil;   he is in hiding,
He is invisible,   for no eye sees him;
Good and evil,   he is here, he is there;
He hurls things about,   he pays no damages,
He makes no amends,   and he is blameless:
Wet and dry,   he comes quite often.

* * *

One Person formed them,   all created things,
His the beginning   and his is the end.

THE PROPHECY OF BRITAIN

The Muse foretells, they will come in haste:
Riches, prosperity, peace will be ours,
And widespread lordship and generous lords,
And after disruption, all regions settled.
Men bold in battle, steadfast warriors,
Keen in combat, unbudging bulwark,
Fighting men will rout foreigners far as Caer Weir:
They will cause celebration, devastation done,
And concord of the Welsh and Dublin's men,
Gaels of Ireland and Môn and Scotland,
Cornishmen and Clydesmen welcomed by us.
Remnants will the British be when they triumph.
Long was it foretold, the time will come,
Monarchs possessing a noble lineage,
Northmen in the place of honour among them,
Amid their vanguard will launch the assault.

Myrddin foretells, they will assemble
At Aber Peryddon, the high king's stewards,
And though not by one means, death will they moan of.
Single-minded they will meet together:
The stewards will seek to collect their taxes;
In the Welsh ranks there'd be none who'll pay.
He is a noble man who will say this,

He'd not come and pay under compulsion.
Mary's Son, great Word, when wouldn't they burst out
Against the Saxons' sway and their bluster?
Away with Gwrtheyrn of Gwynedd's scavengers.
Foreigners will be driven into exile:
None will receive them, no land is theirs,
They know not why they roam in each river-mouth.
When they purchased Thanet through sly deceit,
With Hengist and Horsa, constrained was their power:
Their growth has been base, at our expense:
After secret slaying, churls wear crowns,
Drunkenness springs from deep drinking of mead,
Destitution springs from the death of many,
Desolation springs from the tears of women,
Grief rises under half-savage lordship,
Sorrow springs from a world overturned.
Let the Trinity turn back the blow that is planned,
Britons' land laid waste and Saxons settled.
Let their retreat into exile come
Before the Welsh become homeless.

Mary's Son, great Word, when wouldn't they burst out,
The Welsh, against the taunting of barons and lords.
Nobles and princes alike will complain,
One in voice, one in mind, one in spirit.
Not out of pride would they refuse parley
But to shun disgrace they would not make peace.
To God and Dewi they will plead their case:
Let Him repay, reject the foreigners' fraud;
They did shameful deeds lacking homelands.
Welshmen and Saxons will meet in combat,
On all sides struggling and grappling together
Of mighty war-bands as they test their strength,
And on the slope blades, battle-cries, close combat,
On Wye's banks cry countering cry round bright water,
And banners abandoned and savage assault,
And as food-stuff for wolves the Saxons will fall.
Welsh lords as one band will marshall their ranks,
The van on the palefaces' rear will press hard.
Stewards for their wiles will wallow in blood,
Their blood-soaked soldiers surrounding them.
Others will retreat on foot through the forest;

Through the fort's ramparts the foxes will flee.
No return of war to Britain's land:
Away, saddened, they'll slink like the sea.

Caer Geri's stewards will complain in earnest,
Those in hill and dale, they'll not deny it:
To Aber Peryddon ill-fated they came.
Affliction the taxes they'll gather.
Eighteen thousand strong they attack:
What a pity only eight thousand return.
A sorry tale they will tell their wives:
They will wash their shirts drenched in blood.
Welsh nobles, with not a care for their lives,
Men of the South, will contend for their taxes.
Keenly honed sword-blades cleanly will hew:
No fee for the doctor will come of their strokes.
Cadwaladr's war-bands, boldly they'll come:
Let the Welsh rise, they will do battle.
Inescapable death have they sought:
In ending their taxes, they will know death.
Others they dealt with barbarously;
Never again will they gather their taxes.

In forest, in field, in hill, in dale,
A candle will march with us in darkness,
Cynan leading the charge in each assault.
Saxons facing the Britons will sing of woe,
Cadwaladr, sturdy pillar, with his lords,
Total his shrewdness in seeking them out.
When their people collapse across their beds
In pain, red blood on foreigners' cheeks,
In ending all defiance, enormous spoils,
Saxons will rush pell-mell to Caer Wynt.
Blessed are they, the Welsh, when they say:
The Trinity has saved us from former trials.
Let Dyfed and Glywysing not tremble:
The high king's stewards will not win praise,
Nor Saxon stalwarts, savage though they be,
No delight in getting drunk at our expense
Without paying the fate for as much as they gain,
With sons orphaned and others stiff with cold.
Through the pleas of Dewi and the British saints
Far as Ailego's stream the foreigners will flee.

The Muse foretells, the day is coming
When the men of Wessex become of one mind,
One voice, one thought, with the flame-kindling Angles,
In hope of disgracing our splendid war-hosts.

* * *

With the foreigners daily taking flight,
They know not where they'll rove, where go, where stay.
They will rush to battle like a mountain bear
To avenge the blood of their comrades.
There will be spear-play, incessant bloodshed,
No kinsman will spare his enemy's flesh.
Head will be split open, brains spilt out,
Wives will be widowed, steeds left riderless,
Dreadful the wail before the warriors' charge,
And many a hand-wound before the sides part.
Death's messengers will gather together
When corpses still stand close to their comrades.
There'll be vengeance for tribute and daily payment
And frequent campaigns and the treacherous hordes.
The Welsh must become, through warfare,
Trained troops, united, one band, sworn brothers.

The Welsh will be compelled to make war:
And they'll muster the men of many lands,
And they'll raise the blessed standard of Dewi
To lead the Irish with a linen banner.
And Dublin's clansmen will stand beside us:
When they come to the field they will not play false.
They will ask the Saxons what they were after,
What right they have to the land they hold,
Where did their wayfaring first begin,
Where are their peoples, what land are they from?
Since Gwrtheyrn's time they trample on us:
No claim have they to our kinsmen's realm,
Nor our saints' honours, why have they wronged them?
Nor Dewi's laws, why have they broken them?
The Welsh will take care when they face each other
That no foreigners leave the spot where they stand
Till they pay sevenfold for what they did,
With certain death in return for their wrong.

Paid will be the aid given Garmon's kin
Four hundred and four years after Christ's birth.

Bold warriors, long-haired, battle-hardened,
Will come from Ireland to banish the Saxons:
From Lego a hot-blooded fleet will come.
Baneful in battle, rending the war-bands,
Will come from Alclud staunch reckless men
To drive them from Britain, noble war-hosts;
From Llydaw will come a splendid company,
Warriors on war-steeds who spare not their foes.
Saxons will suffer disgrace on all sides:
Their day has ended, no country is theirs.
Death will befall the dark company,
Sickness and bloody flux and anguish
After the gold, the silver, the courts.
May a hedge be their haven for their bad faith,
May sea, may anchor, be their counsellors.
May blood, may death, be their companions.
Cynan and Cadwaladr, bold our war-bands,
Will be praised till doomsday, fortune will be theirs,
Two powerful lords, weighty their counsel,
Two crushers of Saxons, on the side of God,
Two generous lords, two fine cattle-raiders,
Two ready champions, one fortune, one faith,
Two bulwarks of Britain, splendid war-bands,
Two bears undaunted in daily battle.

Seers foretell all that will happen:
From Manaw to Llydaw will be in their hands,
From Dyfed to Thanet will be their own,
From Gwawl to Gweryd, to the river-mouths,
Will stretch their sway over Yrechwydd.
No return will there be for the Saxon tribes:
The Irish will go back to their comrades.
The Welsh will rise, a fine company,
Armies round the ale and warriors' uproar
And God's princes, who have kept their faith.
Wessex men on their ships, oppression will cease,
And Cynan make peace with his comrade.
The foreigners will be known not as warriors
But Cadwaladr's churls and his chapmen.
Every Welshman's son will shout for joy

That the island-scourging swarm is gone.
When corpses stand close to their comrades
As far as Sandwich, blest will it be,
The foreigners setting out for exile,
One after another, back to the comrades,
The Saxons at anchor on the sea each day.
The Welsh keeping faith will triumph till doomsday:
Let them seek no sorcerer or selfish poet;
None but this will foretell this island's future.

BENEDICTION

Glorious Lord, I give you greeting!
Let church and chancel praise you,
Let chancel and church praise you,
Let plain and steep slope praise you,
Let the world's three wellsprings praise you,
Two above wind and one above land.
Let the darkness and the day praise you,
Let woodland and orchard praise you.
Abraham, source of faith, praised you:
Let life everlasting praise you,
Let birds and wild bees praise you,
Let stubble and grassblades praise you.
Aaron and Moses praised you:
Let male and female praise you,
Let stars and seven days praise you,
Let air and ether praise you,
Let books and letters praise you,
Let fish in the current praise you,
Let thought and action praise you,
Let sand-grains and earth-clods praise you,
Let all the good of creation praise you.
And I shall praise you, Lord of glory:
Glorious Lord, I give you greeting!

II. THE POETS OF THE PRINCES
c.1100–*c*.1285

MEILYR BRYDYDD

POEM ON HIS DEATH-BED

Rex regum, a ruler easy to praise,
  To my highest Lord I present a prayer:
Supreme prince of the blessed sphere high above,
  Good sir, make peace between you and me.
  Feeble, fleeting, remembrance of my having
  Pained you, and repentance for doing it.
I have done wrong in the Lord God's presence,
  My rightful devotion unobserved:
  I will serve, nonetheless, my Lord King,
  Before I am earthfast, defenceless.
Certain the foretelling to Adam and his offspring
  That the prophets once proclaimed:
  Jesus in Mary's womb (her Lord's daughter),
  Mary, she bore, blessed, her burden.
A burden I have gathered of sins heaped high:
  I have lived in fear of its turmoil.
  Lord of all places, how good to praise are you:
  May I praise you, be purged, before I am punished.
King of all glory who knows me, do not refuse me,
  For mercy's sake, because of my wickedness.
  I have often had gold and silk brocade
  From mortal rulers for praising them,
  And with song's gift gone, superior power,
  Impoverished my tongue in falling silent.
I, Meilyr the Poet, pilgrim to Peter,
  Gate-keeper who gauges true worth,
  When the time comes for us to arise,
  The many in the grave, make me ready.
May I be in that dwelling awaiting the call,
  The abbey where the tide beats beside it:
  Secluded it is, its fame undimmed,
  Its graveyard in the breast of the brine.
Fair Mary's isle, saintly isle of the saints,
  Expecting resurrection, it is splendid there.
Christ of the prophesied cross who knows me, he will guide me
  Past the pains of hell, sequestered dwelling:
  The Maker who made me, he will welcome me,
  Amidst the saintly faithful of Enlli's parish.

GWALCHMAI AP MEILYR

EXULTATION

Sun early-rising, summer speeding near,
    Birds' sweet sound, delightful bright weather.
    I am gold-mettled, dauntless in battle,
    Lion before a war-band, lightning my charge.
    I stood night watches, guarding a border,
    Foaming fords, Dygen Freiddin's waters.
    Bright green the fresh grass, water gleaming,
    Nightingale loud, familiar lyric.
Seagulls at play on the couch of the wave,
    Glowing their feathers, clamorous factions.
    Far-roving my mind at the start of summer
    Because of loving a comely lass.
    Far from Môn's slim maid is a host's commander,
    Gentle girl, my secret enchantress.
I have listened to lips in sure seclusion,
    To the soft speech of a distant maid,
    And for noble Owain, splendid fetter,
    They tremble, the English, before my blade.

Gleaming my sword, lightning guards one who's bold,
    Glittering the gold on my buckler.
    Harmonious the waters, warm the day,
    Pleasant melody, songbirds busy.
Keen my mind today in a distant region
    Entering Efyrnwy's countryside.
    Glowing the apple boughs, blossom-clustered,
    Trees finely clad, each man's mind's where he loves.
I love a comely maiden, noble her ways,
    Hateful to me those who will not praise her.
Genilles whets me, though she slay me with a word,
    Not much profit to me, my visit.
    Blessed the one on whom God bestows
    A maid's favour, fair virgin's comfort.

Gleaming my sword, lightning its fashion in conflict,
    Glittering the gold on my warshield.
    Many adore me who've never seen me
    Of Gwent's maidens frantic to praise me.

I saw Angles in death before Owain,
  And by Rhibyll a ruler enraged.
Gwalchmai I am called, foe of the Saxons,
  For Môn's prince I attacked in battle,
  And for a fair one's favour, snow's hue on trees,
  When we fought before Caer, I spilled blood.
A bloody blade my sword, and savage in battle,
  Against England a champion will not hide.
  I saw, from the stroke of Gruffudd's warchild,
  Broken retainers, wreckage of retreat.
At Aberteifi, fierce in battle Owain,
  Blest prince of Britain, land's rightful lord:
Brave men evade him, on hearing him there,
  Before Iago's great-grandson, massacre maker.
Gwalchmai I am called, bane of Edwin and Angles,
  And in a host's hurly-burly I am red of hand.
  And I have witnesses who swear for me
  Of Cynan's lineage, descendants of Coel.
And for her favour who will greet by Breiddin's proud hill
  I will not evade conflict through fear.
  I love May's nightingale, thwarting morning sleep,
  And a gentle girl's eyes, long, white, her cheek.
  I love splendid steeds, long-legged stags,
  Keeping sorrow at bay with hardship's armour.

* * *

Lightning my sword, to defy me is useless,
  I stay my hand from slaying none who confront it.
  I saw a king's rage before Craig Gwyddyr
  When Môn's splendid ruler defended his lands.
I saw at Rhuddlan flame's rush before Owain,
  And corpses stiff in death, and red spears.
  I saw them there in a vale, shattered:
  A hundred leaders were still who'd been heedless.
  Caerfyrddin was breached in men's conflict,
  Loud his onslaught, eagle of Emrys.
Let rulers bring to him royal tribute,
  Prince of Aberffraw and Ynyr's land.
I listened to the nightingale, longing for a gracious girl,
  Maid clad in purple, contemplation's goal.
  No long sleeper, the fair, I know why,
  When apple boughs burgeon with blossoms.

Foaming is a wave beside Porth Wygyr,
Fervent is a lover, high-hearted a lord.
Dreaming of a maiden, dewdrop's fair hue,
It is rare, the night it spared me.

* * *

I love the small bird and the soft sound
Of a woods' constant song, comely its wings.
A maid praises me when she greets me from afar:
Let her think for my sake what she will not dare.
And I have long had in mind (well I know
Her dwelling's ways) a marvel – it is steadfast.

A green wave woke me by Aberffraw,
It assaults tranquil land, it bears riches.
A bird sings in high spirits beside it,
No woodland weaves shelter upon it.
Secluded trysting-place, calm conjunction,
Where resistance to me clears away.
Savage my stallion on Caeaw's field
For a lord's sake, praiseworthy Cynan.
Fair Gwynedd's famed hero is he, all say,
All of Britain's keys his possessions.
I listened to an eagle dining on a carcass:
Gwynedd furnished a massacre for it.
When golden Owain fought for Dinbych's dwellings,
Day in a dale, taking toll of shields,
I hastened in a host against the Angles:
Sadness in England from my hand's path.
My mettle made me worth the choosing
On Cadell's heirs' hill, Tysilio's country.

A green wave woke me by Aber Dau,
It attacks the grey bank, comely its streams.
A little bird's bill sings in high spirits,
Place for my displeasure, best retreat.
Delightful fresh grass when days grow long,
Delightful trees finely veiled, fair their blossoms.
Delighted I drank mead served from golden vessels
In tall Owain's court, bold-natured warrior.
His wine was poured for me by a lord's fair hand
In Caernarfon, near Hiriell's country.

He claimed on my behalf a gift for my hand
On Carnedd's battlefield, from noblemen.
He pours out riches, costly presents,
Bears the praise of Britain's four corners.
Pledges are his from northern Din Alclud,
He is war-leader down in the south.

Mild the first month, bright the day's weather,
Soft the slope, summer cheerful, delightful.
Mild run the waters, glad is green at the bankside,
Of Ogfanw and Cegin and Clawedog.
A sea-wave awoke me in turmoil,
It flows often from Abermenai.
A white comber batters Mount Cyngreawdr,
Maelgwn the king's Morfa Rhianedd.
I crossed the Lliw to Lleuddiniawn's homesteads,
I rode to Efrawg Gaer on a lively steed,
And they asked me, of the kings of Britain,
Which provider hero's most generous?
And I asserted, without hesitation,
He was tall Owain, much pledged of Christendom.
And it's he who'll grant me a maid finely wrought
Who has known me well, long fellowship,
And she will pay me the cost of haughtiness lately
With long dark lashes and long soft cheek,
And in a court of plenty I will be desired
(Tonight I become a wonder, if I come freely),
And if the God of heaven is good to me
Bliss is mine, with the fair one to sleep beside me.

THE BATTLE OF TÂL MOELFRE

I celebrate a noble of Rhodri's line,
Borderland's warden, ruler by right,
Britain's rightful lord, steadfast Owain's endurance,
Of lords who'll not grovel, not hoard up wealth.
Three legions, they came, sea-surge vessels,
Three mighty fleets to press him hard,
One from Ireland, another of men in arms
From the Norsemen, flood's far-stretching trails,
And the third over sea from Normandy
Heading for hard dreadful toil, ill-fated.

127

And Môn's war-lord, how brave his behaviour in combat,
    And their bold defiance was battle's clamour,
    And before him rose a grim wild welter,
    And havoc and conflict and doleful death.
Host on bloodstained host, shudder on dreadful shudder,
    And at Tâl Moelfre a thousand war-cries;
    Shaft on flashing shaft, spears upon spear,
    Thrust on wrathful thrust, drowning on drowning,
And no ebb in Menai from the floodtide of bleeding,
    And the stain of men's blood in the brine.
    And grey mail-coats, and maiming's anguish,
    And corpses piled before a red-speared lord,
And England's onslaught, and engagement with it,
    And them demolished in the shambles.
    And the fame raised of a savage blade
    In seven-score tongues to praise him long.

PLEA FOR RECONCILIATION

    I celebrate a noble of Aeneas' line,
    I celebrate a hero, lightning-bright lion,
I celebrate the kindest of Britain's kings
    And most kingly, splendid Owain, gold lad.
My father celebrated once his mighty royal father,
    With inspired skill his vast bounty:
And I will celebrate a chieftain, leader in combat,
    With sweet poetry's speech, with a song of lineage,
And declare of a lord, Idwal's true descendant,
    He will not forgo vengeance as payment for murder,
And in Cadwallawn's court, by a host's gift-giver,
    May a fitting gift be remembered.
    I have served a warrior, warriors' bulwark;
    I have praised Cemais, Welshmen's haven.
    Owain loved me at his side as a lad:
    Common, after great love, commencing of hatred.
    He gave me from his spoils without stinting
    Firm-fleshed steeds, honourable favour.
And now I know at a stroke a leader in combat,
    Frequent his blades on a pack of grey wolves:
    Hard for me to cope with Goliath's spear,
    Dreadful his wrath on a dapple-grey steed.
Still estranging's anguish pains me like prison,

And the fierce passion of a mighty lord enraged.
And God has created him best of men:
Would I had been slain before I felt his wrath.
And since I take on myself so much of the blame,
 Make peace with your poet, who will not sing basely.
  Son of Gruffudd, boisterous in battle,
  Far-reaching your conquests, past Ewias,
  And I will praise your worth to the full,
  And all, realm's ruler, will praise you.

GWALCHMAI'S DREAM

May God, divine in nature, teach me
As God taught the prophet David:
May God teach me to defend myself
From a cruel ruler, battle-snarer.
May God steer me fearlessly:
 What is due the Lord, that has been heard.
He has proffered one certain atonement as well:
 By heaven's angels it was ordained.
 From Madawg's great fall, leader in combat,
 For a host's bounteous post, I was made strangely fearful.
God will not disgrace me with a wrathful gift:
 I would keep no one from sharing a dream.
 No dim memory for me, though I am grown grey,
 Goronwy's slaughter, shield-bearing hero:
 No lie that I was ground down by his death
 On the grindstone of persistent oppressive grief.
 Sadness for a noble man – where you exist,
 Sleep and bliss differ less when you come.
An attack known so well overtook me,
 I was worn out with dread for the three.
 Gold-natured Genilles, the hour she was taken,
 To leave me was wrong when she was not left.
 Whom the Creator may leave, blest was he created,
 To give food and drink in God's name,
 And clothes to the naked, protection from the cold,
 And a bed and a house and hearth's warmth.
 God and King, you are jubilation:
 Who goes not in your favour, he is humbled.
 And as for me, bereft of my good,
 May God keep me safe and secure,

Keeping your commands till I meet my death,
And may my prayer be fulfilled.

OWAIN CYFEILIOG

THE DRINKING-HORN

Dawn as it rose, they raised the war-cry,
Enemies sending clamorous threats.
Red-speared our men after heavy labour
Launching the assault on Maelor's town.
Fine men I sent into battle,
Fearless in combat, red-weaponed.
Who vexes a brave man, let him beware:
Wrath's expected when he's aroused.

Cup-bearer, what calms me, let it not leave me:
Bring it, the horn, for a drinking bout,
Long and blue its pattern, gold its trim.
Fill to the brim, cup-bearer, with joy
The horn in Rhys' hand at a gift-lord's court,
Owain's court, forever nourished on plunder,
Port for a thousand you hear, portals open.
And bring another drink of bragget
To Gwgawn's mighty hand for his deed.
Cubs of Goronwy, bold prowling in battle,
Cubs quick of foot, courageous their act,
Men who earn reward in every hard fight,
Men of worth in strife, bold deliverance,
Shepherds of Hafren, gladly they hear
The din of mead-horns, plenty on hand.

Fill the horn brim-full for Cynfelyn
Made famously drunk on foaming mead,
And if you wish life for another year
Pay him full respect, as is proper.
And bring to Gruffudd, red-speared foeman,
Wine, with bright crystal enclosing it,
Hero of Arwystli, border's trust,

Hero of kind Owain, Cynfyn's heir,
Hero who stirs, is not stricken by, strife,
   Terror in carnage, torment in pursuit.
   Comrades went to be worthy of praise,
   Companions in arms, armed with keen blades.
They have earned their mead, as Belyn's men once did,
   Well-remembered while a man's left alive.

Fill the horn to the brim, since I have a notion
   That warriors look for sparkling talk,
   In Dehewain's hand, lion of battle,
   Lightning beneath a broad light buckler,
In Ednyfed's hand, heroic lion,
   Valiant spear-thrust, shaven thin his shield.
   Two firm in turmoil, fearless by nature,
   They slash, cutting wind above fair land.
Tall waves my warriors in giving battle,
   Swiftly they'd slash a gold-chased shield-face.
   Deep-dyed their spears after piercing heads,
   Swift in attacking a palisade.
   I heard in Maelor sudden great clamour
   And warrior's harsh cry and sharp anger,
   And they gather around a wine-cup,
   As in Bangor once round a fire of spears
   When two kings quarreled over mead-horns
   At the merry revels of Morfran.

Fill the horn to the brim, since I remember
   Where they fought for the mead of our realm:
   Fearless Selyf, safeguard of Gwygyr,
   Let him who irks him beware, eagle's heart,
And Madawg's one son, renowned Tudur Hael,
   Killer wolf by rights, lightning on lances.
   Two bold ones, two lions in their counsel,
   Two savage forces, Ynyr's two sons,
   Two freely striking on the day of battle,
   Unyielding bulwark, peerless deed,
   Strong lions' stroke, strong-stabbing soldiers,
   Lords of battle, assaulters, red their spears,
   Steady force in attack, hurried flight,
   Shorn their two shields from a single cause.
   The wind cried loud above the sea-bank,
   Source of the swift force of Talgarth's waves.

Fill brim-full, cup-bearer, court not death,
   The horn much-honoured in revels,
Long blue bison horn, high privilege tonight,
    Not too thin its casing of silver,
    And bring to Tudur, battle's eagle,
    The first drink of the dark red wine.
Unless there's fetched of the very best mead
    A goblet of drink, off goes your head,
    For Moriddig's hand, sponsor of songs:
    They spread his fame, before cold burial.
    Steadfast brothers, high-spirited pair,
    Steady courage beneath their shields,
    Soldiers who gave me their services,
    No hot and cold, or shilly-shally.
    Warriors, wolves foremost to attack,
    Battlefield's ferocity, bloodstained spears,
    Bold, Mochnant's soldiers from Powys,
    And both driven by battle frenzy,
    Ever attackers, red their weapons,
    They held their ground against turmoil.
    Praise is their portion, these I speak of;
    Elegy, the two now changed to one:
    Ah Christ, how sad am I from the grief
    Of Moriddig's loss, much is he missed.

    Fill the horn, since they ask it of me,
    Long and blue, with joy, for Morgant's hand,
    Man who merits his own song of praise,
    Bitter his combat, ferocity's thrust,
Worthy man, source of suffering his blade,
    Smooth its sides, sharp its edges.
    Fill, cup-bearer, from silver vessel
    A gift of honour with dignity:
    At Gwestwn Fawr I saw affliction;
    Goronwy's stand was a hundred's deed.
    Warriors firm of purpose performed this,
    Welcoming combat, heedless of life:
A brave man met the enemy army,
    A steward was slain, sea-coast fort burned,
    A precious prisoner they brought forth,
    Meurig fab Gruffudd, strong the prophecy.
    Each man was sweating when they returned;
    Filled with sun were long hill and valley.

Fill the horn brim-full for the fighters,
    Owain's cubs, warriors striking as one,
    Ones who warrant a place of honour,
    Constant where they go bright iron's stroke,
Madawg and Meilyr, men accustomed to conflict,
    Opponents against iniquity,
    War-band's thunderers, skilled in skirmish,
    Strife-seeking men, sturdy defenders.
I have heard that for mead men went to Catraeth,
    Proper their purpose, weapons sharp-edged:
    Mynyddawg's troop, for their sleep in death,
    Had their tale, fear-rousing assailants.
No worse did my warriors in Maelor's strife,
    Freeing a prisoner, praiseworthy feat.

Fill brim-full, cup-bearer, with clear sweet mead,
    For battle's spear-lord, sweating under stress,
    From bison horns splendidly gilded,
    For merit, reward in return for lives.
    How great the sleeplessness lords suffer
    None knows but God and he that speaks it.
    One who swears not, pays not, plays not false,
    Daniel, lord of support, how fine and true.
    Cup-bearer, hard work it is to shun
    Men who shun not death until appeased.
    Cup-bearer, the mead-feast I share,
    Blazing fire gleaming bright, glowing tapers.
    Cup-bearer, you saw rage at Llidwm:
    The men I honour, they will be honoured.
Cup-bearer, you saw warriors' armour
    Encircling Owain, a savage shield.
    When Cawres was plundered, hot fighting perforce;
    Angry plundering is highly praised.
    Cup-bearer, deny me not, I'll not be denied.
    May we be received in Paradise
By the Lord of kings, long be our welcome,
    In the place one sees true protection.

HYWEL AB OWAIN GWYNEDD

IN SUMMER

I love, come summer, a steed's trampling,
Men high-hearted before a brave lord;
Foam-crested the wave, swiftly coursing;
Apple-tree's gowned, another omen;
Bright-shining my shield shouldered for battle.
I've loved what I had not, though longed for,
Tall white hemlock, gently bending,
The hue of fair dawn at mid-day,
Fragile bright form, white, supple, delightful,
As she walks, scarcely bends a rush-stalk.
Lovely little dear, mild her manner,
Little older than a girl of ten,
Child-like, shapely, full of propriety,
She was brought up to be bountiful.
Young woman, more often the fair shows desire
Than unseemly speech comes from her lips.
Beggar on foot, will a tryst be mine?
How long must I beg you? Do as you should.
Without measure am I from love's madness:
Jesus won't chide me, he'll understand.

THE CHOSEN ONE

My chosen, a lovely slim maiden,
Tall and fair in her heather-hued cloak;
And my chosen lore, to watch one who's womanly,
When she speaks, scarcely heard, modest words.
And my chosen part, to tryst with a girl
And partake of a secret, a gift.
A chosen I have, wave's beautiful hue,
Your pure-spoken Welsh part of your wealth.
My chosen you are: what am I to you?
Why be silent? Lovely her silence.
I've chosen a sweetheart I'll never regret:
Rightly is chosen so fair a choice.

COMPLAINT

I love a white fort beside a white shore
    Where a shy girl loves watching seagulls.
I would love to go, though I'm not overloved,
    Longed-for visit, on a slim white steed,
    To see my dear one, soft her laughter,
    To talk of love, since it's come to me,
To speak of my grief, and her great beauty,
    To speak of a maiden, sea-wave's hue,
    Snow's hue, bright cold on a lofty peak.
    Because I was scorned at Ogyrfan's court,
    A prince's wound fell in her dwelling,
    It has taken my life, I've grown weak.
I've become, from passion, like Garwy Hir
    For a fair girl denied me at Ogyrfan's court.

DESIRE

    I love a well-fashioned, rounded fortress
    Where a well-rounded form disrupts my sleep.
    One deeply troubled will visit it,
    Tameless wave sounding loud against it,
    Choice spot, bright, splendid, its features,
    Gleaming bright it rises beside the sea:
    And the woman illumines this year
    In desolate Arfon, in Eryri.
    Who looks not at silk merits no mantle:
    Never a one might I love more than her.
    If her favour came for composing verse,
    Any night I would be beside her.

REJECTION

    I desired today, glossy grey steed,
    To visit Cynlas' fair country on you,
    To seek long talk, before death's extinction,
    With a sleep-marring, joy-barring girl.
And would that mine were a sign, as a worthy youth:
    Her complexion was like blue waves' white crests.
    Full of yearning my mind, amid comrades,

Of longing for her, and she loathes me.
Though I do honour to a praiseworthy girl,
　　Pain gains me no ease. Call this well-bred?
　　Broken, this heart: it has known longing
　　For a slender maid's form, red-gold wand.
Not there today, not worth my sustaining,
　　In the place where once it was, my bond.
Oh God's only Son in the kingdom of heaven,
　　Before I knew suffering, would I'd been slain.

THE BATTLE OF TÂL MOELFRE

When crows were merry, when blood was gushing,
　　　When there came great carnage,
　　When warfare, when houses turned red,
　　When shore red, when court burned red,

When red flame reddened, it flamed to the heavens,
　　　Home offered no refuge.
　　Easy to see its bright burning,
　　The white fortress on Menai's shore.

Perished, the third of May, three hundred ships
　　　In the majestic fleet,
　　And a thousand men fled before him,
　　A beardless warrior at Menai.

EXULTATION

　　A foaming white wave washes a grave,
　　Rhufawn Befr's tomb, ruler of monarchs.
I love, England's bane, the bright Northland today,
　　And the flourishing groves by the Lliw.
　　I love those who gave me my fill of mead,
　　Where the seas reach, ceaseless contention.
I love its war-band and its abundant dwellings,
　　Its ruler happy to stir up strife.
　　I love its sea-marsh and its mountains
　　And its wood-bordered fort and fine lands,
　　And its watered dales and its valleys,
　　And its white gulls and comely women.

I love its warriors and well-trained steeds
    And its woods and strong men and homestead.
I love its meadows and its wealth of small clover
    Where fame had a firm joyful welcome.
    I love its lowlands, bravery's due,
    And its wide wilderness and its riches.
Ah God's only Son, great the wonder,
    Such splendid deer, so much abundance.
    I did superb work with a spear-thrust
    Between Powys' host and fair Gwynedd's,
    And on a white steed, surfeit of strife,
    May I win a release from exile.
I will not, for sure, hold out till it comes:
    A dream says this, and God will decide.
    A foaming white wave washes a grave.

    A foaming white wave, bold by homesteads,
    Hue of hoar frost, as it is cresting.
    I love the sea-marsh in Meirionydd
    Where mine was a white arm for pillow.
    I love the nightingale in privet
    Where two rivers meet, valley of praise.
    Lord of heaven and earth, Gwynedd's king,
    How far from Ceri is Caer Lliwelydd.
    I rode a bay mount from Maelienydd
    Far as Rheged, by night and by day.
    May I win, before my grave, new reward,
    In Tegeingl, the fairest in her land.
    Though I be a lover of Ovid's kind,
    God be mindful of me at my end.
    A foaming white wave, bold by homesteads.

IN PRAISE OF FAIR WOMEN

I greet the marvellous, supreme enchanter,
    Because he is monarch,
    Weaving song in time-honoured fashion,
    Music of praise, such as Myrddin sang,
    For the women who rule my word-craft,
    How reluctant they are for a tryst,
    All of the best in the western land
    From Caer's portals to Porth Ysgewin.

One is the sweetheart whose praise will come first,
    Gwenlliant, summertime's glow;
        Next she that said no, distant my lips
        From her, from the gold-torqued girl,

Fair Gweirfyl, my gift, my grace, never won,
    Won by none of my kin:
        Though I was stabbed with double-edged blades,
        The king's foster-brother's wife refused me.

With comely Gwladus, young bashful child-bride,
    The hope of her people,
        I will whisper a secret sigh,
        I will praise her, while gorse is gold.

Soon, for passion, may I see estranged from him,
    With my sword in my hand,
        Bright Lleucu, my darling, laughing,
        And her man will not laugh when hard-pressed.

        Great stress that concerns me beset me
        And longing, alas, that is constant
        For Nest, fair as apple-blossoms,
        For Perweur, the heart of my sin,

For pure Generys, who relieved not my passion,
    May she not remain chaste,
        For Hunydd, desire till doomsday,
        For Hawis, my choice for courtship.

        I had a girl who concurred one day;
        I had two, the more is their praise;
        I had three and four with good fortune;
        I had five of them, fair their white flesh;
        I had six with no shying from sin,
        A bright girl from a white fort was mine;
        I had seven, with earnest effort;
I had eight as reward, prize for praise I sang –
        Best for teeth to guard tongue.

PERYF AP CEDIFOR

LAMENT FOR HYWEL AB OWAIN AND HIS FOSTER-BROTHERS

While we were seven, not thrice seven would defy us,
    Would rout us before our death:
  Left, alas, of the seven
  Are but three who shun not strife.

Seven warriors were we, flawless, unflurried,
    Unrestrained their onslaught,
  Seven firm men, flight pointless,
  Seven, once, who brooked no wrong.

Since Hywel has gone, battle's eager attack,
    We were as one with him,
  All of us confess the loss:
  May heaven's host be the fairer.

Cedifor's sons, noble children in union,
    In the glen near Pentraeth,
  They drank deep, strong of purpose,
  Were cut down near their foster-brother.

Since treason was brewed, unchristian Briton,
    By Cristin and her sons,
  May none be left living in Môn
  Of Brochfael's bald freckled clan.

Whatever wealth come of holding land, this world
    Is no trustworthy home:
  With a spear, ah savage Dafydd,
  Pierced is war's hawk, tall Hywel.

CYNDDELW BRYDYDD MAWR

TO A GIRL

I saw on a dear, high-spirited girl
A look without love, stately, sedate.
Glowing hue of waves, spume-spreading billow,
Tide surge where river meets sea, short-lived,
Frequent the sending of harsh angry thoughts
Between me and the maid, pride's candle,
So that I am hiding a wounded heart.
Unseemly: the beauty sought Eiddig's bed.

IN PRAISE OF MADAWG AP MAREDUDD

I extol a lord with nine parts of my art,
　　With ninefold spirit, with nine-metred verse,
　　To praise a hero, spear-lord's valour,
　　Roar of sea-surge that gouges a shore.
　　War's bold red spear, fair Cadfan's heir,
　　Long will he reign as our sovereign.
　　Swift-darting spear, perfect chieftain,
　　Mighty Madawg, battlefield's champion:
　　My bard's voice, under heaven, it is not flawed;
　　My bard's words for you, not shameful, not feeble.
　　Keen for war, for fortress, for splendid field,
　　Thick round a bold lion, silver-giver,
　　The thrust for gifts of a throng at New Year's,
　　Swift wave's roar on shore round seagull's feet.
Wayfarer secure in my craft of lyric,
　　Smooth-styled homage, praise that will not pass,
　　Shield-piercing protector of strangers,
　　I drank at your court, splendid Lleisiawn,
　　Superb drink served in a golden cup,
　　Gold bison horns, a lord's drinking-horns.
　　Ever have you shared out to us
　　Small long-striding steeds in silk trappings,
　　Sleek, dappled, stag-bodied, well-foddered,
　　Silver hue of fish, young sea salmon.
　　Famed his bloodstained hand on bloodstained field,
　　Eagle of warriors since he was warrior,

Spear-thrust of strife on white-breasted steeds,
Foremost pursuer, ferocious wolf.
A delight, my devotion to my noble prince:
Let me sing – what? – the renowned war-wounder.
Since I love, since I am lofty of voice,
I will sing of support, of famed portals.
Arise, sing: I will sing my verses:
And I, bards, within, and you, without.

A LOVE POEM FOR EFA

Spirited prancer, fierce passion I suffer
For one I will praise, whom once I praised,
Twin of foam on wind-ruffled water,
Soft-voiced her Welsh, of the valley's court,
Bright as daybreak when it takes its way,
Hue of snow glowing on Epynt's slope.
Disposed to stay distant, bright glances,
The maid prized me not, though they prized me,
The young maidens who conversed with her:
They lauded a love song to Efa.
I would visit, dwelling they guarded,
Powys' lord's resort, if they let me.
When I have gone, there they would be:
Through glass windows they'd gaze at me.
Glowing seagulls would keep a keen eye on me;
Unmanning, the answer they'd send me.
Gladly I'd love them, though they love me not,
They were sprightly, innocent handmaids.
Prudent-minded, long they would ponder:
They were wary of Cynddelw the poet.

Spirited prancer, with passion I plead:
Sprightly gold-mantled maid, far from my sight.
Golden steed so discreet, I am lost:
I've lost discreet words from her who stirs me.
Mind in a whirl, for a girl I am now
Unsettled, sleepless, though I endure it.
She stayed silent, pay for my lasting pain:
I will not stay silent to the one I love.
Hidden beauty, wave's hue round an oar,
Too much for me, though I be not with you.

A bold shining sign, though I beg you,
Since you give me not, despite my song,
Treat me not, maiden, so that I lose sleep.
I'll not grieve you, though I may not have you:
No better tidings may I look for,
But for love's sake I may not blame you.
I mind not, lord's child, not seeing you,
Seeking no payment for what I sing.

Spirited prancer, constant your faring,
Look on the court of Powys warriors,
Court where noblemen come to serve her,
Efa's court, it was made for poets.
Courtly her tall form in cloak of gold,
Modest, sagacious, fair-skinned beauty,
Eloquent princess, splendid her lot,
Hue of fine foam before the ninth wave.
Ninth part of my pain since she was born
No one has ever borne, or the like.
I prize no girl who is hard of heart:
No praise, to spurn me, despite my worth.
And tell there of the torment that is mine,
And speed to me with a kind reply.
For my sake, hide not the way I look;
For her sake I yearn, she trusts me not;
For your own sake, let her not doubt me;
For the Lord's sake, let her not scorn me.
Scorn she caused me before she dismissed me:
Needful was mercy, were that her wish.
Gracious bard am I to her, by right;
Gracious word for me comes not my way.
Though not loved, let me not ever be blamed;
If blamed, not denied benevolence.
Long it pierces me, thought of her loss,
Spoiler of spoilers' spoils in raiding,
War-hardened red spear facing armour,
Lord of Cynfarch's line, before he was gone.
After bounteous Owain, stubborn demand,
Bold, fearless, the raid on his homestead:
They come to her, it is no honour,
Sorrows for the stags of Rheged's hearth.

Spirited prancer, constant your friendship,
Sublime songs' choice gift, chosen singer,
Mead-horn familiar, mead-feast's resort.
Best to go once more to a maiden:
Make no peace with her while hope lingers;
Take no contradictory answer.
I go not to her, worthless long journey,
On the feet of the wind a third time.
Never, like a fool, have I ceased to praise her:
Not a move she makes to relieve me.
And the maid does not prize me, strange turn,
When her hand has been my glad reward,
And no bard in the world, skilled word-craft,
May love longer while hope still lingers.
The slim girl will not come to me, comely form;
She'll not so speed me to her court far off.
Fair innocent, quiet her conversing,
Mild-mannered, to my mind, companion,
Pure refined princess, gently musing,
Daybreak's hue on a desolate sea.

Spirited prancer, constantly ready,
Ready for pursuit that wins reward.
Spirited prancer, brook no delay:
Here and now I am passion-ridden.
Yearning tells me, mead-nourished youngster,
Of one I love, though she love me not.
Weary the shore before the green surge,
Glad is the muse, the breeze is stronger.
Greatly she whets me, hue of a wave's crest,
When her breast gleams next to her bracelet.
Mild look, desired by one who observes her,
Light's hue her look for one who may see it.
I have seen a fine form, bright its cincture,
He has not seen beauty who sees not her,
And beneath a red gem, a red-gold ring,
And above a fair face, curls of auburn.
A custom I keep with one who may keep it,
Proper for one who may not be pursued,
My secret with a maid who may not wish it:
What rashness can't hide, it will not know.

In hiding, my sleep, in long visiting there,
    Morning stolen by melancholy.

Spirited prancer, constantly loyal,
    Sprightly fair form, may injustice submit.
    As a maid's gracious, so she is praised:
    As I honour, so am I honoured.
One who's honoured will bring to fulfillment
    Honour for praise so far as it's heard.
    Do you hear, noble folk, what is said?
    What a maid says will not be disdained.
    In many-hued riches, much am I given;
    She gives me no better: I'm not desired.
When outside of my land I am sought for,
    My ruler, my prince, will be mentioned:
    Kind Llywelyn's bard, so am I called,
    Red blade, enemy of all injustice,
    Renowned, admired throughout my lifetime,
    Savage my rage if I am not prized.
Far off, the lookout of gulls aloof to a poet;
    It is roofed with precious red gold:
    Far-roaming my mind in Caerwys' land;
    Far gone am I, unless rewarded.
    Graceful walker, far-pacing boldly,
    Walk of praise, how long you'll be praised.

LAMENT FOR MADAWG AP MAREDUDD

    I ask of my Lord hope's blessing,
    I ask, I have asked a hundred times,
To compose in my lofty language gold song
      For my lord companion,
To mourn mead-feasting Madawg, sad his loss,
      Who had foes in all lands.
    Door of the fortress, shield-comrade,
    Buckler in onslaught, in glorious battle,
    Roar of heather in turmoil, on fire,
    Router of foes, shield a door-bolt.
    Lord of myriad songs, singers' hope,
    Bloodied, unhindered, steadfast comrade,
    Madawg was called before his death
    The snare of vile, villainous foes.
    Lavish to me, my hope's answer,

Clothing a-plenty, Gascon steed's companion;
Red spear of Brân ap Llŷr Llediaith,
Lavish his praise for piling up spoils,
He evades no raiding war-band.
Constant in kindness, pledged comrade,
Blade of terror in strife, in slaughter,
Blade of bloodshed that loves contention,
Hand swift beneath many-hued shield,
Helm of Powys, land left hopeless,
Demanding, man who wants no child's play,
Courageous, shield of four peoples,
Heir of ancient iron-clad kings,
Generous Madawg, unyielding dread
From his dying, we died with his death;
From his burial, comradeship died.
He was fond of bards' pure bardic verse,
Was the desolate deep's firm anchor,
Was long-welcoming, open-handed, benign,
Was the war-cry for blood in combat,
Was mead-horns' court, blood-right's buttress,
Was a warrior line's golden lion,
Was a lord's blameless powerful comrade,
Was iron-clad hands, iron-crowned.
May his end be, since his death has come,
To make amends for what wrongs were his,
In the saints' light, in the bright passage,
In the blest light of perfect freedom.

THE FALL OF POWYS

On Bryn Actun's field I honoured a hundred,
    My red blade at my side;
    In one ebb, three hundred war-lords:
    May they enter heaven as one.

On Didlystun's field our men were alert,
    Not reluctant for praise,
    Each lord on a sleek, keen steed,
    Each lion, blade at his side.

On Maes y Croesau we blessed noble men,
    Riders of russet steeds;

145

Harriers set out for spoils,
Generous men, red swords ready.

On Trefgalw's field our men's host of horses
        Is heard far and wide,
    Roar of riders on sweating steeds
    Like high wind's roar through a grove.

On Mathrafal's field, downtrodden the turf
        By noble horses' hooves;
    In battle, victorious meeting,
    Thriving land's true prince's banner.

No one knows, save God and the world's sages
        And diligent prophets,
    Golden-torqued golden war-band,
    Our number at Rhiweirth River.

Many a grey mount at Llanfawr abbey,
        Prancers in January,
    And many a man bold in battle
    With Llywelyn, poets' patron.

Many a man and mount at Maesing today,
        Peaceful wide-spreading land,
    And many a man bold in strife
    With Cadell's noble descendant.

At Ystrad Langwm I considered our men;
        They considered what I sang:
    Prince Madawg's host, assault's wall,
    Llywelyn's host, these I saw.

    Llywelyn's portion, onslaught's lion,
    From Rhug as far as Buddugre,
    Many a sprightly mount's rider,
    Many lads along a green hill.

When we were summoned to Cynwyd Gadfor,
        Our counsel was offered:
    Proud warriors, their shields shattered,
    Through the pasture we were routed.

May God allow none who live hereafter
    Two cloaks, since this occurred:
   Madawg dead, great my distress;
   Llywelyn slain, disaster.

   My greetings, Gwaelest Edwy,
   And the court beside the Dyfrdwy,
   And the fair place like a beach
   That has made me yearn more and more.

   My greetings to Cwm Brwynawg
   And the homes and the famous borders,
   And the place where no lord is spurned,
   And the church above Madawg's court.

   Since blessed Madawg is dead,
   Not merry, many a lord;
   Grief-stricken is the world I know,
   And high honours, worthless now.

   Because combat's bull has died
   And my long-handed lord lives no more,
   If a heart will break with sorrow,
   Mine it is will be split in two.

If Lleisiawn's lord lived, Gwynedd could not camp
    In the heart of Edeirniawn
   Without men slain by a warlord:
   Bait for kites, abundant hosts.

In Madawg's lifetime, not a man would dare
    Seize the fair borderland:
   Foolish to think of owning more
   Of the world than comes from God.

IN PRAISE OF OWAIN GWYNEDD

I praise a patron high-hearted in war,
    Onslaught's bold leader, strife-stirring wolf,
   Song of great pleasure wherever he is,
   Song of mastery, fortunate mead-fed man,
   Song of aspiration, swift-winged falcon,

Song of a lofty soul's lofty thoughts,
Song of a hero, deft-handed warrior,
Song of one who inspires praise-song,
Song for my lord, freely he prevails,
Song with words of praise, praising Owain.
He fought against Angles for Tegeingl's lands,
Blood-shower pouring, blood in full flow;
He fought with dragons, rulers of Rome,
Rhun's descendant, red his lance.
Dragons in conflict, dragon of the east,
Fair western dragon, better his fate.
Ardent, shining, was sword above sheath,
And spear in strife, and bloodflow from blade,
Sword held in hand and hand hewing heads,
Hand on sword and the sword on Norman hosts.
And heavy feasting in the wake of death
And swilling of blood and revelling,
Blood on warriors, on warriors' bones:
I heard birds rapacious for flesh,
For the piercing of a spear in flight;
Ravens clamoured on the trail of blood.
They rode on corpses, on a thousand crows,
Riders on Brynaich's men, Owain's ravens;
Massacre's buckets, prostrate carcasses,
A tidbit for them, dead men's entrails.
In throngs we went, for a prize, for a prince's praise,
Many singers, for Owain's bounty,
To Cadell's strong offspring, tall Hiriell,
To a lord of Coel's line, for reward.
Battlefield's spear-thrust, far-spreading fame,
Buckler-bearing, powerful eagle,
Bold defender, resplendent at a feast,
Deeply dyed his spear, broadcasting wrath.
At Aberteifi fallen spears shattered
As at Baddon, clamorous onslaught:
I saw savage troops and stiff red corpses,
It was left to the wolves, their burial;
I saw them abandoned, defenceless
Beneath birds' feet, strong men slain;
I saw their ruin, three hundred dead;
I saw, battle over, bowels on thorns;
I saw dreadful tumult in turmoil,
Troops contending, a rout collapsing.

148

I saw struggle, men falling from sea-cliffs;
    I saw them flung off, enemy's end.
    I saw warriors' spears around a stone wall;
    I saw lances red from Owain's rush;
    I saw for Saxons sorry corpses,
    Sad merciless day, soldiers reapers.
    Victor, prince of the land's descendants,
    At Bryn Deganwy, they followed him;
    I saw at Rhuddlan in a fine red tide
    A brave crowd round one bent on fame;
I saw at Penfro a flawless ruler,
    I saw at Pennardd a fallen leader;
    I saw their fine slaying, fine host falling,
    Where a fine land bears seagulls' bounty.
    I saw grief-stricken troops; I saw rejoicing;
    I saw fierce sally, resounding signal;
    I saw mail-clad men, warriors, routed;
    I saw warfare at Caer, at Coed Llwyfain.
    They were not, Gwynedd's manhood, mere boys:
    You were no coward, shepherd of Britain.

LAMENT FOR HIS SON

In the first wave, famed war-band's bright bulwark,
    You could not be constrained.
    Not easy, death-sentencing blade,
    Dygynnelw, to keep pace with you.

Dwell in the saints' honoured place, gold assembly:
    Heaven's Lord will save you.
    Harsh is the world without you.
    Dygynnelw, God be with you.

He that fashioned him man, form in torment,
    Bore away Dygynnelw.
    With God, no profitless complaint:
    Grave-hidden, splendid end of Cynddelw.

PETITION FOR RECONCILIATION
to the Lord Rhys

I implore God's favour, doubtless your gift,
    Your gifted man am I,
  On your warriors, war's eagle,
  On your land, Lord of the South.

I implore, I plead a great plea to the Lord
    Who made heaven and earth,
  Refuge from your wrath, singer's friend,
  On your gates, on your gate-keeper.

I implore, I plead, a pleader I am called,
    Ever-faithful God's favour
  On your portals, war-wager,
  On your porter, fair land's lord.

I implore your favour, hide not your support,
    Since remorse is proper.
  Court-heralds, call for silence.
  Be silent, bards: hear a bard.

I implore glad favour, gracious men of the South,
    Sure support of singers,
  With your band of shield-bearers,
  And your host of royal sons.

I implore glad favour, bounty's bulwark,
    Kings cannot withstand you,
  On your host, combat's columns,
  On your guard, worthy of mead.

A mead-feast their drink, mead-horns pour it forth,
    Serve it to golden hands:
  Prodigious drinking-bouts,
  Brave warriors and bold monarch.

Britain's regal hawks, your high song I fashion,
    Your high fame I broadcast:
  Your bard, your judge I will be;
  Your support, it is owed me.

Answer what I sing, what I may sing, lord:
  Hear me, since I have come.
 Lleisiawn's helm, bold lion, brave lord,
 Ease your wrath: your bard am I.

I am bard to my lord, green billow's splendour,
  Songfest singers' roads' splendour.
 Plea for refuge, long-feared exile:
 I implore a high lord's favour.

POEM ON HIS DEATH BED

 I beseech, God, true devotion,
  To praise my gracious, bountiful Lord,
Mary's one Son, source of afternoon and morning
   And teeming river-mouths,
  Who made trees and mead and true measure,
  And crops, and God's overflowing gifts,
Who made grass and grove and mountain heather,
  Who made one blest, by righteous judgment,
  And another lost for rejecting grace,
  In desperate need, bitter-hearted.
  I ask of God's Son, since he suffices,
  Atonement for our sin, sinning is wrong,
  And welcome in heaven our haven:
  May we go to the land we long for.

I beseech, God, beseech, resplendent praise
  For the poem I compose.
 There are thousands praise you, High Prince,
 Of your hosts, to your highest bounds.
I would wish, my Lord, with your permission –
  From your love, I believe you;
 You, song-renowned, I celebrate –
 Gift-pourer, let me be faultless.
 More than need it was, greatest grace,
 Lord of the mighty, to save with full might.
 The thought terrifies me thinking
 Of the sinning that Adam sinned.
Foolish exile, I wander your fair land
  With your fair host round me:

The church's bards shine the brightest;
Their support has been my portion.
Pleasant my path, a place I make for,
Hope in the High Judge, fellowship I seek:
King of every people, deliver me;
After wandering the world, bless me.
By leave of the Father most royal
And the Son and the Spirit most holy,
In righteousness' light I'll be blest,
In angels' dwelling-place, pure, most gracious,
In paradise, Prince of heaven, I pray.

Sovereign Ruler, when you were born
Came mercy for us, came redemption,
Came Adam's children from infidelity,
From long lawlessness, from captivity,
Came to call on us what we desired,
Came prowess, powerful abundance,
Came Christ incarnate, Master supreme,
Came in Mary's womb the wished-for Son,
Came the world's five ages from torment,
From deceit, from false dwelling's darkness,
From abiding hardship, from deep sadness,
From the enemy's prison, set free.
And he is our helm, our utmost haven,
Who will judge by our deeds our doing,
And he, heaven's Lord, predestined peace,
Brought us forth from perdition when pierced,
And he rises for us, and his blessing comes,
And he, Lord, will not deny us our good.
And he graciously was given,
In full might, the sun's road's domain.
One whose hand will offer his tithe to God,
He is not denied what is due him.
I am a poet: let me compose perfectly
In my Maker's keeping, Lord of hosts;
I, Cynddelw the singer, let grace reward me;
Let Michael, who knows me, welcome me.

Sovereign Ruler, when I sang of you,
Not worthless the poem I composed.
No lack of fine style in my lyric,
Not lacking, the gift, where I gained it.

152

Not created was I by unchanging God
To devise folly, or fraud, or violence.
Not without devotion, one with faith in God:
No painful wound will he suffer.
Not waking up have I spent my days:
Not sought for, heaven will not be given.
None too great the zeal in my devotion;
None too great reward have I deserved.
Not fitting, the pride I have nursed in my heart;
Not a thought of suffering penance.
In the Lord's dwelling I have longed for,
Freedom for my soul, this need have I pleaded.

Sovereign Ruler, deign to accept,
Worship's plea in harmonious song,
My spoken words flawlessly fashioned,
My poem in your praise, hundred land's candle.
Since you are Master, since you are Monarch,
Since you are Counsellor, Lord of light,
Since you are prophet's heart, since you are Judge,
Since you are gracious King, since you are Giver,
Since you are my Teacher, banish me not,
In your wrath, from your bright land.
Deny me not your favour, creator Lord;
Place me not, bowed low, with the graceless;
Deal me not, from your hand, a vile dwelling;
Leave me not with the dark horde, the loveless.

GRUFFUDD AP GWRGENAU

LAMENT FOR GRUFFUDD AP CYNAN

The One who sustains the moon at its full,
Who sees through to the heart of all things,
By his leave, by his grace, by his virtue our haven,
Radiant is the sun in his court.
And he when our end comes will bear us,
By his favour, to mercy's dwelling.

Lust's sadness, the destruction of our flesh:
　　In the end, the earth will consume us.

　　It is bad for us, how badly we live;
　　Second, the sum of our oaths;
　　Third, deceit in defending wrongdoing;
　　Fourth, wantonness; fifth, exorbitance;
Sixth, close-fisted solicitude for gold
　　And the world's splendour and honours;
　　Seventh, venting wrath by sleight of hand,
　　Sober words while the guts are seething;
　　Eighth is slaying with red-stained blades
　　A foe, the crows' song on his bosom;
　　Ninth, the thief's arrogance, no wonder,
　　Who cannot look on Christ crucified;
The tenth accursed thing is the tameless fury
　　　　Deaf, blind, before the grave gapes,
　　The lord ingloriously unyielding,
　　Long unreconciled in his wrongdoing.

　　God desires to come to his throne
　　Strong and weak, not a place to refuse.
From the stones, from the grave, we will be raised
　　To be cleansed of our transgressions.
　　Death is the scourge of all supremacy,
　　Too great, unwise our contention.
For Gruffudd, triumph's red spear, it hurts me,
　　Who gave me gold and well-trained horses,
　　Cynan's descendant, piercer of vice,
　　Gracious to the weak, Owain Gwynedd's heir,
　　Madawg's descendant, strong princely stock,
　　Song's delight, no dishonour his end,
Joyful in feasting, supreme in dignity,
　　Of the finest princes' lineage.
　　I had mead kindly poured from his hand;
　　Bards led no poor life in his service.
　　I have parted from a man, no joy,
　　Sore hurt, the dead and the living parting.
After a faithful lord, after parting's end,
　　No light burden, man's fragility.
　　No one will be, in five hundred years,
　　Less grudging, so kind, worthy of a feast:

May God not grudge my comrade in feasting
When all gather for the great judgment.

LAMENT FOR HIS COMRADES

Dead, congenial Merwydd, and tears drench me,
    Unstinting, and frequent.
  Man's old age will not await him;
  No longer one's life than a mirror's.

We think on, we mourn a warrior-welcoming lord
    God will not let be lost.
  Dead thousands, blameless songs' splendour;
  Dead Merwydd, dead we all shall be.

Far from Powys it is, hidden thought, for one
    To avenge, Abel's blood;
  Low in a still house of sand
  The red bed of Gwilym Rhyfel.

I have seen a place that pains me today,
    I can readily weep,
  A red grave, precious its sight,
  With Edenawg underneath it.

Since dead is the splendour and strength of Griffri,
    Heavy blow his going,
  Einawn will die, flawless gift:
  Then, nothing good will be left.

LLYWARCH AP LLYWELYN
(PRYDYDD Y MOCH)

A LOVE POEM FOR GWENLLIANT

It is Whitsun, campaign time for warriors;
    A bold man may campaign, bright rising.
    Set off, white-rumped steed, best of the stud;
    Trot briskly, sun rises in splendour.
    Take unafraid the road to the place,
    Foam-flecked, stag-like, fluent your movement,
    Past Tudur's region, Elise's land,
    Renowned Cyfeiliog, sad memory,
Past Cynfelyn's daughter, foe to lords' complexions:
    Though she be noble, she is out of reach.
    Nest spoke to me, nothing will come of it:
    One who readies the warp does not weave it.
Llywarch I am called, war-band's comrade,
    England's bane, invincible, rampart's ruin;
    My shield is long acquainted with combat;
    Foes are acquainted with spears in their breasts.
Any way I may take, boldly croak the crows,
    A raging man on their battlefield.
    Many a sigh for my anguish rises,
    Wends from my passion higher than the sky.
    Waters are wearing along their banks
    A gown of fair leaves, like birds on twigs;
    Cuckoos lay eggs; the trees are lively.
    I know for a girl my cheeks lose colour.
    Usk has borne, fair its rippling current,
    Many hills' leaves to Caerllion's dales.
    Fine steeds, eager, lusty, will bear me
    On praise's course, plea to the sun-hued,
    Gwenlliant's ramparts, of Gwynllwg's line,
    Lovable beauty, light of the border.
    Since no favour comes to me, fevered
    For the gentle maid's shape, daybreak's hue,
    I feel my bruised heart like a fierce flame
    Burn for her as a bonfire blazes.
    Form without flaw in a gown of gold,
    Surely sending the stud's white-maned steeds,

Bearing her suit, her praise will spread
To where the sun sets, where it rises.

ORDEAL BY HOT IRON

Heaven's creator, true to his servant,
I would trust him as I'd trust Saint John.
A hard judge of law's blessing God created:
　　I submit to you for support.
Your truth will shine out, white hot;
Your zeal, to my mind, is not hostile.
Consider, when you judge my heritage,
Scorching creature, who created you.
I entreat Peter for the attribute of Christ
　　Who bore the cross with dignity,
Through the fair intercession of Thomas,
And of Philip and Paul and Andrew.
From the grip of my hand, pale blue blade,
To avoid the burden of murder,
Good iron, bear witness: when Madog
Met his death, it was not at my hand,
Any more than Cain and his kindred
Share in heaven and its nine kingdoms.
For my part, I desire fellowship,
God's favour to me, and escape from his wrath.

ADMONITION

A petition for reconciliation to Dafydd ab Owain Gwynedd

First of October, season day dwindles,
　　Stalks pale, moon high, showing the path,
Turmoil in river-mouths, tide rising,
Winter-time near, sea high-spirited.
The Lord's talents, they were dealt to me
As they were not dealt to my forebears:
News came to me of a mighty lord,
Worthy of my gift, deriding me,
And boldly will he take back a gift for my song,
And harsh his dreadful passion about it.

Patient have I been, battle's rampart,
Famed leader, in remaining silent;
I will not vow, Beli's bounteous heir,
Or be sullen in sulking far off.
I know, where I may strike, envenomed
The tongue's wrathful path no salve will heal:
Wrathful is my talent in turmoil,
Strife-strident in combat, in conflict.
Quiet your rage, refuge of poets,
Blazing because poems were composed:
Look, free-handed Dafydd, war-band-shattering hero,
Gift-giver, that you beware my spear.
Champion defending Teyrnon's land,
Eryri's warlord's ardent warriors,
Ruler of the west, restore me:
To reject my song is to vex me.
Worth more am I to you, noble lord, than many steeds,
Horsemen faring far on your missions;
Better are you, famed master, than the three,
Mordaf, Nudd, Rhydderch, for giving.
Superb ruler, restraining the strong,
Pour out wealth to me for praising you,
Pourer of golden favour, Rhodri's descendant,
And see whether I remain angry.
Drive me not from you, refuse me not;
Leave me not outcast, housed in silence;
Britain's blest ruler, be my refuge
With your gold, your blessing, your kindness.
Your fame will blaze forth, clear proclaiming,
From the warmth of my poem and passion.
I have seen bards hoarsely, no vanity,
Dreadful pain, extolling your valour:
I have sung your praise as they will not sing it,
Mighty warrior, glorious lord.
The wise have no fear of poverty:
Precious song-wise hero am I for you.
I know that God, best of the prophets,
Takes not back, of his grace, his goodness:
Know, Dafydd, Elifri by nature,
It is no easy thing to control me.
If it suits a kind lord to curb my vigour,
With miserly order to anchor me,

Unconcealed will be niggardliness
Where greed to hoard embitters me.
Owain's royal son, carnage of rulers,
Benlli's splendid coastal kingdom,
Do not, soldiers' eagle, be sluggish
To meet me, lord skilled in parley.
Tread not your mantle, your good am I:
Resist me not for any reason;
Do not deal me for gold to other lords:
No other will please though I'm honoured.
Pledge honour for me, confer it on me
As a valiant man will pledge it.
The day has come, highly praised Dafydd,
Noble nature, to win me or lose me.
Let there come, before strife between us,
Angels of peace, peace that will not perish:
May mine be, gift-giver, concord with you,
And good health through long life be yours.

IN PRAISE OF LLYWELYN AB IORWERTH

Sorry Christmas for those allied to England:
    A Welsh lion held them,
    Concord's song, guardian shield,
    Even-handed, bold in battle.

Bold was Arthur, routing these with his war-band,
    Mourning surrounded him,
    In strife's din soldiers' fond soldier,
    As you are today, bold man.

Bold man Llywelyn, open-handed to bards,
    With his numerous hosts:
    Christendom's lord will not soon refrain,
    England's chain, arrogant throng.

Arrogant are any not bound to my lord,
    Man who prizes not misers.
    God made not, heaven's high king,
    Nor will make, his like, his equal.

You made war, Britain's mainstay, gold-speared boon,
    Not easy for your foe;
  For Welshmen, Godiar's fellow,
  England's lair was a tamed land.

Benlli's prowess, when appeased he is gracious,
    A merciful ruler,
  Fearless when he is hard-pressed,
  Valiant, fearsome in pursuit.

Fierce attack, raging battle on Lleon's border,
    Britain's helm, Llywelyn,
  Stern ruler your forebears bore,
  You launched, red-stained lord, the assault.

Llywelyn's assault, renowned helm of Britain,
    Pledge to England he spurns.
  Thousand bards' patron, praise-anointed,
  Ferocious, he makes for the field.

Attacker, assaulter, foreign lord your foe,
    Red-stained your retinue,
  Mine your gift, battle-famed Nudd,
  Yours my song, zeal unconcealed.

Unconcealed your assault, Llŷr's zeal and Brân's,
    And red-shredded your spear.
  There you attacked, warriors' lord,
  Through Tren's river, royal eagle.

Since you have ruled, England uprooting, the Welsh,
    Seizing thousands of spoils,
  Dragon's riches, thrusting prince,
  Ellesmere, mighty lord, is shapeless.

No delusion, since Mold, wolf-pack fortress,
    Rhun's descendant's triumph:
  Towers burnt, each one gutted,
  Mighty flame, Alun's folk in flight.

EINION AP GWALCHMAI

LAMENT FOR NEST

Maytime, day long, giving is lavish,
Trees are not captive, fair-hued the grove;
Birds are tuneful, tame is the ocean,
Hoarse-voiced is the wave, the wind falling.
Flawless gifts are the goal of prayer:
Sanctum tranquil, I may not be silent.
I listened to the waves wearing land away
Around the wide bound of Beli's sons:
Piercing fiercely was the sea in surging,
Great, beside the wave, was grief for her.
Her ways were not coarse, slow to make demands:
Salt were the tears, unstinted the brine.
Favoured by a gentle maid, above the wave's cries,
Stiff-legged I walked Dyfi's head-reaches.
I sang song for Nest before she died,
A hundred sang her praise, like Elifri:
I will sing, with mind saddened, for her,
A song to mourn her, deep misery.
Candle of Saint Cadfan's, clad in silk,
Bright the sight of her near the Dysynni,
Virgin gentle and fair, wisdom sharing,
Woman for whom I was no false lover,
Red earth enfolds her, fallen silent.
Foul bereavement, graveyard's stone tomb for her:
Nest's burial, manifest evil.
Look of a proud hawk greatly gifted,
Fair as gossamer, and blessed with goodness,
Gwynedd's honour, there was need of her.
She was graced with no common nature:
Common were gold coins for praising her.
No painful penance was ever imposed
That is greater than mine without her.
Death afflicted me with infirmity:
Not a living soul feels what I feel.
Needs be does not bid, praiseworthy prayer,
The one parted from her to bear it.
Nest in her resting-place of sacred song,
I am troubled in mind, like Pryderi.

Apprehensive of heart, I know of no help:
    Not without good cause do I say this.
    It is a shroud hidden low torments me,
    Fair girl's hindrance, hoarfrost's hue on Eryri.
    I plead to my Lord, God of heaven,
    What I plead is no frivolous plea,
    A plea for one in a coffin I plead,
    For a slender girl, it must succeed,
    Through the constant righteous prayer of Dewi
    And ten times the saints of Brefi's synod,
    For a girl who is rightly protected
    By the highest claim of the prophets,
    By the power of God, wise his choosing,
    By Mary's and the martyrs' haven.
And on her behalf, a prayer I offer,
    Who gave me bliss to torment me:
    None has been so dear to me as she.
    May she suffer no pain, Peter shield her.
    God will not wish to deprive her:
    May Nest not be deprived, heaven be hers.

PRAYER

    God, supreme worker of wonders,
    Grant us a share of your blessings.
    You formed people for your own purpose,
    And a gifted mortal man am I.
A gift rightly is mine as a man of high art
      With thoughts at the ready.
    A devout man am I at masses,
    Lord God, illustrious lawgiver.
    A bad son am I to you, my Maker:
    Were I good, I would not be doubtful;
    Before burial, hateful behaviour,
    Though I am wicked, be merciful.
From true devotion, tears of expiation,
    May they flow freely along my cheeks,
    Gaining atonement for my transgressions
    Before I go gravewards amidst the graves.
    Before the bitter reckoning comes,
    Before sinful desires disappear,
God will grant me love within heaven's walls,

God will hear my cry in my anxiety.
God make me shun, fierce current of cold,
Hell's wicked flood, ferocious waters;
God make me avoid giving wounds;
God make me stay sinless on Sundays.
God defend me from my intentions:
God, take me to you, great Father of mine.
God, do not punish me for my sins
On the day transgressions are punished.
You will have no end, have had no beginning:
     May I not be sad to meet you.
May I pay him, bountiful Lord of kings,
Upon Jordan's bank for his blessings,
By pangs and anguish upon my knees,
By welcoming penance on my elbows
In a worthless life for the wanton words
     That past measure have come from my mouth.

For five ages' sake you bore, spikes' anguish,
Five bleeding wounds, art's heavenly Lord.
May I bear the pain of the Alps' abode
To go where I have heard that you were.
It was the height of faith to see your wounds
When you were in pain from your piercings.
With support from gentle bright angels
It befits you, Father, to forgive me.
Since you made, Lord, the day to be mine,
By your nails, leave me not to the fiend.
Your cross, rood of wood, royal honours,
Has shielded six ages from punishment.
Emperor creator, from your pleading, it was bloodstained,
I will not be left poor by your laws.
Blessed be the monks in their churches,
Church-loving, kindly, cherishing pains,
Gentle communities, sinless their songs,
Mankind's steadfast unshakable men.
Woe to him that caused them, peril's betrayals,
When Jesus was stabbed in his ribs.
After he came for the end intended
He bore hell's spoils away in his grasp.
And after that, this is what he did,
What is preached in the sermons is true:
He was seen to go, blissful powers,

On Ascension Day: do not doubt it.
God's Son gained, that Thursday, heaven above,
    A small sum of sins is too many,
    The worthy ruler at God's right hand,
    Gracious hero companioned by saints.
    May our end be to dwell on the fringe
    Of the sea in Enlli, so long our hive.

    After speaking, perverse nature, falsehood,
    And after, as well, lovers' lechery,
    After plotting to join in battles,
    After nursing envy of the best,
    After ardently courting a host with oaths
    And a good many causes for sighs,
After scorning too much, after worldly songs,
    After sin committed at matins,
    After quarreling with judges' verdicts,
    After long pursuing worth's rewards,
    After angry abstention from Mass,
    After the attendance on princes,
After the tangled strands of human life,
    After wrathful pursuit in battles,
    May I have from God above, after sins,
    A place of repose, paradise land,
    Place where none are older or younger,
    Place untroubled by wide-spreading want.
I ask God's favour: on the gates of heaven
        May Peter not put locks
    To keep me from my prize, from my own,
    From my inheritance, from my dear love.
    May Michael come to bring me a pledge
    As Saint Cwyfan brought books and learning,
    Like Elfod's coming to Gelau's land,
    Like Cenau's quickly flowering faith.
    Mary and Saint Giles, Martin, Matthew,
    Saint Mark and Saint Luke, the mouth of John,
    To God for my soul, words are needful,
    Intercede, stay firm in your purpose.
    Paul will judge my plea when death comes to me,
    Noble, strong, he'll not ban me from my faithful One.
    Before I lie still, may no grief be mine:
    Good, devotion and faith and grace's gifts.
    Strong intercession will gain great merit

Where it bows, wise God, to your power:
For my salvation, may fervent thoughts
Give praise to the Trinity like prayers.
The good of God's relics will win me pardon
    And renouncing arms.
May a perfect while, the best work,
Before I rest in the grave, be mine.

MADOG AP GWALLTER

THE NATIVITY

A Son was given us, a Son born blessedly,
    Beneath his station,
A Son of glory, a Son to save us,
    The best of sons:
Virgin mother's Son, firm her devotion,
    Pregnant her pledges,
Without fleshly father, he is the Son of grace,
    Giver of graces.

Let us weigh wisely, and let us wonder
    At wonders done;
Nothing more wondrous will ever exist,
    Will lips suppose:
God has come to us, the One creating
    All the creatures,
As God, as man, and God as man,
    With the same gifts.

Great little giant, powerful weakling,
    Fair were his cheeks,
Wealthy pauper, our Father and Brother,
    Author of judgments,
This is Jesus, the one we welcome
    As King of kings,
Humble noble, Emmanuel,
    Contemplation's honey.

An ox and an ass, Lord of this world,
    Their manger is his,
A bundle of hay instead of a cradle
    For our Lord of hosts.
No silk he wishes, no fine fabrics
    Are his swaddlings;
Instead of sendal around his bed
    Were seen tatters.

He is, however, as revealed from heaven
    That performed marvels,
Was the Lord, the one they speak of,
    Books and lore,
And wonder-workers, wise and learned,
    Singular doings,
And the foretelling of holy prophets,
    Lucid speeches.

For a proclamation made to shepherds,
    Watchers of sheep-folds,
An angel appears, and the night like day
    Became bright:
Then were spoken, and were believed,
    Tales of good tidings,
Of God being born in David's town,
    Without a doubt.

To the sound of angels people listen,
    Giving thanks,
Great rejoicing, with many a voice
    Lifted in song:
'To God *gloria, pax in terra*
    To our borders,
Peace to the world, salvation for all
    After death.'

Men of old kept watch, with long memories,
    Because of their fathers,
Accomplished watchmen, men of the East,
    Upon the hilltops:
Each one in turn, they took in order
    A portion of watches,

From night to night, like eager waiting
    For a lord's favour.

They saw a star, of a different hue,
    Having a halo,
With a different goal than the stars above,
    Over their heads:
He was being born then, the good king,
    Certain the portent
That first and foremost was seen by three kings,
    Greatly privileged.

Then they believed, then they go in quest,
    A successful quest,
And their epiphany a star before them
    Sending forth light:
To Jerusalem and Bethlehem town,
    Expecting no tricks,
They came swiftly on speedy horses,
    Proper their fodder.

Alighting in haste, the star instructs them,
    True its instructions,
To the house they go, without door, without frame,
    Windy doorways:
The Son was there, the One who was born
    Beneath his signs,
And his mother resting, her precious breast
    Pressed to his lips.

A man they see, they believe he is God,
    Good is their faith;
They worship him, they do not delay,
    On seemly knees;
They open treasure, they offer gold
    And finer things,
Myrrh and incense, chancel's ornament,
    Song's virtues.

Wisely they turn, by another road,
    Without losses,
Back to their land, from the false king's
    Tricks and treachery.

Herod was thwarted, cruel stroke,
    In his plans:
Sons were slaughtered, innocent, holy,
    Grief for their mothers,

And not grief for them, blessed are they,
    That they are saints
And martyrs for their monarch's sake,
    In their swaddling clothes,
Before as yet good will existed,
    No thoughts of vengeance,
No good deeds, no good words
    Upon their tongues.

Those things were accomplished at the birth,
    Fair miracles,
Of true God's only Son, if one will look
    At the beginning,
The Nativity's night, a night unlike
    Nights of wickedness,
A night of joy for Christendom:
    Let us too be joyful.

A blessed time is the Nativity,
    Fit time for feasts,
When the Son was born, Lord of every priest,
    Of all things Master,
Born of a lady who will do us good
    And prevent our pains,
And make room for us on the fairest height
    As our reward.

BLEDDYN FARDD

LAMENT FOR LLYWELYN AP GRUFFUDD

Christ, great Lord, plentiful grace I seek,
Christ, guileless Son of God, care for me,

Christ righteous, generous, strongest defender,
  Whose body bore the harshest torment.

What pertains to a man I declare:
  Let one that suffers grief be most sane;
Let one by nature the highest in power
  Be the humblest in mind.

Christ came into the world lest Adam
  And his tribe dwell in hell, host held fast,
To fill heaven, the high lord's dominion,
  Place the angel most disgraceful lost.

Great Wales has lost the manliest lord,
  Manly blade, bright hero most brave:
Manly helm not alive, what shall I do with him lost,
  Manly lion, benign, most bountiful?

A man was slain for us, supreme man,
  A man for Wales, boldly I name him:
Manly Llywelyn, most manly Welshman,
  Man not fond of flight the nearest way,

Man staunch in charging a warband's wing,
  Man whose campsite was green-pavilioned,
Manly son of Gruffudd, least grudging of gift
  In Nudd's and Mordaf's resplendent way,

Man red-speared, prudent man, like Priam,
  Man rightly the proudest army's king,
Man swift his praise, man most generous in spending
  As far as the sun takes the furthest course,

Man whose ruin's bitter, most courtly lord,
  Man sorely mourned, most loyal friend,
Man trustworthy, wise, the choicest from Môn
  To Caer Llion, the fairest place.

A man was Llywelyn near Taf's border,
  Manifest ruler, bestowing raiment,
A man who excelled as chief of soldiers
  To Porth Wygyr, tranquil eagle.

The Man who bore the most harrowing dread,
　　Death for five epochs, deepest torment,
May he welcome a ruler most nobly bred,
　　For mercy's sake, greatest majesty.

LAMENT FOR GRUFFUDD'S THREE SONS

Winter-time, most ashen the ocean,
　　Surging billows the sea-birds' perch,
Hoar-frost now a cold cloak on Eryri,
　　Loud the white wave round Enlli's white land.

I grieve more and more in misery;
　　I lead a life of pain, lacking lords.
Three men have I lost, three rightful rulers,
　　Noble brothers of Rhodri's line.

Too harsh were we all before their loss;
　　Too sad has Christ made us, cross of light;
Too strong their passion for raising warbands
　　To support troops on Hoddni's border.

Men crystal-lived, men of great valour,
　　Men who pierced boldly round Ceri's land,
Men who charged in battle, fierce when hard-pressed,
　　They would not let Ystrad Tywi fall.

Owain ap Gruffudd, nobility's grace,
　　Spirited horseman, distributing horses,
Aberffraw's eagle, none will equal his goodness
　　In fostering Gwynedd's fame and honour.

Slain was a man, unselfish his way,
　　Ruler of Welshmen, bold his title,
Llywelyn, proud leader of troops in combat,
　　Red-bladed hawk in arms at Caer Ffili.

Dafydd, fame's spoils before he perished,
　　A Drystan in his ways, shield shearing,
Gwynedd's grief, woe's us, he was taken away,
　　Assault's hawk, giver of red brocade,

Blood-dripping lance, of Beli's lineage,
    Steel-speared, like Arthur, at Caer Fenlli,
Dread lord's splendid rush to redden a gold sword,
    When Gwynedd's men went to Teifi's lands.

Lords of slashing weapons, excelling,
    Mighty war-lords, a thousand war-cries,
Sorely have we grieved for three men's long silence,
    Like Llŷr's sons, praiseworthy power.

To God I plead, Lord, give them welcome,
    Open hand, ruler's glorious gift,
To all the saints, to exalted Cybi,
    To noble, holy, righteous Dewi,

To Mary's great throne, mighty her prayer,
    To the men who were created prophets,
In the parish of lasting joy, pardon's dwelling-place,
    Amid the worshipful saints of Brefi's senate.

GRUFFUDD AB YR YNAD COCH

LAMENT FOR LLYWELYN AP GRUFFUDD

Heart cold in the breast with dread, grief-stricken,
    For a king, oak door, of Aberffraw.
      Bright gold was bestowed by his hand;
      He deserved his gold diadem.
Golden king's gold cups! No more merriment,
    Llywelyn; no blithe garb may I wear.
I grieve for a prince, hawk beyond reproach;
    I grieve for the ill that befell him;
I grieve for his loss; I grieve for his lot;
    I grieve to hear how he was wounded.
Cadwaladr's stronghold, bulwark from spear waves,
    Lad with red lance, gold-handed linch-pin.
He lavished riches, he gave each winter
    The garments he wore for my wear.

Lord rich in herds, he aids us no more:
    May life everlasting be his.
Mine, rage at the Saxon for crushing me;
  Mine the need, before death, to lament;
Mine, with good reason, to rave against God
      Who has left me without him;
    Mine to praise him, unstinting, unstilled;
    Mine ever, henceforth, his remembrance;
Mine, for my lifetime, is sorrow for him,
    Since mine is the woe, mine the weeping.
    A lord I have lost, long may I fear,
    A royal court's lord, a hand slew him.
A lord truly constant, listen to me,
    How loudly I mourn: ah, the mourning.
    A blest lord till the eighteen were slain;
    A gracious lord, low he is laid;
A lord bold as a lion guiding the land;
    A lord eager to create havoc;
A flourishing lord, till he left Emrais
    No Saxon would venture to strike him;
A lord, stone his roof, Welsh people's ruler,
    Of the right line to hold Aberffraw.
    Lord Christ, how sad am I for him,
    True Lord, from whom comes salvation,
From the heavy sword-stroke, his downfall,
    From the long swords that had him hard-pressed,
    From the wound for my prince that sways me,
    From hearing of Bod Faeaw's lord's fall.
Perfect the lad slain by enemies' hands;
    Perfect his forebears' honour in him;
Candle of kings, strong lion of Gwynedd,
    Throne of honour, he was much needed.
    From great Britain's death, support's sad end,
    From Nancoel's lion slain, Nancaw's mail-coat,
Many a tear gliding fast down a cheek,
    Many a side made red with gashes,
    Many a foot soaked in puddles of blood,
    Many a widow wailing about him,
    Many a burdened mind wandering,
    Many a son left without father,
Many a homestead black in the firebrand's track,
    And many a ground ruin lays waste,
Many a sorry cry, as at Camlan,

Many a tear trickling down a cheek.
From a prop cut down, gold-handed prince,
From Llywelyn's death, lost my sound mind;
Heart frozen in the bosom from fear,
Lust for life like dry brushwood shrivels.
See you not the rush of the wind and rain?
See you not the oaks thrashing each other?
See you not that the sea is lashing the shore?
See you not the Judgment portending?
See you not that the sun is hurtling the sky?
See you not that the stars have fallen?
Do you not believe in God, foolish people?
See you not that the world is in peril?
Ah, God, that the sea would cover the land!
What is left us that we should linger?
No place of escape from terror's prison,
No place to live; wretched is living!
No counsel, no lock, not a single path
Open to be free of fear's sad warning.
All retainers, true to his trust;
All warriors, his supporters;
All strong men once swore by his hand;
All lords, all lordships were his.
All counties, all towns are now taken;
All households, all clans now collapse;
All the weak, all the strong, he kept safe;
All children now cry in their cradles.
Little good it did, to deceive me,
Leaving me my head, left headless:
Head cut off, no foe in terror,
Head cut off, it were better not,
Head of a soldier, head still praised,
Head of a warlord, dragon's head,
Head of fair Llywelyn, harsh fear for the world,
An iron spike through it.
Head of my prince, harsh fall's pain for me,
Head of my spirit left speechless,
Head that owned honour in nine-hundred lordships,
With nine-hundred feasts for him.
Head of a king, his hand sowed iron,
Head of a king's hawk, forcing a breach,
Head of a kingly wolf out-thrusting,
Head of heaven's kings, be his haven.
THE LORD GOD

Blessed king, rule over him, Lord of hosts,
    Whose hopes reached to Llydaw:
Aberffraw's truly rightful king,
    Let heaven's blest land be his home.

MEDITATION

The King of glory, worthy his doing,
    Nothing tainted or false comes from him.
If some would not do as he commanded
    Too great their arrogance.
Breaking the commandments and supporting thieves
    And oppressing the weak will not avail.
Evil, in the end, your cunning wrong-doing
    Through pride in wealth, no good is presumption.
Consider, ungodly one, as it is said,
    There will be no arguing with God,
Nothing but truth and courteous peace
    And true mercy, as is fitting.
Examine your life before you go to your grave:
    If you have done wrong, do not wonder
There is need to pay in the presence of Jesus
    Where three hosts will see: it will cause grief.
Woe to those who have faith, if they do wrong,
    In the false world, poor thing that will vanish,
And do not think upon what is needful:
    The excess one has, one will not remember.
Though worldly pomp may be full of pleasure,
    A feast of honour, it causes conflict.
I saw Llywelyn and his hosts, another Merfyn,
    Welshmen from all corners in his train;
I saw rulers of Gwynedd and the South,
    Armies' pillars, gathered together;
I saw men embattled and horses mustering
    And wine and people and playing-field;
I saw multitudes and daily feasting
    And a prospering world, heroes' conquest:
That has gone by like a wave of your hand;
    Everyone leaves, transient lifetime.
The wealthy man will be no more long-living
    Than the ragged who does not quarrel.
Let him consider while he lives, before harsh pains,

What he may seek, what he will despise;
Let every man blest seek the feast that lasts,
    The tranquil joy of faith that flowers.
Let guile not seek, by false accusation,
    Heaven so fair, since it will not prosper.
When one thinks in full, meditation's penance,
    Of the pain of Eve's wicked worthless greed,
Not from his wrongdoing came the Lord of heaven
    To the tree of suffering, pride's destination.
Woe is he unfortunately born, sinful deed;
    It will be torment, seeing the total sight:
He will show the welts and all of his wounds
    And his nails and his blood and his cross.
'This is what I have done: what have you done?'
    Christ will say, heaven's Lord: then would be needed
Purity made ready to meet the Trinity
    Before ruinous sin's tribulation.
Woe to them, the misers and the fraudulent men
    And the evil-minded who will not worship,
To see they are forsaken for their wrongdoings
    In the pains of hell, hidden place of penance,
And see going to heavenly glory
    Those found in a state of grace,
With the joy of the feast that will never end
    In the blest assembly, eternally free.

III. THE POETS OF THE GENTRY
c.1285–c.1525

IORWERTH FYCHAN

A LOVE POEM FOR GWEIRFYL

My mind I have set, besotted my senses,
On a slim, comely, elegant form.
Bearer of all bliss, nine sorrows consume me,
Faint promise, fair sun's hue, won't hinder me.

Besotted, I considered, comber's beauty,
Not convinced to give up the choice girl:
I think of pursuing, hue of dawnlight,
Where the horses of Elenid run.

I look, for her sake, like a hermit;
More and more sorrow's surfeit is mine;
And at midnight it came to me: if one were chosen;
No colour was left in my face at all.

Silent, regal, beautiful, fickle,
Slender fair, frail and graceful, radiant sun,
White of throat in a cloak where green garb was bestowed,
Crowds' frequent tread, thousand bards entreating,

A maiden I saw, so glowing,
Comely, discreet, of a far-famed hall,
Stately, shapely, where one deemed her a treasure,
Her leg so white above her shoe-top,

Fortune's goal for one who was wounded,
Gold-mantled, fair-skinned, slow to reward,
Hue of snow on a slope, swift flow my thoughts,
Lover's happiness where she'd be loved,

Softly spoken, undoubted lady,
Blithe-hearted beauty who would be served,
Blight on cheeks' brightness, unmoved by suffering,
Flood tide's hue, sleep was unsought,

Reward of long woe gently reproved,
Bestowing wealth where it was shared,

179

Deserving supremacy, maiden by nature,
   Accustomed to wear precious jewels.

   When Welshmen were a grief-stricken throng
   Of one mind because of their sorrow,
   By making poems, song that was rewarded,
   For their fair dawn's beauty, earth was brightened.
For a foam-pale face, my weakness she sees,
   For a poem, Gweirfyl, pains have been taken.

GRUFFUDD AP DAFYDD AP TUDUR

THE SILENT GIRL

Gracious maid, whose spell dispels sleep, pain's blanket,
   Be pleased to speak to me:
   Not painless, your lack of answer;
   Not easy, conversing with a mute.

Mute and proud, falcons' offspring, I see you
   If I judge you, passion's language.
   Môn was the name of my homeland;
   Mine, sorry thoughts: I'm feeble.

I'm enfeebled, hurtful yearning's strong spell, for one word
   From a famed stone fortress:
   Fainter and sadder she makes me,
   Fair court's offspring, faint soft glance.

Your glance, crushing frown across me, I'm an exile,
   Goes a mile beyond me:
   Girl who puts thought in shackles,
   Speak a ready word for my sake.

Speak a proper word after passion's storm,
   Since I complain of harshness,
   As recompense, comfort's message,
   Or of your good will, gift named freely.

I've not had freely, answer's needful for trysting,
    Hue of harbour's white wave,
  For recompense, or through any power,
  From her, as yet, an answer.

The proverbial answer, soul's long labour,
    Speaks, on the plaintiff's side:
  It confesses, fair slim darling,
  Clear betrayal, modest beauty.

I'll have no calm day with a meek, soft-voiced maid
    At the fair court of Eitun:
  For me, a mighty lack of sleep;
  Mine, intense pain, above Caer Rhun.

Let her partake, shapely girl so kind, of my torment,
    To pay the price for my sleep,
  In a green place, Eitun's fair earth,
  For the sake of her own soul.

No worthy foe has caused me sharp grief till now
    Except her in Eitun,
  Or thought, or song of longing,
  Or dreadful affliction, save one.

I knew I'd not have my desire: I've yearned
    For a lively dear in Eitun;
  She knew insomnia's art,
  Modest, hostile, graceful form.

Eight nights, last night, from my sleepless turmoil,
    Eight notes went again to Eitun:
  Eight answers went with each one,
  Went in secret, without one favour.

  Often through yearning they've gone,
  Easy terms, muse's ardour,
  From my mouth, radiant words,
  Golden flood, to you in Eitun.

  It was wrong, mocking the current,
  That you sent, spellbinding form,

No message to me from Eitun
While a soul was still found in me.

Surely heaven's Lord will accept
Two souls without a blemish:
A soul to me is the tall fair maid,
And he knows the soul within me.

It's a pleasure, true wisdom that may be taught,
      For a learned man to speak,
   And best for, courteous language,
   Fair wits, full of guile and enchantment.

By long-studied enchantment the fair girl intends,
      Towards the one weak without her,
   Turning more and more haughty in thought,
   Stronger in guile than men's wisdom.

Men's passion, I see truly, candle-bright maiden,
      Has made me slip into madness,
   Sensible man's painful journey:
   The wise like the blind she beguiles.

Guile alters good sense, something long brooded on,
      Like a drunkard drinking deep:
   Hue of marshes' harsh-voiced billow,
   Because of her, no sleep for me.

The first of men was Adam
And a gracious maid, for heirs,
And two of a kind, sound of chiding,
They were called, sorrowful union.

Adam was one, for an apple,
With Eve, though she was guileless,
Who gave to their many daughters,
To their wise sons, the choosing.

After Adam, lord of high passion,
Before Pope's law and his fussing,
Everyone did the deed of love
With his lover blamelessly.

Blameless will be, free and easy,
Well did May fashion leaf-houses,
A tryst under trees, in hiding,
For me, me and my darling.

Guard, dainty form's guileful mind,
A glance, before causing pain:
By gaining learning and vigour
And adventurousness, be first.

IORWERTH BELI

COMPLAINT AGAINST THE BISHOP OF BANGOR

Lord Christ, gracious-hearted sovereign,
    Protector, Patron, of angelic hosts,
Hear me, my Helm, Head of Christendom's rulers,
    Glory's gold talisman, true salvation.
I've been sorely pierced, Arfon's been worthless:
    A master of learning made me doleful
When he clothed, he honoured, strummers of strings,
    Ringing in ears tuned to bardic contention,
And left, mastery of serious themes,
    The learned entertainers stark naked.
And I found it strange, with the signs of favour
    From our lord, too severe the wrongs,
When God did not send instant retribution
    Where bards' compositions were disregarded.
While Llywarch lived, respected by patrons,
    And Cynddelw, defence of princes' honour,
And Gwilym Rhyfel, praise wide-spreading worth,
    And Dafydd Benfras in Môn's great hall,
A bountiful lord, bestower of gifts,
    Would not cause the least slight to poets.
While splendid bards lived, true song's fine servants,
    Perfect in thrice-gifted eloquence,
There'd be no respect, like swine squealing,
    For a harsh willow crwth, broken-gutted.

Listening to so lovely a long-versed lyric
    Of the poet's high work in proper language,
It was harsh to hear the hiccuping of harps
    From hollow wolfskin, taut strings.
When Maelgwn Hir went from the son of Dôn's land
    To Gwalch Gorsedd's feast, to Caer Seion,
Taking with him, splendid intentions,
    Such performers on strings as there were,
He made them, thick crowd of sturdy men,
    Every one of them, swim the river.
When they reached the land, Môn's edge, at ebb-tide,
    The harpists weren't worth a halfpenny.
God's a witness to this, witnesses know it:
    Because of their mastery, learned men's gift,
The poets composed as well as before
    Despite what they'd swum, noble men's way.
From Bangor's choir's lord, honoured with mitre,
    A peer, a prince of the Britons' land,
Worthless companies have had apparel,
    Thrusting tribe, oppressive burden.
Jolly Tudur Wion, bullock-shaped mumbler,
    Beggarly, vexatious his verses,
For knowing English, scoundrel's English accent,
    Had a flowing green-fringed garment:
He had, hateful churl, unseemly occurrence,
    Accursed rascal, fat crows' cuckoo,
Fraudster, leader of foul-speaking horns,
    Mangling mixed language, pied clothing.
Nobility's not cherished by the dregs of tabors'
    Music, the senses of English yokels.
It was a sorry sight, repulsive wretches,
    Giving them clothing not full of holes.
Did his grace not know, master of learning,
    Not like Tutcyn's song, sound claiming fame,
A wise man's public verse would go, dishonour's brand,
    From the English Channel to the Irish Sea?

GRONW GYRIOG

LAMENT FOR GWENHWYFAR

A veil was placed above a ravaged cheek,
Bright, beautiful, clear-voiced maiden,
Too short for the world, the length of her lifetime,
A stone screen's constraint in Llan-faes.

Lofty Llan-faes, above the sea-strand,
Hides Gwen – blithe favour – hwyfar,
Saints' lodging, and friars' privileged ground,
Girl's earth-blanket, long sleep's utter grief.

Long the turmoil of mind in me
Because of God's harshness to her:
She honoured with great goodness readily,
Generous, joyous, dormer's fair-hued sun.

Vile the dormer, after face and form's
Beauty that's hidden by soil:
Painful memories, Rhiannon's gift,
Sadness for a modest, beautiful maid.

For her modesty, core of memory,
Lovely tranquil Gwenhwyfar,
And her fairness of mind, guileless form,
And her bounty, the Lord will reward her.

Lord of heaven, grievous lot the sore loss,
Girl's deep sleep, the world won't regain her:
Earth was placed on a moon mantled in beauty;
Earth has not been placed on a better lady.

Better and better the mind, splendid candle,
Of Gwenhwyfar, the earth's joyful sun:
A large stone screen is the lady's veil,
Harsh tale for her kindred, the grieving for her.

Greatly it grieves, an unfailing gift's taking,
Madog's daughter, of noble rank.

Gravel today, fitting stone, possesses her,
Whose cheek once was decked with fur.

A veil was placed above a ravaged cheek,
Bright, beautiful, clear-voiced maiden,
Too short for the world, the length of her lifetime,
A stone screen's constraint in Llan-faes.

DAFYDD AP GWILYM

THE GIRLS OF LLANBADARN

Passion doubles me over,
Plague take all the parish girls,
Because, frustrated trysting,
I've had not a single one,
No lovely longed-for virgin,
Not a wench or witch or wife.

What's the hindrance, what mischief,
What flaw, that I'm not desired?
What harm if a slim-browed girl
Has me in a dark forest?
No shame for her to see me
Lying in a bed of leaves.
Not a time I wasn't loving,
Never's been so binding a spell
Surpassing Garwy's passion,
One or two each single day,
And for all that, no nearer
To finding a friendly one.

No Sunday in Llanbadarn
I'd not be, as some will swear,
Facing a dainty maiden,
The nape of my neck to God.
And when I've long looked over
The parish across my plume,

Says one radiant clear-voiced dear
To her pert pretty neighbour:
'That lad pale-faced as a flirt,
Decked in his sister's tresses,
Lascivious are his eyes'
Slanting glances: he's shameless.'
'Is that what he has in mind?'
Says the one who is next her,
'He'll never have an answer:
To the devil, foolish thing.'

Cruel the bright girl's cursing,
Poor pay for a love-dazed man.
I'm compelled to call a halt
To these ways, to such nightmares.
I'm forced to become like one
Who's a hermit, an outlaw.
Too much looking, stern lesson,
Behind me, a sorry sight,
Leaves me, lover of strong song,
Head bowed, with no companion.

A CELEBRATION OF SUMMER

Summer, parent of impulse,
Begetter of thick close-knit boughs,
Fair forester, wooded slope's master,
You're everyone's tower, hills' tiler.
You're the source, word of power,
Faithful lord, of the world's rebirth.
You are, inciter of speech,
Every living plant's farmstead,
And growth's balm, double growth's source,
And chrism of woodland trysting.

Well knows, by God who is loved,
Your hand to make green trees flourish.
Precious lifeblood of earth's four quarters,
By your grace, too, wondrously grow
Birds and the fair soil's harvest
And the flocks that soar in flight,
Moorland meadows' bright-tipped hay,

187

Beehives and wild bees swarming.
You foster, highways' prophet,
Earth's full burden, green-laden garth.
You make my bower blossom,
Weaving a fine web of leaves,
And evil is it always
How August nears, night or day,
And knowing by the slow dwindling,
Golden hoard, that you would go.

Tell me, Summer, such this step,
I have the skill to ask you,
What region, or what domain,
What land you seek, by wise Peter.

'Hush, praise-bard, your painstaking verse,
Hush, sorcerer's masterful boasting.
My fate it is, potent tale,
I am a prince,' sang the sunshine,
'To come for three months to grow
Fruits of labour in abundance,
And when roof and leaves have done
Growing, and branches weaving,
To shun the wind of winter
From earth to Annwn I go.'

The blessings of the world's bards
And their good wishes go with you.
Farewell, king of fair weather,
Farewell, our ruler and lord,
Farewell, the fledgling cuckoos,
Farewell, balmy banks in June,
Farewell, sun high above us,
And the plump cloud, white-bellied ball.
Army's monarch, you'll surely not be
So high, crest of sky's snowdrift,
Till come, fine garden unhidden,
Summer once more and fair slopes.

THE RATTLE BAG

As I was, readiest praise,
Upon a day in summer,
Under trees between field and mountain,
Awaiting my soft-spoken girl,
She came, there's no denying,
Where she promised, undoubted moon.
Together we sat, worthy theme,
The girl and I, debating,
Trading, while I had the right,
Words with the splendid maiden.

And so as we, she was shy,
Were learning love for each other,
Hiding wrong, obtaining mead,
A short time lying together,
Suddenly, cold comfort, came,
Blaring, a bloody nuisance,
A sack's bottom's foul seething
From a creature in shepherd's shape,
Who had, public enemy,
A harsh-horned sag-cheeked rattle.
He played, yellow-bellied intruder,
The bag, curse the scabby shank,
And there, before satisfaction,
The sweet girl panicked, woe's me.
When she heard, festering breast,
The stones whir, she'd not tarry.

By Christ, no Christian country,
Hundred curses, has heard the like.
Noisy pouch perched on a pole,
Bell of pebbles and gravel,
Saxon box of rocks making a racket
Shaking in a bullock's skin,
Creel of three thousand beetles,
Commotion's cauldron, black husk,
Field-keeper as old as straw,
Black-skinned, pregnant with splinters,
Its tone's an old buck's loathing,
Devil's bell, stake in its crotch.
Scar-crusted rock-bearing belly,

May it be sliced into thongs.
May the filthy churl be struck frigid,
Amen, who scared off my girl.

IN A TAVERN

I came to a choice city,
Behind me, my handsome squire.
High living, a festive place,
I found, swaggering youngster,
A decent enough public
Lodging, and I wanted wine.

I spied a slim fair maiden
In the house, my pretty dear,
Set wholly, hue of sunrise,
My heart on my slender bliss.
I bought roast, not for boasting,
And costly wine for us two.
Playing the game young men love,
I called her, shy girl, over.
I whispered, bold urgent fellow,
It's certain, two magic words:
I made, love was not idle,
A compact to come to her
When the people had fallen
Fast asleep. Dark-browed was she.

After all were, sad journey,
Asleep but the girl and me,
Painstakingly I sought for
The girl's bed. It went not well:
I had, when I caused a racket,
A hard fall, no luck at all;
I could rise, the price of vice,
More clumsily than quickly;
I bumped, I jumped up poorly,
My shin, and woe to my leg,
On the side, an ostler's doing,
Of a stupid noisy stool.
As I got, penitent tale,
To my feet, Welshmen love me,

I struck, bad to be too eager,
The place was, not one free step,
A trap where mad blows were traded,
My forehead on a table top
Where there lay a loose basin
And a booming copper pan.
The table collapsed, sturdy structure,
Both trestles and all it held,
Raising clamour from the pan
After me, far off they'd hear it,
And clanging, my wits were gone,
From the basin, and dogs barking.

Next the thick walls there lay in
A stinking bed three Saxons
Bothered about their bundles,
Hickin and Jenkin and Jack.
Whispered the scurvy-lipped lad,
Angry speech, to the others:
'A Welshman, din to dupe us,
Is stalking here treacherously;
He'll steal, if we allow it:
Take heed, be on your guard.'

The ostler aroused the crowd,
All of them, dreadful story:
Scowling they were around me,
Searching for me, all around,
With me, sore ugly bruises,
Keeping quiet in the dark.
I prayed, in no bold fashion,
Hidden, like a timid girl,
And by prayer's wondrous might,
And the grace of faithful Jesus,
I gained, a sleepless tangle,
Unrequited, my own bed.
I escaped, the good saints were near:
Of God I ask forgiveness.

REPROACH TO HIS PENIS

By God, cock, there's need to keep you
Under guard with eye and hand,
Stiff-headed pole, with this law-suit,
Even better from now on.
Cunt's net-float, because of complaint,
Needs must your snout be snaffled
To keep you from being indicted
Again. Listen, minstrels' despair.
You're a loathsome rolling-pin,
Scrotum's horn: don't rise, don't waggle.
Noble ladies' New-Year's-gift,
Nut-stick of a groin's cranny,
Snare's posture, goosey-gander
Sleeping in its year-old feathers,
Wet-helmeted neck, milk-shaft,
Shoot's tip, stop your crude twitching,
Crooked blunt creature, cursed stake,
Halves of a girl's rump's pillar,
Stiff lamprey's head with a hole,
Blunt rail like a rod of hazel.
You're longer than a large man's thigh,
Long night's roving, hundred nights' chisel,
Auger like the signpost's pillar,
Leatherhead that's called a shaft.
You're a sceptre that causes lust,
A girl's bare arse's lid-bolt.
There's a pipe within your shawl,
A whistle for daily coupling;
An eye's in your tiny forehead
That sees every woman as fair.
Round pestle, expanding gun,
It's hell on a tiny cunt;
Roof-beam of women's crotches,
A bell's clapper's the rapid growth.
Dull pod, it would delve a tribe,
Skin snare, fruitful balls' nostril.
You're a trouser-load of lewdness,
Leather-necked, like a goose's neckbone,
False by nature, lechery's shell,
Door-nail causing law-suit and trouble.
Mind, there's a writ and indictment:

Children's dibbler, bow your head.
It's hard to keep you in order,
Cold poke, woe to you indeed:
Frequent, rebuke to your master;
Outstanding, the harm from your head.

THE SKYLARK

The lark's sure hours of prayer
Spiral up from his home each day,
World's early riser, song's rich spate,
Skywards, porter of April.

Graceful voice, melody's steersman,
Sweet path, lovely labour is yours,
Shaping song above hazel grove,
Brown wings' gracious achievement.
Yours the spirit, precious task,
And high-flown speech for preaching,
Strong song from the fount of faith,
Privileged in God's presence.
Aloft you soar, Kai's own power,
And aloft you sing each song,
Bright spell near the wall of stars,
Height's lengthy turning journey.
Full measure, you have mounted
High enough: the prize is yours.

Let every good creature praise
Its Creator, pure bright Ruler.
Cease not, thousands hear it, he's worthy,
To praise God as was decreed.
Love's author's means, where are you?
Lucid-voiced in grey-brown garb,
Yours is song pure and cheerful,
Melodious russet muse.
Chanter of heaven's chapel,
Fair is faith, skilful are you.
Full honours, harmonious song,
Your broad cap is brown-crested.

Set a course for well-known skies,
Singer, the wild white country.
One beholds you high above
Surely, when the day is longest.
When you arise to worship,
A gift from the Trinity,
Not a treetop sustains you
Above the world, speech inspired,
But the just Father's graces,
Miraculous providence.

Teacher of praise, dawn to darkness,
Descend, God protect your wings.
My fair brown bird, if you'll bear,
My fellow bard, love's message,
Bring greetings to a beauty,
Radiant her gift, Gwynedd's moon,
And beg one of her kisses
To bring here to me, or two.
Lord of the sky's chartless sea,
Hover by her hall yonder.
Would I were with her always,
Eiddig's rage, my break of day.

The fine's such for slaying you
That none will dare to slay you.
Should he try it, though, fierce turmoil,
Eiddig's bane, you'll stay alive:
Great the compass that's your birdcage,
You're so far from bow and hand.
Stamping the ground, sad the bowman,
His great aim will go awry:
Wicked his wrath, wheel above him
While he with his arrow goes by.

THE MASS OF THE GROVE

In a pleasant place today,
Under fine green hazel mantles,
I listened as the day dawned
To the skilful speckled thrushcock
Singing a polished stanza,

194

Bright lessons and wondrous things.

Far-travelled, discretion's essence,
Love's grey envoy journeyed long.
He's come here from fair Carmarthen
At my golden girl's command,
Wordy, with not one password,
Straight course, to Nentyrch's vale.
Morfudd it was who'd sent him,
May's melodious foster-child.

About him there were hangings
Of blossoms from May's sweet boughs,
And his chasuble, they resembled,
Of the wind's, green mantles, wings.
All of gold, by God almighty,
Was the altar's canopy.
I heard in glowing language
A long, no faltering, chant,
The gospel read, no restraint,
To the parish without mumbling.
On the hill of ash-trees then
Rose from good leaf the blest wafer,
And from the grove's near-by corner
The slim sweet-voiced nightingale,
The vale's songstress, rang sanctus
To the welkin, her whistling clear,
And the offering was lofted
To the sky above the copse,
Devotion to God our Father,
A chalice of bliss and love.

The liturgy contents me:
The dear birch-grove gave it birth.

MORFUDD'S EMBRACE

The girl's figure, form of Enid,
And gold tresses set me aflame.
Bared brow, a lily petal,
Queenly and gentle her hand,
A modest girl, well-mannered,

And womanly, none better bred.
Hands on neck at leaf-hid tryst,
It turned to yearning's injunction,
Something quite unfamiliar,
And I was held fast by her lips.
Comely wine-nursed form's weak bard,
I was long ago her captive.

Doubtful of mind, there is now,
A gift it was, God witness,
A love-knot, though I conceal it,
Between us, surely: I'm bound.
The gracious bright snowdrift arm
Of Morfudd, cheeks like sun-glow,
Held me, it was easy though bold,
Brow to brow in the leaf-house corner.
Well did she, slim, fair, tender,
Enclose me in hands that love me:
Restraining knot of pure love,
The wrists of my true sweetheart.
All mine, for my eager journey,
Brave collar of shy secret love.

Bard's smooth yoke, shapely jewel,
No burden was the dear's bright arm.
Beneath her celebrant's ear
A torque, I can't reject it,
Chalk-hued, like a snow circlet,
Fine gift to deck a man's neck,
The girl put, and one knows it,
Round her bard's throat, slender gem.
Splendid sight in the bracken,
Tegau's form strangling a man.
And then in a faster clasp,
Golden dawn, Oh that necklace,
The enchanter slyly bound me.
Long live the spellbinding girl
Who keeps, tryst's fine arrangement,
Caresses for me like a nurse.

No cause for any to scorn me,
Sun's likeness, between her hands.
Fearless, no coward, bold-browed

196

And black am I, and reckless,
With my faithful girl's two arms
Around me: is mead delightful?
Drunk I was, I have suffered,
Drunk on a strong slender maid.
Bliss for me without vexation,
The darling's arms whitened my neck:
Blissful long-lasting embrace,
They were this once my collar.

A SIMILE FOR MORFUDD

I pursue a soft-spoken girl,
Snowdrift's glow on a field's shingle.
God knows the girl is radiant,
Brighter than a crest of foam;
Hue of a bright booming wave,
Sun's brightness, she is gracious.
She knows she is worth my love-song,
Sun's splendour beside a cloud.
People's dawn, fine fur mantle,
She can mock an ugly man.
Fair Morfudd, woe's the weak trifling
Bard who loves her, reluctant beauty.
Web of gold, man's semblance, woe's he,
Comely his form, loudly moaning.

Great her deceit and cunning,
Above all, and she's my love.
At one time my fair lady
Shows herself in church and court;
Another, proud white battlements' girl,
Radiant Morfudd stays hidden,
Like the land's beneficent sun,
The nurse of warmth's enchantment.
Praiseworthy her splendid task,
Merchant of May's refulgence.
Great the wait for radiant Morfudd,
Mary's mirror, shining clear.

Along the earth, broad its borders,
Comes the sun like a fair-hued girl,

Comely creature of the day,
Shepherdess of sky's expanses.
Afterwards, mighty battle,
Comes thick cloud about her head:
When there's need, we'd know torment,
Of the sun that wears out sight,
She escapes, darkening nearly,
Bitter pain, to night coming on.
Full are the dark-grey heavens,
Sorrow's image, the planet's place;
Hard for any to know then,
God's orb she is, where she goes.
There's not a hand can touch her
Or get a grip on her brow.
Next day once more she rises,
From the world's roof flaming afar.

No different, grief's portion,
Is Morfudd's hiding from me:
After she's come from on high,
Sallying below in sunlight,
She sets, her scowl is lovely,
Behind the frigid man's door.

I've sought passion in a clearing
Of Penrhyn, love's dwelling-place.
There is where is seen daily
The bright girl, and nightly she flees.
Hand's no nearer to touching
In a hall, it's been my death,
Than are, girl praised so dearly,
One's hands to holding the sun.
Not a face that's finer, gladder,
Has the blazing sun than she:
If one this year's the fairer,
Fairer, lord's kin, is our sun.

Why, perverse wish discovered,
Cannot one govern the night,
And the other, splendid warmth,
Fine light, colour the daytime?
If both these faces appeared
Circling the world's four corners,

A manuscript page's marvel,
Night's coming, while the maiden lived.

MORFUDD AND DYDDGU

Woe's me, misery's image,
Without let-up, that I knew not love,
Before the age of marriage,
For a slim gentle faultless maid,
Greatly gifted, loyal, prudent,
Clever, sweet, highly refined,
Conversing like an heiress,
Dainty, artless, truthful girl,
Firmly rounded form, serene,
Talents trained to pefection,
Lovely, lively as Indeg,
Virgin land, a steer am I,
A sweetheart who'll never waver,
A gold wand, glowing her brow:
Such is, worth expansive praise,
Dyddgu of the smooth dark eyebrows.

Quite unlike that is Morfudd,
But like this, a burning coal,
Loving those who chastise her,
Stubborn dear, and she wears one out,
Possessing, highly respected,
House and husband, a gorgeous girl.

No less frequent my fleeing
At midnight for that girl's sake
From one at her glass-windowed place
Than by day, I'm a bold vaulter,
With the crass man, senseless his speech,
Beating his hands together,
Constant outcry, free-flowing lust,
Shouts of stealing his children's mother.

Weakling, to the devil
With his shouting. Why does he howl,
Ah, woe's he, persistent,
Up to God, that she's spellbound?

Calf's long shameless broadcast bawling,
Fool's labour, his book of lies.
He played the freak and coward,
Complaining of the lively girl.
All of South Wales he'll waken
By calling, a sweetheart's kite.
Unskilful, no lack of discord,
Not pretty to hear, not sweet,
A man screeching, raucous horn,
Croaking like crow for his comrade.

A poor hand, nightmarish cry,
Liar, he was at lending.
If I ever, brilliant notion,
Bought a wife, a doubtful step,
Sorry prickster, for an hour's peace,
I'd share, I'd let him have her,
So badly, widow's sad portion,
Sour man, can he play the game.

In one word, I choose Dyddgu
To love, if she's to be had.

THE WIND

Welkin's wind, way unhindered,
Big bluster that passes by,
You're a harsh-voiced man of marvels,
World-bold, without foot or wing.
How strange that sent from heaven's
Pantry with never a foot,
Now you can race so swiftly,
Over the hillside above.
No need of swift steed beneath you,
Or bridge over stream, or boat:
You'll not drown, you've been forewarned,
You'll have free and easy passage.
Stealing nests, while you winnow leaves,
None indict you, you're not arrested
By swift host, magistrate's hand,
Blue blade or flood or downpour.
No sheriff or troop takes you,

Pruner of the treetop plumes.
Mother's son won't slay you, needless words,
Fire burn you, deceit undo you.

Unspied in your wide bare lair,
Heavy rain's nest, thousands hear you,
Cloud's swift-natured signatory,
Fine leaper across nine wild lands.
Godsent you skim over ground,
Roar of oak-crests sorely broken.
Parched nature, tenacious creature,
Cloud-trampler, tremendous trek,
Shooter above on snow-fields
Of loud heaps of worthless husks,
Tell me, persistent hymn-tune,
Your course, north wind of the glen.
Tempest fettering the sea,
Lad romping on the seastrand,
Rhetorician, magician,
You're sower, pursuer, of leaves,
Hurler, hill's privileged jester,
Of wild masts in white-breasted brine.

You fly the length of the world:
Hover tonight, hill's weather,
Oh wind, and go to Uwch Aeron,
Soft and lovely, a clear tune.
Do not tarry, do not steer clear,
Do not fear despite the Hunchback
Jealousy's accusations:
Closed her fostering land to me.
Woe's me since I set my heart
On Morfudd, my golden maiden:
The dear girl's caused me exile.
Run on high to her father's house:
Pound the door, make it open up
Before daybreak to my envoy,
And if there's a way, find her
And moan the sound of my sigh.

You come from the changeless stars:
Tell my great-hearted darling
For as long as I'm in the world

I am her faithful plaything.
Sad-faced am I without her
If truly she's not untrue.
Fly high, you'll see a beauty,
Fly low, chosen one of the sky:
Go to the pale blonde maiden;
Come back safely, bounty of sky.

THE MAGPIE

Sick was I, for a bright girl's sake,
In a grove composing love-charms,
One day, burst of ardent song,
Sky mild, the start of April,
The nightingale on fresh branches,
The fair blackbird in gaps of leaves,
Wood's bard, he lives in woodland rooms,
A thrush on a fresh treetop
Singing briskly before the rain
Golden notes on a green cushion,
And the skylark, tranquil voice,
Dear brown-hooded smooth-voiced songbird,
Straining his strength in soaring
With a song to heaven's heights,
From the bare plain, impending prince,
He climbs in mounting spirals,
And I, slender maiden's poet,
Jubilant in a fresh grove,
The worn heart reminiscing
And the spirit fresh in me
With such pleasure in seeing trees,
Lusty life, bearing new garments,
And shoots of grain and grapevine
After sunlit rain and dew,
And green leaves on the valley's brow,
And the thorntree freshly white-tipped,
By heaven, there was also,
The magpie, world's shrewdest bird,
Building, lovely contrivance,
In the tangled heart of the bush,
With leaves and clay, a proud nest,
Her mate supplying assistance.

Said the magpie, harsh complaint,
Haughty-beaked in the thornbush:
'A great fuss, vain bitter singing,
Old man, you make by yourself.
Better, by word-wise Mary,
Near a fire, greyhaired old man,
Than here amidst dew and rain,
In the greengrove's chilling showers.'

'Stop your noise, leave me in peace,
A short while, awaiting trysting.
Passion for a fair faithful girl
Creates in me this ferment.'

'Pointless for you, serving lust,
Servile old greyhaired halfwit,
Foolish sign of love's function,
To rave of a radiant girl.'

'And you, magpie, black is your beak,
Infernal bird, fierce-tempered,
You have, vain visitation,
More toil and a tedious task,
Your nest like a mound of gorse,
It's thick, creel of withered twiglets.
You've pied black plumage, how pleasant,
Painful sight, and a crow's head;
Motley you are, a fine colour;
You've an ugly court, a hoarse voice.
And every outlandish language
You've learned, black and speckled wing.
Then, magpie, black is your head,
Help me, if you speak so wisely:
Give me the finest advice
You have for my affliction.'

'I'll give you proper counsel
Before May comes: act, if you will.
You've no right, bard, to the fair girl;
For you there's but one counsel:
Solemn verse, become a hermit,
Foolish man, and love no more.'

Here I swear, God's my witness,
If I ever see the magpie's nest,
Because of this I'll leave her
Not an egg, no, nor a chick.

MORFUDD GROWN OLD

God grant the long-maned friar,
Drooping crow, long life and much grace.
They deserve no peace who revile
The friar's shadow figure,
A lord whom Rome may honour,
Bare feet, hair a nest of thorns.
The world-roaming robe's a snare,
A crossbeam, the spirit's blessing.
Mass-priest, eloquent preacher,
Kite, well he sings, of fair God,
Much privileged his charterhouse,
A ram of heaven's ruler,
Wise words fluent from his mouth,
Life from his lip, Mary's magus,
He spoke of, tough-minded talk,
Her hue who deceives but seldom.

'Put on, head of a hundred lords,
A shirt of cambric and crystal;
Wear long, not undressed for a week,
On smooth flesh the dainty garment:
A noble girl, Deirdre's story,
Blacker she'll be, double grief.'

Grey baldpate, rightly praised friar,
Of a girl's beauty, dark his words.
As a young fool, were I Pope,
I'd not break off with Morfudd:
Now at last, wrath's accusations,
The Creator's disfigured her
Till there's not, once in fine health,
One grey lock more lacking lustre.
Betrayal in store, beauty harried,
The girl's hue's less lasting than gold.
Queen of the land of no sleep,

Face and form men's betrayal,
Lusty was she, one sleepless lifetime,
A dream is she, how swift life's passing,
Besom on a brewhouse floor,
Pale elder almost leafless.

Tonight I'll not, sickness-stricken,
Sleep a wink unless I'm there:
It's love's harsh pangs for a girl,
Familiar thief, like a nightmare.
Enchantingly was she formed,
Pale bandit, an enchantress.
Old arm of an Irish mangnel,
Cold summerhouse: she was fair.

LOVE'S JOURNEY

Has anyone for a mistress' sake
Trekked as I have, love's compulsion,
Frost and snow, such transgression,
Rain and wind, for a radiant face?

I had naught but sheer exhaustion,
Never had two feet more grief,
Making for Celliau'r Meirch,
Golden lure, across Eleirch,
Wilderness country, directly,
Night and day, and no nearer reward.

Oh God, it's loud was a man's
Calling out in Celli Fleddyn.
For her sake, a declaration:
I proclaimed my love for her.
Bysaleg, hoarse and low its sound,
Seething flow, narrow river,
For her sake, very often,
I'd cross through it every day.
To Bwlch, proud and free I went,
Mine is deep pain, Meibion Dafydd,
And beyond it to the Camallt
And the slope, for the fair-haired girl.
Speedily I forged ahead

Through the forked gap of Gyfylfaen
To cast for the fur-clad maid
An eye on the fine valley:
She won't wander here or there
And stealthily pass me by.
I kept at it and would not rest
Throughout Pant Cwcwll in summer,
And all about Castell Gwgan,
Gosling's stoop when it spots a stalk;
I've run past Heilin's dwelling,
Lope of a hoarse weary hound.

I've stood below Ifor's court
Like a monk in a choir corner
To seek, with no favour promised,
A meeting with comely Morfudd.
Not a knoll or deep hollow
Either side of Nant-y-glo's glen
That my passion does not know
By heart, quick-witted Ovid.
Easily may I speak low,
True goal gained, at Gwern-y-Talwrn,
Where I caught a glimpse, dear favour,
Of slim girl under dark black cloak,
Where eternally is seen,
No grass tufts, no trees growing,
Our bed's shape beneath fine boughs,
Crushed leaves there, like Adam's pathway.

Woe's the soul goes unrewarded,
Exhausted, with no recompense,
If it wander the self-same way
The wretched body wandered.

THE RUIN

Broken hut, with gaping holes,
Between upland and lowland,
Sad are those who saw you, they thought,
Once as a festive dwelling,
And see you today, battered house,
Beneath shattered roof and rafters.

And once near your cheerful wall
There was a day, pain's chiding,
Within you, more delightful
Than you are now, sorry house,
When I saw, brightly I praised,
A fair one there in your corner,
A maiden, a noble darling,
Shapely girl, lying with me,
Each one's arm, bliss the dear's embrace,
A bond around the other,
The girl's arm, fine-grained snowflakes,
Beneath her praise-poet's ear,
And my arm, simple tactics,
Beneath the comely girl's left ear.
Ease and bliss in your greenwood,
But today is not that day.

'I complain,' shelter's magic speech,
'Of the wild wind in its passage:
Nursed in the east a tempest
Pounded along the stone wall,
The wailing, a wrathful path,
Of the south wind unroofed me.'

Did the late wind cause havoc?
Well it threshed your roof last night.
It ripped your lathing awry.
The world's a perilous illusion.
Your corner, my sighs' meaning,
Was my bed, not a sty for swine.
You stood proudly yesterday,
Snug above my dear sweetheart;
Simple tale, today you have,
By Peter, no roof, no rafter.
Madness plays many a trick:
Is this torn hut such a fancy?

'The household long since went under
The cross, Dafydd. Its ways were good.'

GRUFFUDD AB ADDA

THE MAYPOLE

Green birch whose hair's unsightly,
You're long exiled from the slope.
Fine lance fostered in woodlands,
Green veil, you've betrayed your grove.

Lodging for me and love's envoy
Was your close, in May's short nights.
Frequent once, it's a foul journey,
The tunes on your fine green twigs;
Songs of all sorts, roads' signpost,
I heard to your bright green house;
Herbs of all kinds grew under
Your leaves among hazel boughs,
When for a maiden's trysting
You dwelt last year in the grove.

You contemplate love no longer;
Deaf stay your branches above.
Completely you've forsaken
The green field, despite the cost,
From the hill and height of honour
To town by a swift exchange.
Though your resting-place be good,
Idloes town, crowded concourse,
Not good, my birch-tree, to me
Your rape, your region, your dwelling;
Not good for you there, long of face,
Your place, for bearing green leaves.

Green-plumed each city garden,
Was it not, birch, a foolish thing
To bring you there to wither,
Sad pole, near the pillory?
In leaftime, did you not come
To stand in the barren crossroad?
Though you're pleasing there, they say,
Better, tree, the brook's heaven.
Not a bird will sleep or sing,

Shrill chirp, on your gentle branches,
So constant, dark woods' daughter,
People's noise about your tent,
Fierce wound, and grass will not grow,
With the town's trampling, beneath you
More than once on the windswept way
Of Adam and the first woman.

You've been made to deal in trade;
You look like a market-woman:
Fair-goers, gleeful language,
Point their fingers at your pain,
Your old fur and one grey garment
Amidst petty merchandise.
No more, while your sister stays,
Will fern hide your bold seedlings;
No privacy, no secrets,
No shelter beneath your eaves.
You'll not shield, high piercing look,
The primroses of April:
You will not think of wishing,
Fair warden, for the valley's birds.
God, it grieves us, land's lean coldness,
Sudden shame, that you're ensnared.
Taller than noble Tegwedd
You tower, fine is your crest.
Make your choice, captive branches,
Foolish is your city life,
To leave for the fine home hillside,
Or wither there in the town.

THE THIEF OF LOVE

I've gone eight times, painful cry,
To the wood there, painful journeys;
I've been out like one who's witless
Keeping house without a fire:
Easy for me, fine prowess,
By true God, before day dawns,
To flee for Gwen's sake briskly
To the far side of the wood.
Woodland dawn makes me angry,

A man on foot there for love;
Hopeless am I, I'm in ruins,
From the wood's sun: it once poured wine.

If from houses some spy me running
In her region where pain's my reward,
There am I, battle-netted,
An arch-thief, says greybeard's serf.
I'm no thief in a hayloft
Shunning the dazzle of day:
I'm the thief, a wound binds me,
Of a fair girl, not a dark horse;
No thief of a ram tonight,
Thief of a maid, sweet moment;
No thief of cows' enclosure,
Thief of her, wave's hue, under boughs;
Thief of a wondrous enchantress,
Thief of painful miles, not mills,
Thief drawn by a maid not mine,
Thief of pure love, not purses.
I'm thief of not one hoofed yearling;
There's no warrant out on me.
It's love's thievery compels me:
I'm thief, pain-fettered, of a girl.

GRUFFUDD GRYG

THE APRIL MOON

April moon, hideous hue,
Sad your look and your complexion,
Noble of a pale-faced mirror,
Stark moon, one would think you're slain.
Your disappointing colour
You change each day, angry face,
Blush before wind, rushing course,
Blue and grey before rain rages.

Pallid crust, sorry circle,
I languish, are you in love?
Sky's clout, your silence is famed,
Are you unwell, wench? Hear me:
Which of your tribe, troubled tale,
Have you lost, flinty florin?
There's no day, mirror's semblance,
You don't heave from cheeks of ice
Your sighs that suppress ardour,
A thousand of them, or three.
Each sigh, strong expiration,
Would shatter a stone in three.
And each night, wan and warm, awry,
Wretched wheel, you spend weeping:
Errant erratic planet,
Platter, tearful chimney dome,
How is it you weep in air,
Worn page, thin, pale, and crumpled?

You broke the bond with Saint James,
Rain's region, you're dishonoured.
You hurled me on Harry's shore,
Still hold me, my opponent.
Were it not for James', most precious,
Power, my lad Jenkin and I,
We could not, though we swam the heavens,
Sorry hindrance, come home again.
Sad is the lord who's seen you,
I've paid for your rage, by God.
You wrenched me, often wretched,
Cold flood-path, off a clear course:
Windlass of tide's ebb and flow,
Third of a worn stone handmill,
Deceitful land's dark covert,
Ball flaming with Michael's fire,
Flat stone of the seething sky,
Sharp spindle whorl's wide compass,
You've been a lantern growing dim,
A pale eye, magnet of showers,
Windy Troy, wandering fort,
Sky's cairn, bald crown of April,
Cold weather's twirling taper,
Lead buckler of pale bare spring,

Deeply cleft dish of tempests,
You arrive, and I'm driven wild.
You've taught clouds to crowd around me:
Come down, shower's coverlid,
And let another, foul colour,
Frigid moon, assume your place.

Worthless cold sky of April,
I have a pledge, and no doubt.
Hate for a lad has never
Fashioned a worse end to spring,
Sign of the ill-starred journey,
Fresh shame to spring, frigid wind.
Choicest month, with cheeks glowing,
Come with the sun, summer's ray,
Bring one ship a fair true course,
Safe from cold skies in April.
May, magic Kai, rising woods,
Because I'll sing your praises,
Bring me, fair month, a straight road,
Bring Saint James of Galicia's bounty.
No unlovely April, calm,
Moon of May, pilot your poet.

LAMENT FOR RHYS AP TUDUR

Gwynedd is like, they're saying,
Wild with grief, sad if it's true,
A crwth and a bell, man's groaning,
Worth many pounds, and a harp:
The crwth where there was strong rhythm,
It loved setting songs to Jesus,
Scant will be, from day to day,
Its attraction lacking its strings;
The harp of golden lineage,
Night and day, once a nightingale,
Lacking hands, promising curve,
Lacking song's tune, lacking fingers,
Ploughbeam's form on its carved wood,
Will give, I believe, no pleasure;
Each matin bell, bitter chance,
From the clergymen's cloister,

If its chain-rope is broken
And its tongue, strong prophetic song,
None will love, resounding confines,
Its peal amid pulpit and choir.

And thus, praise that's due to mead,
Instead of the wine does Gwynedd
Lack Môn's lord, lack frequent singing,
Lack God's church's right, lack bells,
Lack the Lord God's hand, lack tongue,
Lack music, lack good fortune,
Lack feast, lack divertissement,
Lack Rhys, kind lord, lack free favour,
Lack bright beauty, lack dawnlight,
Lack talent, lack worth, lack all,
Lack more honour, mighty flood,
From Richard, buckler's eagle,
Sanctum, golden spear's shaft,
The King, he spread fields with Angles.

Were not his bright deeds, Môn's praise,
And his eyes like an eagle's?
He paid heed to what I needed,
Sweet lord, was his reward not fine?
Did he not show, good stock's vintage,
Wisdom at the court of France?
Was he not merry and modest,
Like Elffin, bestowed wine, noble Rhys?
Is not Gwynedd, faultless style is mine,
Empty of a dark brown eagle,
Of Rhys, lad sadly taken,
Gold chain, Tudur's heir, bearing sword,
Worthy keeper, and it grieves me,
War's victor, of Snowdon's stags?

There is in Gwynedd, yearning look,
Men murmur, unless God save us,
No strength for us, nor assurance,
No banquets, no mighty lords,
No conjunction of true passion,
No pursuit of song, no art,
No wooing of pure maidens,
No making love, there's no mead,

No tree-ringed tryst with a fair,
No birds in woodland birches,
No hillside joyful, no boughs,
No delight except Eiddig's.

Gwynedd, privileged dwelling,
Hear this and obtain my praise:
Here is my oath, wine-blest face,
Eight-hued fame, for your hand, Gwynedd,
With passion, I know sorrow,
Pain and pledge, that you'll never have,
Twenty laments for war's master,
Lord's gold praise, a man like him.

DAFYDD'S WOUNDS

A marvel is poor Dafydd,
Gwilym Gam's son, faultless man,
Bold fellow, sorrow's bedmate;
He's made weak by a hundred wounds.
And still the wearisome lad
Nurses song, slave to swooning.
Lengthy, feeble work, his moaning,
God's mother, it is, says he,
Wretched torture for a Welshman:
It's a marvel that he's alive.

In all quarters, quaking cheek,
Mary hears how he's wounded:
Pains numerous as stars are
Consuming Dafydd's whole body.
Woe is me if bitter pains
Afflict the master poet:
Not pain of thousands clashing,
Not rash's pain, but weakling's pain,
Not back pain, proper burden,
Not sharp pain, but sickliness,
Not frequent pain, not fevered,
Not strong pain but frustration's pain.

Weapons, song-weaving's master,
Are firmly planted in his breast:

It is ten years to today
Dafydd has said, splendid singing,
That perhaps a hundred weapons
Were within him, strokes of steel,
Arrows, vexing frustrations,
And he's been in agony.
A mighty weakness he suffered,
In men's judgment, from such pains.

A big lie, deceitful bard,
Dafydd has told, talking nonsense.
Were it Arthur, great bulwark,
Who made haste to attack a host,
The truth is, if all those pains
Hurt in a hundred places,
The war he waged was savage,
Truth is he'd not live a month,
Much less, the fine lad's slender,
Love's servant, frail as he is.
Ah me, if a Welshman from Môn
Stabbed him with spear, isn't it woeful,
His golden hand on its shaft,
Sharply in his shattered bosom,
Scarcely an hour of morning
Would he live, his colour's poor,
Not to mention, no sweet notion,
Swooning from so many wounds.

Sadness is the death of him;
Weapons have killed his fine colour.
By my faith, this quick-witted lad,
However adept in boasting,
A shrewd foreigner could make
Grieve, with a stiff reed arrow.
And he's in danger, sorely tried,
Of death from Morfudd's weapons?

THE FICKLE GIRL

Maiden of noble breeding
Amid sweet white wine and mead,
You are well-mannered, well-made,

And you, fair girl, are fickle.
What warrants being fickle
When our compact's lasted so long?

Though you're well-born and clever
And have riches in your grasp,
Be not proud, my lime-white girl:
Better not, it's not fitting.
It's likely, dare I say,
The proud will become the humble.
Despite the fine lads' slanders,
Trust them not, until you see;
With a frown, lest you be scorned,
Refuse me not, hue of snowflakes.

If you regret loving me,
What's been, slim girl, will be buried.
Although, wise prudent dear,
Cold care, you love another,
May God, and Dewi and Non,
Make your heart glad to have him,
And for me, precious jewel,
What God wills, my lovely dear.
Let me not, from being angry,
Crook a finger at your friend.

There was a day, in fine style,
Tranquil gem, when you listened,
Many a kiss and greeting,
Many a nod, noble girl,
Many a sign, gold-haired moon,
And many a tryst on hillsides,
Many a garland in birchwoods,
And many a clasp of my hand,
And today I know, she's untrue,
By Saint Dwyn, I'm not acknowledged.

You've been vexed, dear, with him you loved:
Woe's me, if you're too prudent.
Try hard, dear, to curb your wrath;
Love God, redeem your promise.
Beware of being judged as,
Deceit's bitter, a player at dice:

Though winning a little moment,
Wretched is greed, the world turns;
It could be, lime-white beauty,
The world will turn for the proud.
If you, fine-looking woman,
Indulge in fickleness,
Beware, girl, though they greet you,
The course that the man once took,
Loosing the ears, strong and hollow,
Long scowl, before grasping the horns.

Since, before knowing your fault,
Grave word, you choose another,
Farewell, my slender sweetheart,
Since there's nothing else for me;
Farewell, my deceitful darling,
I'll hide, dear, what once I had.

THE YEW-TREE
above the grave of Dafydd ap Gwilym in Strata Florida

Yew-tree for the best of fellows
By Ystrad Fflur's wall and grounds,
God has blessed you, bliss of trees,
Growing you as house for Dafydd.
Blessed Dafydd foretold you
Before you grew out of grief;
Dafydd, after you had grown,
Did you, it was from boyhood,
Honour, a green-leaved dwelling,
A house, every beam bearing leaves,
Castle shielding the dead from cold wind
As well as, once, woodland branches.

Beneath you there is in silence
A close grave, would he'd not gone,
Beehive of swarming angels,
He's been brave, he was in the grave,
And skill of song, measured well,
And Dyddgu grieved when he was silent.
Her bard fashioned a green dwelling
To grow lavishly while he lived;

And you now, chosen branches,
Grow straight and true for a lord.
The tripod's like a good aunt
Gently tending his resting-place.

Be not crooked, not neglectful,
Yew-tree, on top of the grave.
Goats will not taint you, or ruin
Your growth at your father's foot;
Fire won't scorch, fierce greeting,
Joiner won't cut, passion won't wound,
Cobbler won't peel, while men live,
The bark that cloaks your dwelling.
Fuel gatherers or churl
Will not chop, timid-hearted,
With an axe, green your burden,
At your base, for fear of blame.
Leaves are the roof, a good place is yours:
May God preserve your wonders.

CHRIST THE KING

Who's the One deserves the crown?
Holy God, his breast wounded,
Christ, honoured king of heaven,
His pure body the bread and wine.
It's he, in our fluent language,
We should name as One and Three,
Father and Son, in the mass,
And wondrous Holy Spirit.

Certainly the best of men
And good was his baptiser;
Good the gentle, faultless maiden
Who nurtured him as a boy,
Bearing grievous care for a time
Before his anguish for the world's five ages.
All of the Jewish people
Cast scorn upon his five wounds,
Put on his brow, harsh binding,
A hundred-spiked circle of thorns,
And bleeding every thorn-tip,

218

Torn the skull of Mary's son,
His whole body full of wounds,
All pierced, and his breast bleeding;
And he was taken, life over,
Hastily down from the cross.
For Christ, there, there was sadness,
Speedily placed in the grave;
And once again four foemen
Stood guard upon holy God.
Joyful were throngs in his land,
Oh Mary, mighty the Rising,
And all of us, with one aim,
We can ever be joyful.
Judas, since he'd not deserved it,
Bears the blame for selling him:
An unblessed man was Judas
When he sold, for gain, the Man.

Because of his hands' torment
And because he rose from the earth,
Let us ask our God on high,
Where for us he purchased heaven,
Ask the Father, dear Saviour,
Jesus is called full of grace,
That God care for us, bring us home,
In his favour, all men to heaven.

MADOG BENFRAS

THE SALTMAN

I've borne, from costly compulsion,
A load of salt for the sun-hued's sake,
Exchanging, expensive task,
Places with the noble saltman.

I spoke to the fierce bold buck,
Confessed Eiddig's long memory;

I complained to God, presumed
The state of the dark watchman,
Frantic lad, lest I be noted
Conversing with the far-famed hand.
The gaunt old fellow obtained
My tame steed and worthy saddle;
I had in turn, clever notion,
Sore burden for my thin back,
The basket, complete with salt,
Of hairy old hide to carry,
And a cudgel made of pine,
A strap of shiny leather,
A pouch holding mouldy meal,
An old cap, cups to measure,
And a soft cushion of green grass
Between my cold back and the framework.

I found a way, closely guarded,
From dunghill to big dark house,
Stood with the nasty basket
Beneath my arms, filthy load,
Shouted 'Salt', shoulders coated,
Praised clearly the creel of sea-salt.
There rose a volley of oaths
From the ill-mannered servants:
They mocked me with metaphors,
Hounds howling in the kennel.

What with churls' music, and hounds,
And myself part of the turmoil,
The fair goddess awakened,
Free with wine, wave's sprightly hue:

'Faithful Mair, tell me, maiden,
Please, as you're good and dear,
Quite plainly, shepherds' combat,
What the noise is from the hall.'

'There has come, into senseless snares,
Someone who's like a saltman,
And the household, barren brawl,
Resounding tune, deride him,

220

And he, steadfast rebuttal,
Will not let one insult pass.'

'What is he like, clamour's cauldron,
What says he to the foolish churls?'

'An adulterous man disguised,
That's the sort, I imagine.
Never, I know a man's lust,
Was such a look on a saltman,
Or such clothes to thwart exposure,
Spies at work, as those on him.'

'Without anyone knowing,
Amiable maid, my own course,
Ask the man with his basket
To come across the threshold here.'

'He'll come,' the maid said, love-minded,
'God knows he will come for me.'

I brought the hump of a basket
On my back, frigid my thoughts,
Into, passion was patient,
Her bedroom, sprightly fair-faced dear.
The maid led me to the bedside:
I greeted the splendid girl.

'Put down your deceitful pack,
Craftiest of men, you are welcome.'

From the bright of skin, much kindness
Was mine, with no selling of salt:
The kiss, day-radiant girl,
Disputed, for one another.
Long life to the sweet-voiced gem,
In love's name, graceful beguiler.

IORWERTH AB Y CYRIOG

THE BROOCH

Iorwerth, poor ardent youngster,
Never was he in bad grace.
It bears gold and precious stones
Set in a clasp of silver:
Upon his breast, straight away,
His shirt will make it welcome.

May the wise chaste girl be honoured
Who gave the fine red-gold brooch:
Because of her, I've no lover;
It's sad that love's not her lot.
With words of praise I will gild
Her eulogy, summer's radiance;
January cold's nine snowfalls' snow,
I'd gild her praise, dawn's radiance;
Euron's offspring, silver's lustre,
I'd gild her praise with proper fame.

The never-wanton maiden,
Black of brow, she's finely gowned,
Gave me, there's a lovely favour,
The sparkling, bright-blazing gem.
Affectionate gesture she's made,
Love's pledge, it's a wondrous jewel.
It's a collar of glass on cloth,
A tiny precious trinket.
A curse on any who come
To beg me to give the trinket:
I'm a smith of Arabia's gold;
I'll not give my goods out of fear.

No need for the breast to bear
Something to draw plague from it.
I'm happier from the shrinking
Of bloated belly, gaping skep:
Rare now would be its roaring
Through the virtues of precious stones.
They're worth gold, they work wonders,

And they're exceedingly strange.
Here's a stone in my bosom,
It's uncommon, that does me good,
A physician who'd do as Myddfai
Did, with a mead-nourished man.

Pleasantly healthy, this heart:
She with her brooch has healed it.
The better she's been to me, I've loved her,
The better it's been for my breast-bone.
Would not linger, where it was strongest,
Rheumatics, with the tall girl's brooch,
More than stay, consumption's lord,
Frost or snow in sunny weather.

LLYWELYN GOCH AP MEURIG HEN

THE COAL-TIT

Sally, benevolent bird,
Set out, treble-voiced coal-tit,
Fair the girl who keeps me from sleep,
From the south to my sweetheart:
Make for Meirion, flawless gift,
Bright your song in May's young thorntrees,
Swift your flight above hedge bridge,
Rider of close-branched birches.
Soon-wearied wing, crooked grey bill,
You are a bird of four colours,
Green and blue, watchful gold servant,
White and black, stitching the leaves.
Companion to young people,
Though tiny, maker of tunes,
Master of secret missions,
You are fleet, little grey-cheeked bird.

Rush like the wind, fervent course,
To my gold dear in Meirionydd;

Work, master of eloquence,
Your wings above the woods' darkness:
Bear a message to a beauty,
Bid Dafydd's wife a good-day.
She was my sweet: for my sake,
Gold her chamber, beseech her,
White wave's brightness of Meirionydd,
Not to enter, day or night,
My second soul, broad gold-decked forehead,
She was gracious, Eiddig's bed.

This as well, fine sprightly squire,
Woods' bard who outflies the falcon,
Fortunate owner of two
Lean legs, trees' fellow-farers:
You should be bold, I'm eager,
Be bold this once to my love.
Tell her, faithful bard of a bird,
Woods' seer in time of torment,
That I with a song of praise
Am in Deheubarth, brother,
In my heart seven sorrows,
Shaft of yearning for her sake.
Since I've not seen, clear-voiced bird,
By bright wall her fair image,
Plead my praise that will conquer,
For a month, it's a wonder I live.

LAMENT FOR LLEUCU LLWYD

For blithe bard, barren summer,
And a barren world for a bard.
I've been stripped bare, grief's comrade,
For choosing this month to tryst.
There is in Gwynedd today
No moon, no light, no colour,
Since was laid, sorry welcome,
Moon's beauty beneath hard ground.

Fair girl in the oaken chest,
I'm bent on wrath, you've left me.
Lovely form, Gwynedd's candle,

Though you are closed in the grave,
Arise, come up, my darling,
Open the dark earthen door,
Forsake the long bed of sand,
And come to meet me, sweeting.
Here is, all-consuming grief,
Above your grave, sun's radiance,
A sad-faced man without you,
Llywelyn Goch, bell of your praise.
Wailing bard, I am walking
A foul world, fierce passion's slave.
Dear one, whose worth grew daily,
Yesterday over your grave
I let tears fall in torrents
Like a rope across my cheeks.
And you, mute maid's fair image,
From the pit made no reply.

Silent, sadly lacking love,
You promised, speechless maiden,
Mild your manner, silk-shrouded,
To stay for me, pure bright gem,
Till I came, I know the truth,
Strong safeguard, from the southland.
I heard no word, straightforward speech,
But the truth, silent sweetheart,
Model of Indeg's maidens,
Before this, from your fair mouth.
Hard blow, what care I where I dwell,
You broke faith, and it grieves me.

You are, my cywydd is false,
Truthful, words sweetly spoken:
Mine, sorrow's fluent language,
Is the lie, eternally sad.
I'm a liar, skimping prayer,
I've spoken with lying voice.
I will leave Gwynedd today,
What care I where, bright beauty:
My fair flourishing sweetheart,
By God, if you lived, I'd not go.
Where shall I, what care I, for sure
See you, fair moon's pure blossom,

On Mount, Ovid's passion spurned,
Olivet, luminous woman?
You've secured my place completely,
Lleucu, fair wave's comely hue.

Radiant glowing-fleshed maiden,
Sleeper too long under stone,
Rise to finish the revels,
To see if you wish for mead,
To your bard who laughs no longer
For your sake, gold diadem.
Come, with your cheeks of foxgloves,
Up from the earth's dreary house.
A desolate trail the footprints,
No need for deceit, my feet leave
In faltering from passion
Around your house, Lleucu Llwyd.

All the words, Gwynedd's lantern,
I've sung, complexion of snow,
Three groans of grief, gold-ringed hand,
Lleucu, praised you, my treasure.
With these lips, deft my praise-craft,
What I'll sing, life-long, in praise,
My dear, hue of rivers' ripples,
My love, will be your lament.

Lucid, sweet-spoken Lleucu,
My sweetheart's legacy was:
Her soul, Meirionydd's treasure,
To God the Father, rightful pledge;
And her slender, fine flour's colour,
Body to sanctified soil;
Girl far-mourned, flour-white favours,
Worldly goods to the proud dark man;
And yearning, lyric of grief,
This legacy she's left me.

Two equal gifts, sad custom,
Lovely Lleucu, snowdrift's hue,
Earth and stone, bitter grief's gem,
Conceal her cheeks, and oakwood.
Woe's me, how heavy's the turf

And the soil on beauty's mistress.
Woe's me, that a coffin holds you,
And between us, a house of stone,
Church chancel and stone curtain
And earth's weight and gown of wood.
Woe's me, pure girl of Pennal,
A nightmare, your forehead earthfast,
Hard oak's lock, bitter grief's grip,
And earth, lovely your eyebrows,
And heavy door, heavy clasp,
And the field's floor between us,
And firm wall, and hard black lock,
And a bolt – farewell, Lleucu.

THE SNOW

Sorry crop of high spirits,
This is my musing, I'm old,
While snow through January
Locks the lid on Gwynedd's land,
Pride's cold look, on me there stream
Tiny writs, testing moving:
If truly it stays on the hill,
Snow won't allow it, white shutter.
Great pain restraining gladness,
Mary knows, colourless walls,
Frown worse than the shire's sheriff,
Round mantle on fallow moor,
Fierce stream, frigid its surface,
Chalk-coloured white coverlet,
Long it's encompassed each spot,
Sky specks, mountain of fodder.
Cold came on each grove's fullness,
Large crop, like a maiden's skin,
Since the plug, pale appearance,
Was pulled from the salt-pit's paunch,
To salt with swift-hurtling snow
Broad earth's flooring, huge larder.
Enduring it's no delight,
Fine flour of heaven's elders,
Fine snow of mist and hoarfrost,
Winnowing sheet, no path left bare,

Sign of wrath, weir of rush-tips,
Cold froth on heather's rock-path.

If rain comes on its thick roofing,
Pale-bellied earth's burden's bane,
Sharp from the sky, here's a warning,
Flood will keep me from Cardigan:
Hard for me to ford the Dyfi,
A hindrance for stags today.
I'm no wretched wanderer;
I'll not leave, no need, till summer
The place that's been like paradise,
The courts blessed and comely,
Long-lasting my eloquent language,
The sons of Meurig, lord of song's wall.

From Hywel's house, noble line,
To Meurig's, no wastrel lineage,
My role, together with my lords,
Is this, I'm their old kinsman,
To read law, needing skill with words,
And *Brut*, ancient tale of Britons,
Wear, from each one's gleaming hand,
Handsome presents, green garments,
Loudly mock the frenzied throng,
One hears its roar, dunghill minstrels,
Eloquence have I been given,
Smoothly compare Lleucu Llwyd
To a fine garden's lovely rosebud,
Bounteous Mary, or the fair sun.
Delightful for a frail old man,
A fine time comes on Sunday,
Listening after Christmas
To cooks' heavy strokes on meat,
Din of greyhounds, I've no doubt,
Shaggy-haired from their shackles,
Lively crwth and bagpipe in concert,
Peacocks' beaks, in harmony,
And sanctus bells and laughter,
And the men calling for wine.

My prayer, my blessed lords,
My hearts, they will not leave me,

Their old uncle, lively nephews,
To contend with ill-health alone.
A building, there I'll remain,
I'll construct between their houses,
Amidst the place of my praises,
The gab of Cae Gwrgenau's wine.
They've given a rousing banquet:
May I not outlive these two.

CONFESSION

I grasp, compassionate God of heaven,
For your mercy and welcome, reverend Ruler,
High above in the sky your ramparts,
Salvation of the dead and the living, Helm of gladness,
King and Conjuror of every kind of weather,
Creator, Emperor, great blessed treasure,
Holy clear-minded Spirit, mighty shield,
Encouraging Father, open-handed Son.
When war betides, sea-surge's Master,
And the great swarm of people, and the three hosts
On the slope of Mount lordly Olivet,
Bands of angels will be your vanguard.

I have fashioned eulogy with falsehood,
You fashioned sea, glass-hued cataracts, and trees;
I've committed constant violence deserving your punishment,
You made heaven and earth, towering summits;
I have had no regard for heaven and churchmen,
You created the world's and Christendom's crafts;
I have fashioned love-messages, drunken in judgment,
You formed water and holy fire and banksides;
I have shamefully insulted an honest man,
You made foul and fair, humble of mind;
I have compared in a false-praising cywydd
Lleucu to Mary, hue of snow-covered land;
I have committed adultery not admitting it,
You made the Vale of Hebron and its rivers.

I confess to you, world comprehender,
The wrongs I have done, eloquent speaker,
Mighty Prince, powerful, without reproach,

Of lofty dawn and the mid-day hour:
I have uttered packs of oaths every day;
I have taught obstinacy, remorseless power;
I have broken the Ten Commandments, faith's comely treasure,
Goldsmith's law, steadfast his governance:
You broke, you shook, worthy Lord's offspring,
Earth's mountainous grave, mild bright Governor;
Tower of pure faith's perfect meaningful language,
You broke the gates of Hell, soggy bogland.

For your crown of thorns, for your punishment,
For your love, listen, Lord, to my verse,
For your pierced feet and their flowing red blood,
For your grievous wound from the bronze lance,
For your certain death upon your bier,
And the wisdom that rose on the third day,
By the time of my final mortal day,
Bountiful gold Father, befriend me.

IOLO GOCH

BARD AND BEARD

Is it you, beard, scared away
The girl who gladly kissed me?
You've been too thickly planted,
You're a large crop on my flesh.
Harsh and Irish, black and sharp,
As I look at my reflection
My countenance has become,
Chinful of grain, all hairy.

However completely cut
And whatever way it's shaven,
No smoother, there's no denying,
Than a skate's rough-surfaced tail.
The fair girl likes but little
My lips, because of my beard;

Always harsh was the cheek's edge,
Painful bristles, harsher daily.
A woman's gain if a crone has
A troop of toothless carding-combs:
There's on my cheek, they tell me,
Stuff with a thousand small teeth.
It's a slowpoke hedgehog's coat,
Chin's burden, it's like a muzzle,
Vexing tips of holly, prickles,
Goads of steel poking a girl.

Old sow's bristles, whence have you come?
You are a crop of gorse-shoots.
Sharp and tough is every hair,
Sticking a girl, stiff heather,
Resembling, so harsh they grow,
Tiny thistles' thousand needles.
You're like the frozen stubble,
Unbending, stiff-tipped arrow-quills.
Make off, so deeply disgraced,
Chin's thatch like a steed's clipped mane.

If it makes my chin look oldish,
With hot water, out it comes by the roots.

THE PLOUGHMAN

When, a free time, the world's people,
Christendom's vigorous throng,
Before the Lord God, great desire,
Fine bold words, disclose their doings,
Atop Mount, where there'll be judgment,
Mighty Olivet, all of them,
Joyful will be, concise story,
The ploughman, plodder of field.
If he gave, the good God is gracious,
Offering and tithes to God,
Then a good upright spirit
He'll render God, he'll merit grace.

Easy for the fair dale's ploughman,
Trust hereafter in the Lord God:

Alms, through keeping faith strictly,
Lodging, he'll deny to none;
He'll pronounce only on ploughbeams,
Wants no quarrels on his patch;
He'll not wage war, bring lawsuits,
Oppress a man for his goods;
He'll not treat us too harshly,
Not press claims, longsuffering.
There's no worth, by the passion,
No life, no world, without him.
He finds it far more pleasant,
I know, old unflurried way,
To follow, I can't much fault him,
The curving plough with the goad,
Than be, when taking a tower,
An Arthur, a plunderer.
We'd lack, save for his labour,
Christ's sacrifice to nourish faith,
Or the life of, why complain,
Pope or emperor without him,
Or king, fine wine-serving ruler,
Sound his sense, or living man.

Plain-talking old Lucidarus,
He expressed this perfectly:
Blest he, free of hardship after,
Who holds a plough with his hands.
Low-slung broom-splitting cradle,
Fine creel cutting strips in a field,
Its praise is proclaimed, comely treasure,
Crane that opens a bright furrow,
Fluent basket of fallow ground,
Noble coulter-bearing framework,
Grain's surely gained from its craft.
It seeks crops in soil that's fertile,
Faultless colt gnawing the earth.
A fellow displeased with pebbles,
Lad who flays, his leg in front,
He wants his knife and his table
And his food underneath his thigh;
His head keeps at it daily,
Clear street under oxen's feet.
Often will I sing its hymn:

It likes to chase the plough-chain,
Root-smashing fruit of the valley
Stretching an unbending neck,
Powerful lord's train-bearer,
Earth-scattering wooden shank.

Hugh the Strong, fine nation's master,
King rewarding praise with wine,
Emperor of land and seas,
Constantinople's gold keeper,
He put his hand, after ruin,
To a splendid strong-beamed plough.
Hale-living lord, he never,
Sprayer of tilth, sought bread,
Except, good was his teacher,
By his own hard labour, land's bard,
To show, greatly gifted eagle,
To proud men and humbly wise,
A single craft, no false word,
Stands highest with the dear Father,
A sign that this will triumph.
Ploughing, it is wisdom's way.

The Lord God's hand, best of men,
Mary's hand be on every ploughman.

PORTRAIT OF A MAIDEN

I love, she is lovable,
Rowan-berry coral cheek,
Proud sweetheart, she poured out mead,
Splendid fort's gracious daughter.
Glowing-cheeked flawless branch,
Foam's spray on freshwater rapids,
Bright flourishing white hemlock,
Straight-bodied censure-shy dear,
Skin's fair hue like sun on tower,
Rush body no man has known,
Hue of light snow on pale rock,
Lustre of rock-rippled water,
She's caused me great pain, many moans,
Supple bough, red-cheeked Llywy.

Moon's face hue of January snow,
She's mild and fair, the dawnlight.

Fine the untamed maiden's looks
And her taste, shape of Iseult.
Graceful, well-fashioned was she,
Not bashful, by Saint David:
Brow decked with wrought gold well-moulded,
Gold-hued hillcrest's primrose hair,
Eigr's colouring, radiant prize,
Slim dark eyebrow like Mary's image,
Eye like a splendid clasp's jewel
Resembling the Tiboeth's stone,
Ready smile like rime's gossamer hue,
Dainty nose, faint its sneezing,
Sweet little teeth, and a pretty
Delightful lip that sips wine,
Long throat, fair all its flowering,
Swan-like, smooth and slim, rounded,
Thumb that numbers prayer-beads,
And arm, and apple-ripe bosom,
Slender hand white as her glove,
Long dagger, soft pretty finger,
Pink fingernail upon it
And a gold ring here and there,
Goddess' side's smooth lovely shape,
Belt befitting its softness,
Rounded leg snow on hilltrail's hue,
Pale under skirt of scarlet,
Below fur miniver slim ankle,
White foot shapely though it's short,
Speaking sweet soft-laughing Welsh,
Graceful pace, lovely Welshwoman.

If a finger's crooked abruptly
Before her, round pebble's eye,
Pale-nailed rush, frail miracle,
She'll sway like an ear of barley.
Smooth-browed snow-comely maiden,
White border on fine gold sleeves,
Blest is she, white is her cheek,
Who wears, my red-lipped lady,
A white head-dress, wise peerless girl,

234

Cambric pennon, pure-browed peahen.
Who could, though a master-builder,
Paint with lime my dear's appearance?

God's fashioned her, gold son's purpose,
By Peter's image, for his Son.
I've piled up song, strengthless state,
Love's brush: was I not brash to
Imagine, generous question,
I might sleep with my modest-eyed girl?

LAMENT FOR DAFYDD AP GWILYM

'Charmed was, yesterday, Dafydd's life,
Blissful man were his day longer,
Rhyme intertwined, fine word-craft,
Gwilym Gam's son, knot of song.
He shaped praise in strict pattern,
A good practice in a man.
Well-furnished am I, I'll fashion
A lament for love of him.
The shires' gem was he and their crest
And the land's bauble and its beauty,
The mould and the means of pleasure,
Setting me free for fine gifts,
Hawk of Deheubarth's daughters,
Without him, let it turn to chaff.
Every clear-voiced singer's cywydd,
Because he has gone, complains.'

And you, hound, be quiet, cywydd.
The world's not good, will not last long.
While Dafydd lived, skilful song,
You were an honoured pastime,
And because of this, after him,
To call for you's not fitting.
Let praise woven of couplets
Be tossed away to the loft.
Words' architect, he has gone;
Alive, everyone's instructor.
Great my grief-stricken complaint,
Bardic lore in him was wondrous,

And he was love's tailor for a girl,
And harp of court and its household,
And bursar of bards and their praise,
And trident of strife and conflict,
And wretched without relief,
And disdain's been the man's undoing,
And bards' roofbeam, the world's saddened,
And never will he rise again.
Mighty master, keen, bright-voiced, bold,
And monarch, he's gone to heaven.

THE SHIP

Hard for me, a single welcome
On the ship, cold is its deck,
Flood's saddle, hollow its boasting,
Prisonhouse of the bitter beer
And the dark ale, harsh cold gaol,
And the bright cold puked-up cider.
Good luck, golden covenant,
To my lord and all my comrades;
No chance, fiend's calving frenzy,
Of good luck on the ship's deck.

Much punishment, it pained me,
To live in her, thin frail man.
She would rock, rickety thing,
On her side, cold her shudder,
Foul house for me, seas' cheesehouse,
Cramped castle, the sailors' coffin.
Foul dame, often steering off-course,
She's a loathsome Noah's ark,
Oaken soot-pan, rough her furrow,
Round-walled, pale-smocked, spry old cow,
Coal cart, no proper clean court,
With canvas sails, swag-bellied.
Snooty hag, scabby-lipped boards,
Wide-nostrilled, rope-reined saddle,
Kneading-trough's breadth, new moon's shape,
Like an old churn she lurches,
Mobile tower, swollen apparition,
Stiff screen seven cubits high,

Bucketing sea-splashing mare,
Bowl unsteadily bouncing,
Scabby-wooded gaol, crab-gutted,
Broad mare, all watch her from France.
She'd make faces in seaweed,
Skate with its bite in its breast.
More than a mark her rental,
Crooked basket of bobbing cork;
She'll wallow, Arthur's confession,
In the hollow of stone like a wall.

And so, fine renunciation,
I'll nevermore go to my doom,
Cold black belly, bleak shelter,
To her, old sea-going cupboard.
Stupid slut, she's been in Greece,
Broad anchorage, black, frigid,
Sow's graceless outlandish sty,
Chest-swelling, mast-bristling seed-dish.
Broad creaking sled for gravel,
She'd leap furrows, bare cold mare,
Ill-famed, dung-soiled waggon womb,
Cold serpent like Sir Fulke's stallion,
Stout barrow, she pours out yeast,
Stone-bellied snake, salt negress,
Harrow stroking the ocean,
Hunchbacked hind of the sea.

Many times, surely, cold border,
When the wild bare sea was in flood,
I sent greetings, splendid lord,
Golden helm, to the Cilmael,
Where Rhys, court like Lazarus', was,
Robert's son, noteworthy kinsman.
There I'd have, ungrudging gift,
A drink of his foaming gold bragget.
It's there, praiseworthy comfort,
I'd be were I where I'd be.

THE HORSE

By great God, sorry grey horse,
You're in wretched condition.
A fine sturdy straight-legged courser
You once were, too bad you're not still.
You've been the best of racers:
Sad and bitter for me to see
The place you were raised empty,
And your manger without food.
What will I do, to bear me,
For a large and splendid steed?
Hard for a gaffer, walking
Without rest, without a gift,
Without a horse, unless I ask
I know not who in Is Conwy.

'I'll give you advice in need:
Go to generous old Ithael
Ap Robert, the lord's a fine lad,
Ruler, two choirs' archdeacon.
Bards have stayed with him, Ithael's pleased,
On their rounds, getting together:
You needn't, he won't thank you,
Wait for kinsman or go on rounds,
Or entreat, dear requirement,
Or ask, only seek him out.
You'll have of him a fine stallion
From his fair wine-pouring hand.'

It was true: is there one like him?
Prince of the church, when he heard
My horse was dead, great to me was
The sadness after its loss,
He sent back some of his choicest.
It was grand, to choose a colt
And lead a fierce grey stallion,
Beautiful, noble, full-grown,
Firm round hooves bound in rope,
Fast-moving, large his muzzle,
Breastplated: were York's lord to buy him,
Three marks for him would be scorned.
This is the top-notch grey horse,

Wide-nostrilled, round-hoofed, big-bridled.
I'll be his foremost poet,
Not the last to have from his hand.

Here's the field, and here's the horse,
Now mine, posing a challenge:
What good is this, I insist;
I'm attempting to tame him.
How will I swiftly, boldly,
Get up on his back, for fear?
A mounting-block's needed, spry deed;
Heavy's one bent like a hunchback.
I must beware of shepherds
And order any surprised
On the road to get clear of me.
Let those who'd dare have warning,
At a distance, not to say boo:
That's a word known to cause trouble.
I must beware of Henllan's
Mill, dried-up weak-roofed hag,
Like a flabby sow, its clapper,
Gulping beans below the road,
And on winter nights, its mill-race,
And its rocky road, and its ditch,
Must avoid the ford full of snares
Of Glyn Meirchion and hollow Coedfron,
Must fear the close sunken roadway
And its steep slope above the church,
Dreadful road to Dinbych fair,
Thornbrakes and bristling hedgerows.

Be what may, for me, I'm slow,
Whether I fall or don't fall,
God's full blessing on, sure pillar,
The man who gave it, best of gifts.
Ardour's high feast, Uchdryd's heir,
Alive in the world's a treasure.
Lantern of sense, and its sanctum,
The far-away heartland's eye,
All Tegeingl's patron-saint's day,
Renown, Eingl's land's angel,
Great exceller of all others,
Is his compared to the rest.

More cheerful his countenance,
My Nudd, more bounteous than any,
Saint's sensible way of talking,
Precision like a tuning-string,
Plumes of a foam-laden, wine-hued bird,
And the look of an archangel.
My magnanimous foster-father
Is Ithael presently to me,
My third cousin, and my comrade,
Incredible thing, and my serf.
Ready tribute from Ithael
Is swiftly on hand for me,
Fine pension, hawk of high lineage,
The old man still supplied with steeds,
And having on every feast-day
Gifts and welcome, an easy life.
Tranquil praiseworthy man,
Some know, well he pays for poems,
He gave red gold and silver,
I'm a rider, and steeds and gold,
And food and drink at his table,
Ricard's heir, how high in regard.
God grant him, so all of us say,
Let it be true, a long lifetime.

A PILGRIMAGE TO SAINT DAVID'S

I wished to do my soul good,
I'm growing old, it was needful,
Go where Christ was crucified,
Although my two sorry feet
Be settled here in fetters.
The feet had no wish to go there.

It's just as worthwhile for me
To go three times to Mynyw,
As to go, splendid status,
In summer as far as Rome.
I knew where I wished to be,
Godly it is, that dwelling,
In Dewi of Mynyw's manor,
By the cross, it's a splendid place.

In Glyn Rhosyn's the lovely spot,
With olive-trees and grapevines,
And esteemed music and manners,
And clamour of men and clock,
And glad harmony, bright radiance,
Between the organ and bells,
And a huge heavy gold thurible
Pouring incense to spread perfume.
Fair heaven of heavens made public,
It's a fine town, Rome's estate,
Wales' calm comely paradise,
Lordly town, paradisally ordered.

Saint Patrick was reluctant,
Displeased with God, angry time,
For demanding this, disrespectful,
That he from the place he had made
Go far away from Mynyw
Before Dewi's birth. It's good:
A saint for us from heaven
He was made before his birth,
Holy saint when he was born,
Splitting the stone, his faith awesome.
He gave their sight once again
To the leper's eyes, diseased badly,
His godfather, worldly kinfolk,
Blind and flat-faced, great was the praise.
His father, Sant: no denying
That he was prince of the saints;
Beneficent merry-eyed saint,
Non was, his flawless good mother,
Ynyr's daughter, great her kin,
Comely nun, splendid the story.
But one food entered his mouth,
Cold bread and cress and black water,
The whole length of his lifetime,
A course of the very same kind
As had entered holy Non's mouth
Since he was conceived: he's sovereign.

All the world's saints, shared journey,
Came to the fine synod once,
On the same day to listen

To his sermon, and the core of his creed.
A hill rose, no disaster,
Under Dewi of Brefi's feet,
Where he taught a choice multitude,
Where he preached in choice language,
Six thousand, seven-score saints,
And a thousand: oh the congregation.
He was made, purity honoured,
The head of all the world's saints.

He worshipped God beautifully:
Heaven's province was his sanctum,
The warm invigorating bath,
It ends not, will last forever.
Boldly it was he permitted,
The black Lenten fast's good grace,
To the Britons, famed in the *Brut*,
The herring, specially favoured.

God had transmuted, fierce anger,
Two diabolical wolves,
Two old men from enchantment's land,
Crafty Gwydre and Odrud,
For committing, wicked feat in times past,
A sin their hearts were set on,
And their mother, what was her fault,
A wolf-bitch, a curse upon her.
And splendid Dewi relieved them
Of their long pain and outlawed state.
God provided for his altar;
His net worked a great miracle;
He drove the wild birds in flight,
My fair lord, to the houses;
And the swift nimble antlered stags,
Wondrous servants, would attend him.

Tuesday, the first day of March,
He lay down in the grave to die.
At his grave, a good ending,
A fine choir sang Gloria,
Heaven's angels were on the riverbank
When his funeral was over.
The soul of a man, special ground,

Who is, not in vain, buried
In Dewi of Mynyw's churchyard,
It will not be condemned to hell's pit.

If, in a book of blank paper,
As on a long summer day,
One like a notary public
With ink and steel-pointed pen
Each day should write, a blessing,
His life that was open to all,
Scarcely, however accomplished,
A short while, could he record
In a full year and three days
All the wonders that he did.

SIR HYWEL OF THE AXE

Did anyone see what I see
In the night, don't I do rightly,
When I am, greatest pain ever,
Sleeping, part of growing old?
First thing I see is, truly,
A glorious fort there on the shore,
And a fine masterful castle,
And men on decks, and a wall,
And blue sea by a stone rampart,
And foam round a stern tower's womb,
And music of flute and bagpipe,
Lively sound, and noteworthy men
Engaging in dance and carol,
Enjoying pleasure and praise,
Maidens, none of them uncomely,
Weaving the lovely bright silk,
Proud men playing, in the great hall,
Draughts and backgammon at the dais,
And a grizzled man, fierce-natured,
Twrch Trwyd of strife, giving wine
In a gilded golden goblet
From his own hand into mine,
And a lovely long black standard
On the tower, good soldier was he,

With three beautiful white flowers
Shaped the same, silver-hued leaves.

Strange that there's not an elder
In Gwynedd, land of great feasts,
Who's capable of knowing
If I were where I wish to be.
Fortunate, one says, are you:
Wise are you in your dreaming.
The splendid wall that you see,
The good dwelling you'd come to,
And the bright fort on rocky heights
With red stone at the croft's corner,
This is Cricieth, well-constructed,
An ancient building that is,
And the strong grizzled spear-splitting man
Is Sir Hywel, lightning's mangnel,
And his wife, Sir, golden-girdled,
Hywel, war's lord at our need,
And her handmaids, fair of skin,
They were weaving by the dozen
The beautiful bright-hued silk,
The fine glass letting in sunlight.
When you saw, in your vision,
A standard, finely designed,
Sir Hywel's banner is this:
By Beuno, in his pennon
Are three fleur-de-lys, field's iris,
On sable, no ignoble sight.

The son of red-speared Gruffudd
Is so made he makes for his foes,
Whetting a spear in their blood
Savagely, gold-footed chieftain,
Army's carver, splendid red H,
Quick to the fray, red-shielded,
Tusks of a fierce-tempered boar,
Old bone that we have need of.
When pride's harsh reward, the bridle,
Was put on the French king's head,
He played barber like Erbin's son
With spear and sword, hard fighting:
With his hand and its deftness

He shaved off both heads and beards,
And he let, soon as he could,
Blood over feet, sad for some.

Dear he'll be to Lionheart's heir,
Many his bards, praised his table.
He's warden, eighteen-tined stag,
And steward of the stout fortress:
Bold warhorse guarding the stronghold,
Long will this man guard the land,
Guard the folk in a fine keep,
Guard the castle, he's worth armies,
Guard two bounds, long field's warden,
Guard both lands, guard troops, guard fame,
Guard the sea-bull and the seastrand,
Guard the tide, guard the homes, guard the land,
Guard all countries, guard the bright tower,
And guard the fort: good health to the man.

LAMENT FOR ITHAEL AP ROBERT

Wondrously sprouts of pestilence,
This hour, broke the Earth's surface,
And on it they breed terror
Wondrously, hard-sweating globe.
There's shaking, cold tremor of fear,
With fever, the ague's hot fit.
A tempest came, it was Tuesday,
Long day between the end of March
And April, no blessing for us:
Thursday was terror's beginning
Between the new day and the night.
Little-known is what caused it.

A great blow, the death of Ithael
Ap Robert, comely man, fine man,
Who gave us red-gold garments
A-plenty, and silver and gold.
Efficacious stone, burning bright,
Pure precious pearl, large and lustrous,
Angles' magic angelic gem,
Tegeingl's butterfly, fair and holy,

His land's friend, provider of feasts,
Naid's Cross and soul of Gwynedd,
Angel's brother, youthful appearance,
Good and bad, it stabs every heart.
None on him would pass judgment;
Passing on was his single fault.
Awesome man, Ithael of clerics
Was the best, gracious old man:
This world scarcely possesses
A generous man, since he died.
Woe to them, minstrels, in wind and rain,
Now that the earth has grown darker:
It's not known, though it be brief,
Tempest or any weather
Till today, unjust, unseemly,
Like to this, ah my tall lord.

Holy God is sending angels
As escort, greatest of tasks,
To fetch him, it was agreed,
For praise of the thousand thousands,
As, plainly from heaven, God did,
It was good, after the passion,
When hell, vast desolation,
Was harrowed, desolate marsh,
And the broad earth, fair and brown,
Oh such a chill, was shaking.
It was then that he sent Jesus
Back, his beloved son,
And like this a host of angels,
Exalted lord, welcomed him,
To bring him, no strife, no fuss,
In good health home to heaven.
That was a well-furnished funeral
God provided him by his power.

Not less was the uproar now
That assembled, before sunrise,
To escort without a pause
The apostle's worthy body.
Never so many wise men
Assembled in this island:

It's this made the weather frigid,
Hail come from the cruel moon,
The black earth, heaping of dust,
Shake, how great was the quaking,
Mother of all warm prospering crops,
Cold cloak, so heavy its burden,
When they set out, fragile dream,
For the church, holy fragrance,
From Coedymynnydd, with him,
All his family mourning,
And the angels, God's good folk,
Before the lord's host's tumult
Were making a mighty murmur
Between roadway and the sky,
Noblemen managing horses,
Thick hoofprints trampling the turf,
And the sound of sturdy musicians,
And laymen, and a huge crowd,
Hearing, so sad was the din,
Bells and stray bards and vibrations,
And monks' treble, and turbulence,
And sober preaching brothers
Chanting a psalm, pure voices,
And a solemn litany.

Woe for two thousand, after
He entered the church, comely praise,
And the lighting, woe for many,
Of shining candles' fine torches
Like lanterns, bright will-o-the-wisps.
Numberless were in the temple
Proud noblemen, worthy crowd,
Some wringing fingers, sad sight,
Great affliction, like a death-grip,
Some pulling out on all sides
The hair of their heads like grassblades,
Maidens, dear their dignity,
Some faltering, some fainting,
And paupers, woeful people,
Moaning more than other folk,
Many a squire in the rear
Still crying out, woe for the weak,

Many a tear on a woman's cheek,
Many sad nephews, many nieces,
Many feeling long life is worthless,
Ah that he were alive and well.
Frequent loud cries, hundred clerics' bells,
And clamour until vespers:
Around the corpse in purple
The convent, filling the choir,
Was beautifully singing
Sacred songs, splendid interment.
The cross-shaped church was shaking
With the echo and the solemn sound
Like a broad ship at anchor:
Shrinking it shivers on the sea.

Woe for you, Iolo, woe for his household:
From the gold robes to the black pit.
Fine gravel or grit was cast
Upon him as a cover,
With many a cry, great outburst,
Of all round him, as though in battle.
It's known in all courts and churches
That the earth has split in three.

Too much keening would suit poorly
Such a man, heaven for us,
When he has, generous elder,
From God a fair life and estate.
Better silence than harsh keening,
Bitter loss, for a fine stag.
Here is what would do him good,
To worship Christ without complaining,
Give a resting-place, fine occurrence,
To his soul, lamb of God was he,
With Elijah, sacred footsteps,
And Enoch in great glory.
They'll not come, the two grave saints,
From Paradise, they are brothers,
Till Doomsday, the right hand's life,
Comes in the last judgment.
Then shall we see our leader,
Woe and wind, steady strongpoint:
There'll not be atop Mount high

Olivet, perfect ruler,
A finer lord archdeacon
Than Ithael of noble birth.

SYCHARTH
in praise of Owain Glyndŵr's estate

Twice have I pledged before now,
Fair pledge, pledging a journey:
Let each, as much as he may,
Redeem the pledge he pledges.
A pilgrimage, sure of success,
A great purpose so precious,
To go, swiftly sworn promise,
It's a blessing, to Owain's court.
There speedily I will go,
No trouble, there I'll settle
To add honour to my life
With him, exchanging greetings.
My lord can, of noblest line,
Kind gold head, welcome a gaffer:
Praiseworthy, though it be alms,
Blameless course, to be good to the old.
To his court in haste I'll go,
Of two hundred the most worthy,
A baron's court, place of fine manners,
Where many bards come, where life's good,
Light of great Powys, Maig's land,
Promise that can be trusted.

Look at its form and fashion
Enclosed in water's gold round:
Isn't it fine, a bridge on the moat,
And a hundred-pack-wide portal.
There are coupled beams, couples' work,
Every couple is coupled,
Patrick's belfry, French creation,
Westminster's cloister, comfortable close,
Clasped the same way each corner,
Gold chancel, all in concord,
Joists bound breast-to-breast above,
Face-to-face like a dungeon,

249

And each, like a knot tied tight,
Is interlocked with the other.
Eighteen mansions' nine-plated buildings,
Fine timber houses atop a green hill,
On four marvellous pillars
Nearer heaven is his hall.
On each thick wooden pillar
A sturdy loft atop the croft,
And the four lofts, delightful,
Interlinked, where minstrels sleep:
The four bright rooms were converted,
A lovely nestful, to eight.
Tile roofs on each frowning house,
A chimney where smoke could flourish,
Nine halls in matching pattern,
And nine wardrobes for each one,
Fine shops with splendid contents,
Well-stocked shop like London's Cheap,
Cross-shaped church, comely lime-white walled,
Chapels with fine glass windows.

On each side a whole bakehouse,
Orchard, vineyard, near the white court,
Fine mill on smooth-flowing stream,
And his dovecot's bright stone tower,
A fishpond, sunken enclosure,
What's needed for casting nets,
Abounding, no argument,
In pike and splendid whiting,
And his bordage land and live birds,
Peacocks, high-stepping herons,
Fair meadows for hay and pasture,
Grain-rows in well-tended fields,
Our patriarch's rabbit park,
Ploughs and powerful horses.
Close to the court, still finer,
Deer graze in another park.

His serfs do each task that's proper,
It's what a manor requires,
Bringing Shrewsbury's best beer,
Liquors, the foaming bragget,
All drinks, white bread and wine,

His meat, fire for his kitchen.
Bards' haven, wherever he be,
He'll have all there, even daily.
Fairest wooden court, faultless lord,
In the realm, God defend it,
And the best wife among women,
I'm blest by her wine and mead,
A knightly line's bright daughter,
Dignified, benevolent,
And his children come, two by two,
A fine nestful of chieftains.

Very seldom was seen there
Either a latch or a lock,
Or someone playing porter.
No need, no hunger, no shame,
Never parched throats at Sycharth.
The best Welshman, brave achievement,
Owns the land, Pywer Lew's line,
Slim strong man, the best of homesteads,
And the court, delightful the place.

LAMENT FOR LLYWELYN GOCH AP MEURIG HEN

'Oh fair God so good to man,
Did anyone see Llywelyn
Son of noble Meurig Hen,
Poetry's paternal uncle?
Where is he?' Who is it seeks him?
Ask no more; he'll not respond.
'Those here are Meirionydd's
Loving maidens and young men.'
God knows not the court poet:
Strong teacher, he's entered grace.
Wondrously he went at the last
To Rome from the shire's domain.
Never went man, by God's choice,
Whose leaving was more lamented.
To Paradise, to sing for
Mary, he's gone, wondrous lord.
One must take there naught but credit;
Not unsightly, to have a glad soul.

A great matter, if the master-bard's dead:
Mary knows the poems will not perish.
When there's a call for, the custom,
The voices within the great halls,
First called for, authentic work,
From the performers, sweet verses,
Is the old redhead's love-song,
The crowd listens, like a bell.
There's harmony in no poem,
True it is, where young men may be,
There's pleasure in no word-craft
Or any tune from finger tip,
Save the pure-voiced songster's cywydd:
No cywydd's wanted save his.
Not one word, coarse craftsmanship,
Is found misplaced in the poem.
Not Tydai, the Muse's Father,
Or lovely old Culfardd's skill
Could fashion pure song like him,
Bold and brilliant his song-craft.
Rightful refined master-bard,
Song's prophet, how greatly lamented,
High-road and guardian of praise,
Judge of all fine compositions,
He was Ovid's cywydd's prime master,
Experienced, expert, was he.
My great sworn friend was inspired,
For all sweet rhymes the song-book.
From smooth-lipped Taliesin,
In sleep, not poor his harvest,
He learned, what a disciple,
Fervent praise of the Bible in song.
Greatly gifted, no lack of strength,
Fine instructor, he's taken learning
To the place of widespread peace.
And let the song go with him,
No need for it in summer:
Well he knows what pleases most.

No one, precious fellowship,
Would sing a thing in Gwynedd
Save what the two of us fashioned,
He and I. An Amig was he,

Amlyn am I: not too many
Old ones left on the face of Gwynedd.
Song's pure teacher, sweet strong language,
Well-grounded: who now knows a thing?
And I bear a long yoke alone:
I know not how, unsleeping,
To thresh grain, or to weave praise,
With one flail, ah, what ill-fortune.
The same kind as the turtle-dove,
Weak am I, and the same feelings:
The mild bird will not come down,
Not sing on green birch, pure voice,
When its mate, it's cruel I survive,
Is dead, I am dumb-founded.
I, I've no wish to sing ever
With him gone. What will I do?

I have prayed, earnest fashion,
To Peter. I'll sing for support,
That Llywelyn be brought, good man,
Heaven's high master, to the stronghold,
Amidst, civilized people,
Heaven's prophets, mighty are they.
The Prophet David will delight in
Reciting Lleucu Llwyd's songs.
David was God's own poet,
Praised the Trinity and the One God:
My lord composed the psalter's
Poems, every syllable.
He was unchaste in his lifetime,
Sinful in the ways of love;
Harpist, lord of a war-band,
Loving man, he was repentant.
God forgave him, fruitful sorrow,
In the last years of his life,
And he will forgive his bard
His folly, unlovely failing.
An open court, high office,
Is a poet's wherever he comes:
No door, no gate, none complain,
Shuts against him, it's unfitting.
Not easy to keep, grave penance,
A poet out of Paradise.

DAFYDD BACH AP MADOG
WLADAIDD

CHRISTMAS REVELS

Cadwaladr's splendid son, he keeps roads open,
    Elyston Glodrydd's offspring,
    And in his court, noble stock stirring,
    There are obedient boys,

And favour and drinking and a gracious household,
    And crowds in succession,
    And upholding of a lord's honour,
    And never will he be begrudging.

Let no determined man on a stormy day,
    Purposing to please,
    Go, though so foolish his faith,
    Or come, beyond Dafydd's court.

I have seen a court, and a dozen courts,
    And no court have I seen so worthy
As the court I prize for its ruler's sake,
    Not lightly I'll praise it, like Celliwig:
Heaven's bounty on earth in Bachelldref,
    Where there is a song-fest each Christmas,
And a crowd of kinfolk, and a lake of liquor,
    And the luminous honours of Meurig's homeland,
And reading books of a royal clan's lineage,
    And praising exalted pedigrees,
And knowing the law's three tongues and clauses,
    And the grounds of each functioning language,
And the sound of strings and a deluge of drinks,
    And reciting of well-known poems,
And numerous foods, sweet provisions,
    And thick sugar-coated dishes,
And keeping open house for the whole Isle of Honey,
    Clearly none could suppose that there is a court
Like the genial court for honour and grandeur,
    And good-natured well-mannered nobility,
And presiding each day in much prosperity,

And great merriment without one harsh word,
And feeding lively horses on hay and oats,
 And taming young stallions, mountain steeds,
And slender greyhounds, snatchers, graspers,
 Snub-nosed dogs, butchers of meat,
And a chorus of peacocks, and the crooning of doves,
 And swans trumpeting like swans,
And the descant of birds, well-drilled their trilling,
 And seemly language, untroubled speech,
And a red-hued lance of Cadwaladr's line,
 And a blood-gushing blade with a fine gift of meat,
And many a minstrel and merry fiddler,
 And much merriment on a polished floor,
And musicians' swaying, and children chirping,
 And the turmoil of servants with food,
And the cup-bearer weary, and the kitchen's upheaval,
 And three kinds of wine for the thirsty.

Three customs there are, merriment's country,
 At Dafydd's high court, blameless boldness:
Whoever you are, whatever you sing,
 And whatever the thing you are known for,
Come whenever you wish, take what you please,
 And once come, stay as long as you like.

Stay, Dafydd, a princely lord in your courts,
  And your many castles:
  Your word will last three stag lifetimes;
  Your fame has crossed every land.

GRUFFUDD AP MAREDUDD

LAMENT FOR GWENHWYFAR

I

Gwynedd's sun, it's a grave, not alive a lady,
    Past conceiving, her peer.
    An honoured name is no more;
    Moon's glow, it's cold sleep tonight.

Harsh cry breaking in, base in broken earth
    To place blackbird-hued brows,
    Gold girl who wore rich garments,
    Sun's complexion, pouring mead.

    A slender form wore, stone roof,
    Earth's cincture, after fine fur;
    Tender cheeks, hue of dawn-rise,
    Hard for me to live long after.

    A tomb was fashioned, fine shape,
    Dear, of marble around you;
    Mourning for you has fashioned
    For my heart joyless torment.

Comes to this heart, rippling streams' fair hue,
    Torture, sorrow's anguish;
    For strong Gereint's comely heir,
    Soul's misery, much too much.

A grim task, to confine, ah fair Gwenhwyfar,
    Harsh in me, grief for you,
    Flesh most comely under greensward,
    Deep pain, church ground, frail blossom.

I know a lad slain by yearning's pain, Mary,
    Dead Pentraeth's gold candle,
    Left weak by, sorrow's poison,
    A gossamer face, wine and mead nursed.

    World was not granted, heart's sadness,
    Harsh cold ground, beauty's gold moon,

Lament bred after many sighs,
Tears plain, a lovelier sight.

Sorrow stirs memories, moaning and tears
    For three regions' beauty,
  Since she's entered the land of peace
  Who pained me, the Lord's haven.

  Sad to enclose a pale moon
  In stone chest, death's doleful ebb;
  Many the face lined with woe
  For a sage girl, Dindaethwy's gem.

  Many a one, yearning's bold foe,
  White-tipped shallow foam's hue,
  For a tranquil well-born maid,
  By God's violence, were saddened.

Where were fur and green gown, where red garb and blue,
    There's death-stricken torment.
  Where there was gold round her cheeks,
  Where purple, the chancel hides it.

Gowned, wine-pouring's sun, near Cyrchell's white strand,
    In a fresh grave's close cell;
  Woe's he, since she's in heaven,
  Who loved her, from bitter longing.

Woe's me, Mary's pure treasure, tears shake me,
    For Welshmen's gold beauty;
  She's gone, in a hidden bed,
  Slim maid, beneath a marble house.

II

  One and Three as one, dreadful there rises
  A spear full-length through this grief-stricken breast:
Cheek's brightness hidden, dread of sleep frightens me
  For a rough ford's pale foam's splendid hue.

  Ah long grim hardship imposed as penance
  By her brief fleeting life and its leaving;

Ah wait one night, a short while, and spare her,
  Bright maiden's death, she was dearly loved.

  Ah strong Lord of nine orders, grief slays me;
    Gwenhwyfar mourning, I complain as well:
Struck by sorrow's force from the dying day
    Of my much-praised love, there's no life for me.

  Since she's gone, mine is down-hearted yearning,
    To bright Caergybi, famed gift-giving lord,
Splendid flawless form like fair dawn in beauty,
    Many a cry and moan on the strand,

    Many a groan for my woe, constant longing,
    Many a tear on the cheek by the ford,
Many a long wail, it's no sin to mourn her,
    And laboured sobbing, distress in full flow.

    I care not, with dawn's hue in earth's sleep
    Beneath a marble choir, queenly her beauty,
Cause of grief, since there dies, the grave concerns me not,
    Snowy dale's glow, since no life is left.

    My pale girl's set apart in cold ground,
    May pure faithful Mary befriend her;
Sharp pain, shining treasure, blow of bitter grief,
    To bind rippling ford's hue in fresh oak.

    Perished are all my high spirits,
    I'm witless, with her taken, fellowship's plaint;
Splendid the hall before the grave's distant earth,
    Under stone roof's stern lock, a much-sung maiden.

    Gone Welshmen's moon, snow-hued complexion,
    A maid sleeps long, truth will not spare me;
Unconcealed conflict it is that afflicts me:
    Strange to one who hears me that still I live.

    For your crown of thorns' sake, fine assurance,
    And your pain, Mary's Son, on the bloodstained rood,
Welcome a gracious girl, honour's felicity,
    To the feast, and the life free of sickness.

III

This is sickness of a heart that's stricken,
I'm worn down, pain is apportioned me,
This is sorrow whose sighs are not hidden,
This is worthless hope for a long-lasting life.
No joy had I, just a painful day
For a fair-formed dear, hue of highland snow.
It's a lovely maid's wretched death that is mourned;
It's the long wretched plunder that no more will be seen.
Fair was, before the close earthen grave's constraint,
The maiden's brow beneath burnished gold.
Shapely and graceful, fine generous woman,
Superb was her complexion, skin sapphire-pale.
Chaste was she and discreet, correct refined manners,
Gracious in costly garb, honouring truth.;
She set the ploughbeam, anger's not concealed;
The young roe's motion's extolled afar.
Paper-white wine-pouring fort's harsh exchange,
Her ways were ointment for one to be tended:
Wretched the sight, lingering welcome,
Of the ways of death, dreadful demand.
Where there was before perishing, cherished thought,
Silk and sendal deserving high praise,
Where was bountiful beauty, tears will be wept,
And purple and red, here's the grave's mound.
Strange it is I still live in a wicked world,
Harsh warfare, unjust, why am I tormented?
After the forfeit imposed upon me
Of one so much loved, venomous cruelty,
Woe's the tortured rage requiring penance,
Woe's the fool deceived like a blind man.
Gentle modest Gwenhwyfar is called
To God's mercy where she will be loved:
And I while I live will feel the wound
Sundered from her, none will wonder,
And she, hue of pale wave gaily breaking on shore,
Her radiant form will be celebrated.

IV

High-pitched sighing, a corpse thrice over,
 A heart breaking,

For Gwenhwyfar I know sorrow's force
    Through heaven's harshness,
For one fair of face and Gwynedd's sun
    And beneficence,
For purity, for a moon-pale face
    Of noble lineage.
A splendid bard, schooled long and well,
    For her renown,
I sang her praise, my blessed right,
    She was my life.
Woe's he left alive in a world of penance
    To live in pain
After a fair maid, hue of breaking wave,
    Honour to serve her:
Fine wine-taverns, thousands will judge
    The state I am in.
She was coral-cheeked, lovely and tranquil
    Before she was silenced,
Was the fairest sight, radiant white hand,
    Before she was placed
In the deep grave far off, to waste a face
    With too much wailing.
Not shallow, for a sleepless lad yesterday
    To honour her;
Not unworthy, such a jewel's hue,
    Ever to praise her;
Not a wonder, and wealth it was
    To extol her.
Ah, the sad tale, seeing the cold end
    Of a comely-hued Deirdre,
Ah, for the loss of a second Luned,
    Glowing jewel,
Ah, the heavy heart and uttermost sadness
    That earth is over her.
You've done to your servant great outrage,
    Resplendent Mary,
Gowning a maid with fine-woven green clothing,
    Agony to me,
Covering the loveliest countenance, pale skin's radiance,
    Close to the sea,
Wave's brightness, river-mouth's white crest,
    Cybi's fair region.

Woe's one who gave and who lost,
    Look of grove's snow,
Love for her in a bitter turning,
    Too much keening is mine.
Great God divine, Mary and the martyrs
    Implore you,
By your pangs and your lengthy passion
    And your cruel nails,
Care for snow's beauty, piercing gold word,
    Lord of lords,
Bring her of your grace, One and Three are you,
    Even now to your land.

GRUFFUDD LLWYD

IN DEFENCE OF PRAISE

Oh God, is a man sinful
To take gold in return for praise?
Good the role, as good the reward,
If God displays no displeasure.
May one freely take from an open hand?
If it's freely and sinlessly given.
Elucidarium, handsome work,
Has said to me twice over
That for me a sinful burden
Was singing snd selling praise.
Shame on his stern pronouncement,
But I disagree with the sage,
Since I know not, of us complaining,
By what right, or who he was.
Why put a curse upon us
Far off, if he'd give no support?

Threatened, I'll not despair:
I am no frivolous minstrel,
I'm not an ill-mannered jester,
No, and I know how to sing.

And I'm not, though I'm a poet,
A fairground bard, unlovely boast.
The Holy Spirit inspires me,
Flawless name, who dwells in me:
He will prevent, my gold treasure,
Treachery against his bard.
Great the blessings of books of learning:
By God, no less are the muse's.
The hand of God, from true grace,
Gives the muse to his servant:
Wise for a bard, fluent praise,
To compose song that's fitting.

And I publicly, where I come,
Am always bard to good people.
The sons, mine their ready gifts,
Of fair Meurig, Mary bless them,
I would get, amiable men,
Gold from them, Ynyr's grandsons,
Descendants, they do me honour,
Of splendid Gwên, who once gave wine.
Their mother, unblemished stock,
Came of Edeirniawn's princes,
The pure line, light of a lamp,
Of Y Rhug's lord, true greatness,
Heir of Owain, brilliant bulwark,
Brogyntyn, he'd shatter hosts.
They have honoured me for praise,
Noble lords, at their banquets:
Ungrudging Hywel, generous ways,
Splendid Meurig, I'm their fame's steward.
Whatever at Hywel's court
I'm given, he's open-handed.
Without stint comes to a bard,
Dyfr's way, he'll not repent it,
From the wealth, I'm his poet,
Of Meurig Llwyd, what I receive.
He guides his kinsmen, brave band,
I'm joyful, guides not backwards.
Sublime, the men's true talent,
Is the bounty of Ynyr's line:
To achieve the highest merit
Is my two lords' single thought.

Golden the course of my journey,
They're Alexander's griffins to me.
There are our golden falcons,
Above the rock, mighty lords.
The rock's called for its repute
A stage of heaven, a slope drinking.
I've cast praise, loud and constant,
To the summit of Nannau's rock;
Surely the rock should send me
Pure gold for beautiful words.
A trade, without rousing wrath,
I make with humble patrons:
Readily I give a greeting,
My treasure, in exchange for gold,
And readily they give me
Solid gold atop the hill.
No sin's mine, when I consider
Wealth for wealth, I'm a happy man.
I have gold from Meurig's sons
Without one hour of anger:
I've had their perfect presents;
From their poet they have 'Good day'.

SENDING THE SUN TO MORGANNWG

Fair sun, upon my errand
Run, while you're sunshine's wheel.
You're the fairest planet running
In God's possession, fair sun.
Sunday's fame, excellent light,
Yours is a lengthy journey
From east, fair weather's sky-road,
Finest of hues, to the west.
You were rounded full of grace,
On every side you're glowing:
Your glow, by God the helmsman,
It goes throughout the whole world.
Sun so fine, from your lively hue
The moon derived its colour;
Ruling power, spherical rowel,
Round wheel, great your gift and grace.

Bright-complexioned gem of light,
You are the sunshine's empress.

Praiseworthy planet I love,
Blessed are you, through the summer
You're above, place of flawless day,
All of Morgannwg daily,
Ungrudging folk, strong and gifted,
From Gwent, where the men are good,
To, where you know how to fly,
Glyn Nedd, fair princes' region.
For my sake, sun, cheerful curtain,
Keep from that wine of a land
Too much rain, danger to bridges,
Extreme frost, and too much wind,
Baleful stars, and harsh fury
Through the trees, and long-staying snow,
And whirlwind's far-faring force,
And hoarfrost in early April.
Display, day's exultation,
Morgannwg's pennant each day,
And when afternoon's full of light
Come and visit beside me.
If you go beneath cloud tonight,
Thick curtain, in western regions,
Gracious homestead's grand likeness,
Come once again to the east:
Appear for my sake, sure in mind,
In the zenith before mid-morning.

Go on my errand, and carry
With you to Morgannwg's men
Good days, dwelling-place of love,
From me, and bring my greeting.
Turn, no need to command you,
About the great whitewashed halls,
Splendid, by God, your story,
Send sunshine's drill through the glass.
Seek each place of habitation,
Meadow and wood, where there's mead,
Each mansion, fair is your range,
And the glades, and the orchards.

What sort of land? A radiance.
A poet calls it Paradise.
Corner opposite Cornwall,
It's my court of wine and mead.
Place where many folk make merry,
A good place for households and wine,
Place that resounds with welcome,
Place of brave lads, place of pure maids,
Easy place for a bard, lively crowds,
To see, lovely bright daylight,
The best bards truly claim it,
A fine woman wearing white fur.

I send, with fair weather's lord,
Fine feasts, this land a title,
In the words of a true lover,
'Countess, queen of every land.'
If there were a proclamation
That none would be free to give,
Nobody, wealth apparent,
From Morgannwg could say no.
If banned to a blithe-singing bard
All the world, and he was outcast,
He'd find, with no sign of a frown,
His provision in Morgannwg.

OWAIN GLYNDŴR

Sad world, fragile existence,
Everywhere under the sun.
It's full, and no one's joyful,
Abundance on the one side
Of goods for some, not needed:
Quite often it's the churls possess
Gold and silver, they'd give nothing,
And riches, a hard, hard world.
The Welsh, so great their suppression,
Sorry nation, like drunken crows,
I could, I'd crave no favour,
Call them a cauldron of guts.
The lowest in his manners
Is highest, great is my groan,

And the highest before mid-day
Will be lowest and most humble.
Sack's arse once, magical hood,
Is sack's head now, devil's codpiece:
The scrawny kites of wrongdoing
Become hawks at every turn.

It's this that creates, old and new,
The wicked world. What's to come?
The earth is growing feeble
Till there's neither grain nor tilth.
Britons were once the strongest,
The foremost tribe known to men:
They're now, at the age of Caw,
Nothing but chewed-up leavings.
Three emperors overseas
Once came from them: one was
Battle's king, Brân the rightful lord,
The great champion Beli's brother;
Constantine once waged war there;
Arthur, none could be his equal.
It's a certainty there once
Were kings of our famous country,
Five score ruling London's court,
Crowned heads, stags of the island.

Are there noble knights, bold question,
Oppression and shame, for Wales,
Save for Dafydd, shattered shield,
Great magistrate and master,
Of Hanmer, mild grey-haired noble,
And Grigor, a Saint George, Sais,
Since was stretched out, snare of battle,
The deep-biting lightning-bolt spear
And pennon of splendid Sir Hywel,
Renown of Otiel, gold his spur?
Time was there was fierce unyielding
Conflict, till he was brought down,
Where near Provence was tested
A strong lion, guarding prince's host.
Last knight, victorious custom,
Strong courage, steel was his crest,
Of Ednowain's splendid lineage:

266

While his seed and his stock continued
No lively generation
Was without one in the nest,
A bright pledge, if there's a fine task,
Golden, upon his stallion.

Which man now, when he has gone,
Has the task? It continues:
Owain, I know no greater prince,
Lord of Glyn divided Dyfrdwy,
Noble heir of the bountiful line
Of Sycharth, well-favoured fortress.
He comes of, ever old his stock
Since time immemorial,
A Welshman, faultless father's mother:
Wearing scarlet-bordered garb,
And harness of the best gold,
And fine fur, he's a strong baron.
If he is healthy and free,
He will win, when he pleases,
Boots fashioned, comely buskins,
Of fine leather, sturdy bold stag,
Jousting in a tournament,
Bruising bodies, downing a hundred.
He will sit in public view
At the high board, fair boardful.
He'll not suffer wrong or lawbreaking:
He will shine bright amidst earls.

POEMS OF UNKNOWN OR
UNCERTAIN AUTHORSHIP

THE SNOW

I don't sleep, don't leave the house:
Because of this, I'm in anguish.
There's no world or ford or hillside,

Nowhere clear, no ground today.
No girl's promise will lure me
Outside my house into snow.
It's a plague, flakes on the gown
Stay as if one played dragon.
My clothing is my excuse
That looks much like a miller's.
Isn't it true, after New Year's,
Everyone's wearing fur garments?
January, first of the flock,
God's at work creating hermits.

God has given a whitewash
To the dark ground round about:
There's no undergrowth not garbed in white;
There's no bush without a blanket.
Fine flour's the fur on each branch,
Sky's flour like April blossoms,
Cold white screen on the greenwood,
Load of lime subduing the trees.
Illusion of wheat flour's there,
Level land's metal mail-coat.
Cold grit is the ploughed ground's soil,
Earth's skin thick-caked with tallow,
Foam in too thick a shower,
Fleeces bigger than a man's fist.

Through Gwynedd they came stinging,
Bees from heaven, white they are.
Where will God drive such a plague?
What's a fit place for saints' goose-down?
Twin brother to a chaff-heap,
Stoat-shirted, it can leap heather.
The dust has now become snowdrift
Where once were small paths and praise.
Is it known in January
What kind of crew's spitting down?
Heaven's white angels, no less,
Are engaged in architecture.

See how the plank's been lifted
From the floor of the flour loft.
Silver dress of ice this while,

The world's coldest quicksilver,
Cold cloak, its stay's a let-down,
Cement of hill, ditch, and dale,
Thick steel shift, a landslip's burden,
Pavement greater than the sea's grave,
A huge fall's on my region,
A pale wall from sea to sea.
The earth with its four corners
Had all of its brain outside.

Where will it tarry? Cold white plate,
Magic plaster, who'll restrain it?
Who is there dares to shame it?
It's lead on a cloak. Where's the rain?

THE BOWER OF BROOM

The girl, her form and hue finer
Than the countess' gown of gold,
Two tales I know, woe is he
Who can get no tryst and see her:
I am not free to venture
By day to a splendid moon;
God forbids sleight, flawless face,
Beneath someone's wall at night-time.
No trees where a well-mannered lad
Could have a tryst in green birches:
Long my wait, lovely image,
For summer without a tryst.

God to me and my flawless woman
Has given shrubs dressed in choice gold,
Twigs just as good in winter,
And blithe leaves like a summer house.
There I'll fashion to charm her
A bower of slender young broom,
As Merlin, love's craftsmanship,
Made a glass house for his mistress.
On Dyfed, they say, there was once
Before a concealing curtain:
Now, beneath the green branches,
My court is exactly like that.

If a dear comes to my dwelling
She'd be countess in that court:
Here for her, and I'll praise her,
Is this, spirit's paradise,
Shrubs with interwoven branches,
Early leaves on tender twigs.

When May with its green livery
Comes to dignify fresh leaves,
Gold will flourish on the grove's
Threads for whoever owns it:
Lovely the shrub and lavish
Grows the thick gold of its crest;
God has, flawless the weaving,
Showered gold upon the twigs.
Let the fair be glad a poet
Has a grove from paradise:
The flowers we love the best,
This crest is summer's hoarfrost.

Here for me and my sweetheart
Is this, fresh saffron's fair field:
I keep a house, a fine building,
Formed of Arabia's gold.
The Lord of the firmament's tent,
Cloth of gold, its roof speckled,
From paradise a kind angel
Embroidered it in May's bed,
Gold gossamer, wondrous bees,
God's butterflies, beads of sunshine.
Bliss, on a vineyard-like hill,
To have the fresh twigs gilded,
And the tips of bushes seen
Like the stars, golden buttons.

Thus have I, all of one colour,
May's blossoms like tiny birds.
See what a glad thing it is
That the grove's veiled like an angel.
I guard the grove and the clearing,
Courtly custom, for a girl:
My bond's good, I'll not go from
The grove above with the speckled gold veil,

If I'll have, till summer, one tryst
With a gold-haired girl in the greenwood.
Let her come where we'll not be parted,
Fair slim girl, beneath fresh broom.

THE STARS

By God, girl, I had to leave
The groves of this year's Maytime,
Walking a comely hill-slope
And woodlands, my fair-haired girl,
Till I drank on a hill above
And saw our bed beneath birch-trees.

Love is rash, mine's a stirring tale,
A rashness transforming people.
I spent, mine's sorrow enough,
Half the night, a wretched journey,
Bent on having, bountiful favour,
A girl's kiss: I'd won her consent.
I crossed a lawful roadway;
I was night-blind on the bare moor:
A long trail last night, too dark,
Sorry course, for a slender maiden,
Many a foul long-ridged pathway,
I walked, a tall sturdy lad.
I stumbled through nine thickets
And along bare ancient walls,
And from there into a stronghold
Of demons, horrid companions.
I sallied from the great green stronghold
Into bogs on the high mountain's brow:
It darkened, this wasn't easy,
The black headland facing me,
As if, brief battle's betrayal,
I had been locked up in gaol.

I blessed myself, harsh outcry:
It was high time, and quite cold;
I composed, becoming numb,
A cywydd to ward off devils.
Bright scales wrapped in cloth of gold

271

Were once in a stone coffer,
And mine is the like misfortune:
Till last night, frustrated tryst,
Strong hissing, I had never
Been in that pestilent marsh.

I vowed to visit, sworn price,
Llanddwyn, if I were rescued.
Mary's Son, joyful faith's treasure,
Will not sleep when he may save:
He saw how a true bard suffered;
God was gracious, lit for me
The zodiac's rush candles,
Fair downpour against distress.

With courteous swiftness the stars
Appeared for us, night's cherries:
Gracious and bright was their light,
Sparks of seven saints' bonfires,
Flaming plums of the cheerless moon,
The frozen moon's swollen berries.
Kernels of the hideaway moon,
They are seeds of fair weather,
The lustre of the moon's large nuts,
Hue of our Father's sunshine pathways,
Fine weather's familiar portent,
Eagle of all balmy days,
Like flints from the sun's bright surface,
Like great halfpennies of God,
Comely frost-covered red gold,
Heavenly host's crupper jewels.
Sunshine drives rivets for shields
Through the heavens, deep vexation:
Each pair was artfully pounded,
The wide grey sky's clash of arms.
The swift wind won't dislodge them
From strong peg-holes in the sky.
Wide their space, wind won't circle them;
They are the vast sky's embers.
Backgammon pieces and board,
Brightly worked, firm air's surface,
Pins, I am fascinated,
In the firmament's great head-dress,

Fair lights of praise like bright paths,
The sky's cover of clover,
They've done good in a long history,
Frost's gilding, air's marigolds,
A hundred altars' wax candles
For the long service of the sky:

Good to see them, holy God's beads,
Without a string, all scattered;
They revealed hill and dale wisely
To me, the fool down below,
The roads to Môn, and my own road:
Pardon, God, my whole intention.
I came before sleeping a wink
To my dear one's court at daybreak.
I'll not boast of my hardship,
Just this, to a generous girl:
Henceforth there'll be no striking
Of the sharp axe against stone.

THE SKULL

Unsullied skull none will praise,
Hollow dried-up head, fine symbol,
Hidden reproach, foe of the fair
Bold wanton's brittle beauty,
Your countenance isn't worth gold,
Clod of the sad earthen body.
Who set you, it wasn't courteous,
Simply to grimace at me,
Out of foul spiteful hatred,
There on the wall, dreary wretch?

'There's no nose, just deprivation,
There is neither lip nor tooth,
There's no ear, from vile flailing,
There's no brow or passionate look:
Naught remains of eyes but dust
And holes' likeness full of darkness,
Or hair, none has such a mantle,
Or thin skin upon my face.'

Much mortified is our land,
Cold sight, looking upon you.
Make, to conceal your forehead,
Your way to your bed of clay.
Leave off chilling other folk:
Allow me clever cywyddau.

'I have, no return to the grave,
Long lain in a field's belly
In pain, concealing my favour,
With the worms hugging me tight.
I'll not leave, though I may not drink,
My place, exemplum to my parish:
From my niche I preach better
Than Saint Austin, or as well.
There's no man wise in hoodwinks
May see me and laugh at all.
Woe is man, who'll invite me,
Face of pain, that he was born:
Clean contrary to feasting
The sight of my naked pate,
Where once could be seen like silk
Auburn hair in small ringlets,
A glowing, soft, smooth forehead,
Falcon's eye and comely brows,
Lip skilled in conversation,
A fair, sweet, neatly-shaped nose,
Pretty gums' honeyed language,
Clever courtly tongue and teeth,
Having on the lovely earth
A girl's faith in great passion,
A tryst among young birches,
Ah Jesus Christ, and a kiss.
For an earthly tare, worthless,
By God, how great is man's pride,
To fashion a sinful burden,
A strange place for vanity.
Busy weed, scanty lifespan,
Consider your day: be not proud.'

THE SWAN

Swan, upon your comely lake,
White-robed as a holy abbot,
You're the glow, bird, of the snowdrift;
Angel's hue, you're a closed hand.
Very solemn is your service,
Delightful your well-nurtured youth.
God has granted you for life
Lordship of Lake Yfaddon.

Two means to keep you from drowning,
Splendid gifts, were granted to you:
To be a master fisherman,
See your skill upon lake water,
And you're able to fly far off,
Up above the high hill-breast,
And look down, noble white bird,
To survey the earth's surface,
And scan the lake-floor below,
And harvest shoals like snowflakes.
You ride the wave superbly
To waylay fish from the deep:
Your fishing-rod, handsome fellow,
Is indeed your long lovely neck.
Warden above the lake's centre,
Bosom the colour of foam,
You gleam on a stream's ripples
In a crystal-coloured shirt:
A doublet like a thousand lilies,
A splendid waistcoat, you wear;
You've a jacket of white roses,
And a gown of woodbine blossoms.
You are a beacon for birds;
You're white-cloaked, a cock from heaven.

Hear my complaint, gentle fellow,
To you, and come to my aid.
There's a girl of noble birth,
A fair lady, lives near you.
Go in haste, best of creatures,
Messenger white under wings:
Swim as I ask, unhindered,

And to Cemais make your way;
Keep your mind on asking for her,
The moon's hue, of Tal-y-llyn.
The girl's name to be greeted,
This truly, in verse, is her name:
There's W, bright and sprightly:
What word has D, Y, and N?
Seek out her chamber softly,
Greet with a bow the fair girl:
Disclose to her my anguish,
And how frail the state of my health.
Bring, for the fair one I'm woeful,
Glowing creature, cheerful words.
God keep you from all misfortune,
Fair head, you'll have your reward.

LOVE'S ARCHITECT

I loved a tall fair maiden
Ever, with never a tryst,
And just when, I know distress,
I had hope she'd give me gladness,
The girl I courted murmured
To me, rejecting my plea:
'I'll not love one who's a rover,
Ignoble, no goods to his name.'

When I heard this light-hearted spite,
I thought I understood her.
I made a house to love her in,
No fool's work, beneath a birch-tree,
Laid out a stately circle,
A building, my plaiting of praise,
With its leaf roof, tender twiglets,
Like tiles, at the thick grove's heart,
And in the sweet spacious house
Two true tenants speaking one language,
Two thrushcocks, loving their tune,
Comely, brown, speckle-breasted,
Two poets, glowing passion,
Pure songbirds of Paradise.
From its roof, seven songs each day

Suitable for the woodbine,
And the seven, harmonious sound,
I'll take note of on the hillside.

For my splendid girl I desired
To keep house, and this construction.
If I can't get the fine young woman,
My own age, to the birchwood bank,
I'll swear, by way of forfeit,
Never more to build for love.

THE VIRGIN MARY

We pray to Mary, who gives life,
Goldsmith of true salvation.
Rightly is she called a queen:
Heaven hears a cry by her favour.
In hell is found her power,
Above and across the world:
Right when in pain, when in need
In the Channel, to name Mary;
Right for Mary, whom I name,
To be named a light-bearer.

Gabriel, through the bright sky,
Brought the pure saint a greeting,
Ave, for the sin of Eva,
And Mary, great goodness, agreed.
There was a blessed conception,
Of the Father's word, in her womb:
Good was the maid, glad confession,
In her flesh bearing heaven for you,
Of her goodness bearing her Son
And bearing her Father who made her.
The Trinity, under the sun,
In the fair sun were dwelling.
Humbly let us go seek him,
As God he was born, as man.
Mary sang God lullabies
And bore him, holy virgin.

As the prophecy foretold,
To Egypt she brought Jesus:
The lions were light-hearted,
And the serpents, with the pure saint.
Great abundance, Mary noticed
On the day the sun was strong
A tall tree with luscious fruit
On its crest, and Mary craved it.
His golden love asked Joseph
For some from the top, bright gift.
Then wrathfully, in few words,
Did Joseph respond to Mary;
The joiner would not fetch the fruit
For the Virgin on her journey:
'Ask the other, tall fair maiden,
Who made you pregnant, pure saint.'
It bowed to the level ground,
That tree, by the Son's wonders:
She had from the top her fill
Of the fruit, she and all her household.

No one could tell in few words
The Son's wonders to help Mary.
Oh that I could, it was fitting,
Have sung of seven score works,
And sung them purposefully,
With each word praise of Mary.
Let us go to our land in prayer
With 'Mary' our only word.
The Virgin does much pleading,
She will not desist from that:
Mary plucks us from the briers,
And after this life, with her
We'll have bliss, singing to her,
Have heaven: let us sing to Mary.

THE SALMON

Salmon, lad of the ocean,
God granted you grace and skill:
You're the fairest creature fashioned,
By Saint Mary, in the sea.

278

Curig's hymn, prince of the wave,
Protects you amid seaweed
From meshes at the tide's edge,
From hollow snares of weir-men,
From a stab and blow, breast split,
By the trident of a poacher.

Best of servants, sea-trotter,
You're brine's boar, a shining torque,
Sail fast on the ocean crest,
Swim the waves, do not dally,
Take care, fish, you're unnoticed,
And go, staying out of sight,
Where dwells the girl fair-coloured
As the tern upon the wave.
No rocks, no coracle-men,
Second Llŷr, will restrain you.
Once above, lord of two colours,
The rippling ford and the slope,
Resplendent glass, turn to look:
You'll see a splendid mansion,
A pond in a place or two,
And level ground, and orchards.
Keep watch there, catcher of gnats;
Summon the man's bed-fellow.

If you see a dark-browed girl
With a pure white complexion,
And two roses in her cheeks
A crimson red in colour,
And a fine hand, white as flour,
Wearing a ring, I'm wretched,
And slim arm like a sunlit cloud,
And her breasts like the sun shining,
Two breasts as white as the snow,
More gleaming white than seagulls,
Go sometime beside her there
And give to her my greeting.
If she'll come, under gilded hat,
To the bankside, Luned's likeness,
Draw nearer to my linnet,
And make a leap near her white breast.

I'll die of longing: welcome
The sprightly girl, spawner's mate;
Spin a story like Mordred
From the lake to western snow:
Tell, let wise words come to mind,
The fair one how I'm yearning;
My heart, since I see her not,
In my lean side is aching
For love of her, lively woman.
And what's the use? She's so false.
So chaste is she, the goddess,
Though she's wooed, she's not possessed.
The twining vine would promise:
Never a promise is kept.
She did not wish my praises,
And she'll trust neither weak nor strong.

Courteous salmon, chief justice,
Go once more to the fair one:
Ask her if it would be lawful,
Slender girl, to take my life.
Let her choose, the fairest she is,
Slim Dyfr, from Dover to Menevia,
To take my life, love-sick man,
Or decide to leave her husband.

THE NUN

I have grown lean in loving
A devout and dark-eyed girl.
If I woo her for someone else,
By holy God, I'm witless.

Is it true, maiden I love,
You don't wish for summer's fresh birches?
Will you not still the singing,
Stars' hue, of psalms in your house?
You're a nun with saint's devotion;
You're one much loved by the choir.
For God's sake, no more bread and water,
And think how you loathe the cress.
Stop, for Mary's sake, telling your beads,

And the monkish Roman credo.
Spring's no time to be a nun;
Grove is choicer than cloister.
Your faith, fair best of women,
Is clean contrary to love:
Better the ordination
Of mantle, green gown, and ring.

Come to the outspread birches,
To the wood's and the cuckoo's creed,
There no one will deride us,
To win heaven in the grove.
And keep Ovid's book in mind,
And have done with faith's excesses.
On the hillside we will shrive
Our souls amid the woodbines:
God's willing, blameless welcome,
And the saints, to pardon love.

Does a well-born girl do worse
Winning a soul in woodlands,
Than behaving as we have
In Rome and Santiago?

A VISIT TO FLINT

On Sunday last I came to,
I'm a man the Lord God made,
The town, double-walled, lopsided,
Of Flint, may I see it in flames,
For a wedding, without much mead,
A feast of shifty Saxons.
I was intent on gaining,
For skilled work, a grand reward.

I began, I boasted boldly,
Singing an awdl to the clan.
They scoffed, rejected my voice:
It was grief that I gained there.
Easy for dealers in barley
And corn to scorn all my craft,
And they laughed about my song:

Well-prepared praise, it was worthless.
John Beisir talked of pea-plants;
Another talked of manure.

To the board, and there'll be boredom,
All summoned William Piper.
He came, customary demand,
Clutching, not like one worthy,
A sad bag, gut-stuffed belly,
A stick betwixt arm and breast.
He grated, strange sight, vile noise,
Stomach swollen, and eyes staring,
And body twisting to and fro,
And cheeks huffing and puffing,
Coarse manners, his fingers playing
A glutton's skin for the feast's coarse guests.
Shoulders twitching, amidst the rabble,
Beneath his cloak like a fly's arse,
He was snorting, and his head
He was snaffling to his nipple.
His behaviour's like a kite,
Keen his delight in preening.

The wretch blew, uncouth the cry,
The pouch swelling and yelling:
It sang with a wasp's buzzing,
Devil's pouch, pole up its rump,
Nightmare cry, old goose being slaughtered,
Sad bitch's harsh cry under chest,
Shrill pouch for screeching one tune,
Mouth's gristle wheezing music,
Crane's monotonous complaint,
Goose honking under an apron.
In the hollow pouch were sounds
Like a thousand cats' sinews,
Worthless goat with a single note,
Dirty, diseased, and pregnant.

When it ended, frigid girl's song,
This squeal, it would quell passion,
William Beanbroth paid the fees,
Not a lordly hand's largesse,
Penny pieces, where they offered,

And small halfpennies at times,
With me turned rudely away
From the foolish feast, empty-handed.

I renounce, with solemn vow,
Churlish Flint and all its offspring:
Its long furnace will be like hell,
And its Saxon people and piper.
May all my prayer be their death;
My curse on them and their children.
If I go again, ever,
May I not come back alive.

LENT

The day of Eiddig's delight
Came yesterday, harsh oppression,
A day that burdens a bard
Like the world's end, Shrove Tuesday,
Start of the Paradise road
To draw all who are burdened.
For forty days there's pardon
For praying with piety.

Ah Lord, as long as a year
Each two hours imposed this season:
Long for me, I'm in exile,
Three days of the life I lead.
The anchorite's Roman creed
Is mine, like a lean scribbler:
Faithful am I in devotion,
Faithful the girl, she'll make love
By setting us, like Fridays,
Mortifying acts for Lent.
Farewell, my slim-waisted girl,
All are chaste, till Easter Monday.
I'll not go out, I'll not meet her,
A single night until then;
I'll not beg a kiss, sweetheart,
More than God, of my modest dear.
Woe's me, enduring the precept,
Her silent and in good repute:

The damask-cheeked won't consent to
Recompense till Easter-tide.

When Easter brings green woodlands,
She'll come each day for a tryst:
Then the day will come for us
Brimming with exultation,
May and summer where she is,
And cuckoos like Gwgan's daughter,
And each birch-grove with soft fine hair
Green-gowned upon the hillside,
And on the street of thorn-stems
Linen shops like London's Cheap,
Green and fresh like dewy gardens,
Wine berries and ridges of wheat,
Clear sky and blue-crested ocean,
And close screen in the green grove,
A lonely spot, a clearing,
A slim fair limb of a girl,
An end of all my penance,
And grief ebbs, and the world turns,
And my curse from this time forward
On the chilly windy spring.

SIÔN CENT

THE BARDS

False words, false is the yardstick,
Welshmen flee, a foolish path.
Why the old man's pretty language?
To prove how a bard performs.

Two sorts of fluent muses
The world holds, brightly arrayed:
Christ's muse, no mournful topic,
On a true course, honest muse,
This was theirs, full of blessings,

Prophets and masters of praise,
Holy angels in Hebron
Fashioning infallible verse;
The other muse, foolish singing
That trusts in a filthy lie,
This was theirs, impudent men,
The bards of Wales' pretension.

If they praise the life of a soldier
Singing for a foolish robe,
The graceless song's a satire,
It's a lying cywydd he sings:
Claims there was noble vintage,
And mead, where there was mere whey;
Asserts too, high table's words,
The fierce taking of French castles.
A Roland, a bold Arthur,
He slays lion-like in the fray.
Their feuds, woe that men won't see them,
And their evil ways, and their aims.
A poor man's praised, lying song,
More than any, churlish region,
More than earl above gold paving,
And more than great emperor.
The simple man loves eulogy
And trusts it like oath on relic:
Oh God, who's the more foolish,
The man, or the best of bards?

If he sing to a maid fondly
Or bold wife, by the true Cross,
No Mary in three countries
Or the sun's been bright as she.

He declaims, without skill, that he's a
Lord or a prince of gold praise:
He's a boor, all belly and claw,
Tattered and scabby and crumpled.
In full cry there's no spectre
Or hound could be worse than he.

This is a muse, weak its claim,
From an infernal furnace.

A good spirit, like a sober sire,
God save it, speaks no falsehood,
No smooth-tongued fraud, no folly,
No false song, no fabulous lie.
There's the dictum in the dictates
Of Thomas Lombard, guard of truth:
Every lie, whenever or why,
However small, is sinful.
So testifies the steadfast
Good sense of Alysanna's book,
Or Durgry's book, much sought for,
Precious title, only look:
These bards, with their dreadful falsehoods
For frenzied slander of folk,
Weapons in mind, fitting promise,
All of them have become Jews.

If there's a Welsh, I submit,
High bard or humble poet,
If he knows how to answer,
Let his lip make answer now.

REPENTANCE

It is in my mind to pray
To God and to his Mother:
High time for me, Saul's pledges,
To cease worldly wantonness.

I've borne, without amending,
A hurtful burden of sins:
Pride in the midst of many,
Foul work, it was a wicked life,
And with pride my habit's been
Empty praise and defamation;
Envy has filled to the brim,
Perverted faith, my body;
And wrath too, where it entered,
Unhappy load, was no less;
Sloth till the grave, I was foolish,
Lazy was the life I led.
God weed a man, greed was worse,

And drowning in begrudging;
Gluttony, fornication,
Again were two enemies.

Three enemies come to man
To offer means for mischief,
The foul world, and the devil,
The flesh, tending Judas' crop.
Woe's the man, I knew his fault,
Wanton, who did not govern
His life, before going to his grave,
Well, prepared for its finish,
Chastizing heedless mischief
And the body's deceit as well.

I acknowledge my own disease:
Of God I'll beg forgiveness.
I'll confess every secret,
I'll attempt to tell in full,
Rash excess, fearless and endless,
How I lived when I was young:
Straying in birches and ferns
And green woods above a valley,
Hearing and speaking wrongly
Of love's doings, enchantment's round,
Touching wrongly, clear concord,
Seeking good, hating its source,
Audacity and envy,
Looking wrongly at a fine girl,
Praising, unblest, unbridled,
Beauty, breaking marriage vows.

Wantonness brings on a man
Revenge if it's long followed,
Unless he makes atonement
To God before his day comes.
Let no one look for, foul marshes,
Repentance after his death.
I'll weep, I'll call on Heaven
And Mary before I die,
To gain a bright blissful dwelling
For my soul in need. Amen.

THE PURSE

My velvet purse, my parson,
My gold coffer, my lordly means,
My precious saviour, my seer,
My comrade with but one language.
No better saviour, grace giving,
Nest of gold, than you on earth.
None pays off foreigners better:
Many thanks, my purse, for this.

I've owned horses, been respected,
Baubles, weapons, gorgeous shirt,
Brilliant jewels, heavy rings,
Chains, nine bundles of brooches,
Improved on, clever fellow,
My land and my station in life.
Abundant my kind in Emlyn:
Many thanks, my purse, for this.

I've studied Solomon's book,
And the seven arts and speaking;
I've studied heavenly things,
Church's lamp of serene learning;
I've studied to use, people's mead,
With bold strokes, battle's conquest,
Awdl and cywydd and englyn:
Many thanks, my purse, for this.

Claiming connection with me,
Plenty of undeprived people,
Nine times more, blows to my bliss,
Than my true kin, came calling:
Eight kinds of kin, surely, are mine,
A life full of sworn brothers.
All the vagrant, all the paupers,
All minstrels, all hard-up seamen,
All broken men come begging:
Many thanks, my purse, for this.

Fine is wealth, says famed Gwenddydd,
Fine for us is every day,
A worldful of food, of drink,

And all served in fine fashion.
I'm greeted with friendly names,
Sweet words in public, true Menw;
I'm honoured in every market,
Throned at each feast in my land,
And with reverence I'm welcomed:
Many thanks, my purse, for this.

If a theft is traced surely
To me, and I'm brought to court,
If trial or verdict come,
I know I'll gain acquittal:
Forty will swear, quite tamely,
Falsehoods, three Sundays, for me;
Friendly are the officials,
All of them, questioning me.
You're my herald, my gold jewel:
Many thanks, my purse, for this.

I've had much love from women,
I'd get what I sought with a gift,
Had love's envoys in Is Conwy,
Had a million, if I so wished.
I've no need to leave the tavern
All my life, if I see fit,
Such grabbing at the elbow
For me, bringing me to mead.
I've respect, act of homage:
Many thanks, my purse, for this.

For gold I'll have, I take pains,
The whole world, full of pleasure;
I'll have all Wales, none missing,
Its houses and castles and land.
I'll have love in Paradise,
Have God for my flesh, solemn thought,
Life for my name, heaven for my soul,
And gain Papal indulgence,
With all the foe's war over:
Many thanks, my purse, for this.

THE VANITY OF THE WORLD

Mortal flesh is full of grief;
The world, cold thing, 's a sermon.

Today a blithe man of gold
Has brooches, rings, and jewels,
Abundant scarlet and camlet,
Handsome silk, if it's in vogue,
Splendid drinking-horns of gold,
Wine, and kestrels, and falcons.
Mounted on Gascon stallions
He'd ride ahead, and all bow.
To ask for a good farmhold
On his lands is an offence;
He gets a weak man under
His thumb, and seizes his place,
Takes his farm from one who's blind,
And takes another's acres,
Takes the grain under the ash-trees,
And takes an innocent's hay,
Collects two hundred cattle,
Gets the goods, and jails the man.

Pointless the frantic plotting
Of frail clay, dead in a day.
From bare earth he came, dark cold,
Cold, he will go as ashes.
He'd not give two good cows,
Yesterday, for two from God:
Today in earth he's worthless,
Has nothing of all his wealth.
Pain fills him when he goes there,
Housed within gravel and grit:
His bed will be much too base,
His forehead next the roof-beam;
His strait-fitting shirt the shroud,
His sad cradle soil and gravel;
The porter above his head
Earth black as a nightmare;
His proud flesh in the oak-chest,
His nose a pale sorry grey;
His coat of mail black with grime,

Its fringes all have rusted;
His gown wood, long annoyance,
His shirt without sleeves or shape;
His sure course into this earth,
His arms across his bosom;
And ways empty, where was wine,
His cook departing his kitchen;
His hounds, in the hollow hall,
And his steeds, in doubt about him;
His wife, from the wine-pouring hearth,
Quite rightly, weds another;
His stately whitewashed mansion
A small coffin foregoing the world.
And the wealth of the land leaves him
Down below with empty hands.

When in his handsome coffin
He hastens from court to church,
No pretty girl will follow,
No healthy man, past the grave.
No slender wanton will slide
Her hand beneath that blanket.
Grief will not long continue
Or lie a month on his grave.
When for an hour he's lain there,
This man with long yellow hair,
Should he notice, dark is the house,
A gross toad will tend his bedside.
Under the edge of the stone
More fat worms than fair branches;
Around him in earth's sad shroud,
More coffins than great stallions.
The choir priests detest dealing
With the three executors:
Three hundred pounds in payment
They receive for poor services;
His kinfolk will be quite pleased
If they complete three masses.
There the soul will not possess
Mansion or rank or faction,
Or fine ornament, or idol,
Only what it did for God.

Where are the towers? the town?
The many courts? the singers?
The turreted houses? the land?
The high offices for merit?
Where's the tidbit? the new dish?
The roast? the cook who serves them?
Where's the wine? the birds? the boughs
Carried throughout the country?
Where's the wine-cellar? the kitchen
Below the slope? Where's the mead?
The journey to England? the gear?
The fine bards? the high tables?
Where are the huge noble hounds?
The flock of swans? the stallions?
The full wardrobe? the treasure?
Possessions on land and sea,
The great hall newly enclosed,
The manors and the mansions?
Worthless is the smallholding,
Merely seven feet, man's end.

The body that once wore purple
Lies in a chest next the choir,
And the soul will not know then,
Dim-witted, where it will go.
For the wrongs and the heresy
Committed in his lifetime,
It's too late on the dark day,
As I'm a man, for repenting.
Not one, then, of the hundred
He'll reward, that nap's too long;
Not one fellow will follow,
He'll not conquer, not bear arms,
Not court a girl, not be greeted,
Not attend council or court;
He'll not have mead for a spree,
Not leave the grave to revel.
I'd not give a head of leek
For his corpse in the coffin.

And the soul, shuttled shamefully
Between ice and fire, freezes,
Where he's compelled, no shelter,

To a sure compact with cold.
What good then's a hall of ice?
Beware, the pit is frightful:
Pools, and infernal ovens,
Cauldrons, dragons, fiendish forms.
See each beast, Christ is mighty,
Horned and tusked and glowering;
The hand of every devil
Holds a crooked cooking fork;
And the murk of smoke the like of
Flood-tide treachery razes all paths.
May Christ, the whole place is wretched,
Keep people from going there.

Learn that there's a worldly state
Leads many to the devil.
Trusty Saint Benedict says
God gives only one heaven:
Just one may, eloquent words,
Be had, if helped by Mary.
Let no man for the pleasure
Of lust find his heaven here,
Lest he lose, say praise's masters,
Eternal heaven through God's wrath.
Day without night is displayed,
Health without drawn-out illness,
And the gaily coloured face of
Heaven's land, better than wealth.
The world will not last, nest of twigs,
And heaven will last forever,
Without death, all men at one,
Without end. Amen, Son of Mary.

LLYWELYN AB Y MOEL

THE BATTLE OF WAUN GASEG

We started out well today,
Ready war-band, on the hill-brow,
Powerful, flawless gold people,
With fine determined mind,
Bent on gaining, splendid sign,
The greatest fame for Owain.
We met, before foolish complaints,
Before setting off for the battle,
Declaring our aim of sharing
Profit if the foe were slain,
Everyone of staunch nature
Swearing, before seeing their men,
They'd never flee, they'd earn praise,
The field despite the onslaught.

And so, after a war-song,
As we vied for a famous name,
Look there, we saw upon us
Loosed amidst us, sad the turn,
Along the fern-covered slope
Horses, more than a hundred,
And with them, case for complaint,
A blaring ardent war-cry,
A summons, gold gift's harsh strain,
A vile French badger-ward mocks it,
Ape jaw, playing a tabor,
From a horn louder than a gun.

Base behaviour, frustrated course,
We, after all our speeches,
Our resolve upon the moor
Lasted not an hour in battle,
No trial of arms, attack scattered,
Or mail-coat, before we fled.
The host whose wrath we'd roused
Chasing us there in great numbers,
Hot they were to pursue us:
They pursued us across nine streams,

The treasure of Caer Wysg's soldiers,
Pursuing goats, gaily clad.
Bitter turn, blow to our pride,
It hurt us to see, I'm a witness,
At Waun Gaseg, unstained bundle,
Our soldiers' spears on the grass.

As for me, sorry vanguard,
I took the lead from the fray,
Heading in quite a hurry
For a gorge, great host behind,
All pointing at me fleeing
When they recognized me there.
Stupid on a mountain's long slope
Is a white-clad man, ill-fated.

After this, unanswered summons,
Henceforth they may come when they like:
I'm damned if they will see me
White-clad in the vale of the Waun.

THE WOOD OF THE GREY ROCK

By God, Wood, you are lovely,
Of the Rock, Llech Ysgar, grey mound.
Round of leaves, Irish rabble,
God's blessing upon your boughs.
Closely ranked is your array,
You're a fort, a place for sport.
Cosy croft's close of bracken,
Strange in summer if a man,
He'd praise a sure love-envoy,
Could do without you, to my mind.
I've cherished your fortresses,
Handy for ransoming Saxons,
Your interwoven branches,
Your hillsides, haycocks of leaves,
Your unconstricting caverns,
Your flawless sanctum from constraint,
Your unblemished form, your brushwood
That, perforce, I've always walked.
Better far than bard's roaming

For a man who'd wish for wealth
To seize a Saxon and strip him
Under your boughs, fair's your dell.
My paragon, my partner,
You're my prince, my paradise,
My patron saint and my surety,
My manor-house and my haven.
To me, long trust, you're like earthworks
On a hill's brow when I've been trailed.
Perfect nurture, it's been splendid
Having you to safeguard me:
Cosy mantle's lovely close,
Fine snug coppice firmly woven,
A greensward underneath it,
Soft fertile earth and hewn stones,
The Father's flawless garment,
Dark canopy overhead,
A place for my rest in safety,
Your branches on high unlike
A churl's hut that's roofed with turf,
Faultless, after having oat-cakes.
It was sweeter, lovely purpose,
For a joyful boy and girl
Forthwith, at the end of roaming,
To lie amid small young trees,
And listen, such pretty trilling,
To a nightingale's pure-voiced song,
And dispel rage and turmoil,
And break leaves, awesome their lore,
And gaze, the world's radiant mirror,
At the stars, wondrous miracle:
Wondrous, exceeding short-lived,
To me was a praised day of trysting.
And, fitting sight, I beheld
The slope's forts from this border,
Where one need not, bracken's fullness,
Lurk by day, no bitter place,
Place of hard paths, remote place,
Where no Norman host goes by night.
Wide circle above the roost,
For Owain's men you're London,
Tall trees' grove full of outlaws,
Wider than moon's face or seas.

Perfect blessing amid your favour,
Full reward, Owain's handsome host,
Perfect state, through the moon's phases,
God let your soldiers succeed.

LEWYS GLYN COTHI

AFTER A PILGRIMAGE

My full intent in Britain
Was to be a pure anchorite,
And wear a cope each Thursday
Like Saint Antony and his hair.
I was, they said, a hermit
Or a wolf in his coat of fur;
John of Beverley crowds called me,
Or a stag from upland streams.
I'm a person doing penance
By three roads to Peter and Paul:
I've been walking to seek them
From Môn to the town of Rome,
Broad Burgandy, the Rhine valley,
Italy, Lombardy too,
All Germany, and Brabant,
Swabia, Flanders as well.

I was a mild fanatical
Brother to Merlin the Wild Man
With his feast in the Caledonian Wood
And his grizzled beard on his bosom.
My beard's wild like a maiden's hair
And white and speckled like rush-tips,
And across the edge of the jaw
Was a woodland grove, all shaggy.
I'm a man, so that none know me,
With a hedgehog piercing his face,
A chin that needs to be sheared,
All of its wool fresh holly,

Steel flax that's filling both cheeks,
Cheek overflowing with heather,
Points of needles to wean me,
Furze muzzle, bundle of reeds,
Eaves of thick-coated white oakum,
The burdened cheeks of a bear,
Mist that encircles the chin,
Nest of breath like a gorse-bush.

My intent here was to hasten
To make myself fair-faced with steel.
Wiliam Fychan the warrior,
Gwatgyn's son, Tretower's bound,
White fort's captain, what better stag,
Above Ystwyth and its castle,
From ancient Gwallter Sais' breast
He's issued, long his ash-spear,
From your grandfather, Earl of Hereford,
From Gwgon's blood, a line of dukes.
My role as his court's envoy,
Before this, in Paulinus' town,
To ask Peter to prevent mischance,
And Paul, and pray for Wiliam,
To walk upon your behalf,
With bare breast, the three stations,
And to wish, with my hand outspread,
By God, Wiliam, to see you.

I'm as much of a bogey
As a beast that hasn't been sheared:
Master Wiliam, if it please you,
Have the chin that's snow-hued shaved.
When your courageous barber
Trims the thick hedge to its roots,
Not three days out of the seven
Will pass without a thorough shave.
I'll not now, like Gwenhidwy,
Let a beard grow on my lip.

THE COVERLET

Angharad of the Silver Hand's gold
And wine were once had by the needy:
I'd have just as lavish gifts
From Elin, Môn's merry daughter.

She's the lily on the lawn,
Sun of gallant Llywelyn;
Prysaeddfed's planet is she,
She's Hwlcyn's radiant offspring;
She's the Non of ancient Ynyr,
Non of Nannau's line and its men,
From Meirion's Meurig's branches,
From Cynddelw's great leaves in Môn.
Saint Catherine for wine-streams
Is Elin, Llywelyn's daughter,
And, like the oil, from Elin
One is given five kinds of wine.
She's open-handed to many,
Elin of feasts, Elen of the Hosts.
Derfel's blessing to Elin,
Gwynedd of the wine's noble bough.
She's praised, Llywydiarth's daughter,
From her region through Aber-arth.

Too much, by Saint Garmon's church,
For Môn is my uncouthness.
Let my plaint go to Gwynedd's sun:
I'm complaining about mongrels,
So treacherous were, so base,
Mobs in the town of Chester.
It's they who plundered my dwelling
Of my fine bedspread and bed,
And they have left me barer
Than salmon swimming a stream.
I'm naked without much blushing:
Nine churls have my coverlet.

Elin's giving me again,
Free-handed, a speckled cover,
A tapestry of vine-leaves,
A small torch broad as the trees.

In my coverlet are nine colours,
Nine birds there are on its cloth,
Nine stags lying down to rest,
With nine hinds in like fashion,
And twelve leaves of varied green,
And ten dark-blue in colour.
A hundred were green and white,
A thousand red and yellow,
Girl's handiwork's tiny pictures,
Oaks, and a clearing with birds.
A sky will hide one's forehead,
The cloth's a dapple-green sky.
The gift won't leave till summer,
No cold night, no frost for me.

Elin gives for my bare bed
Every night a green banner.
Mahallt, Hywel Selau's child,
Because of words that praised her,
Gave a coverlet, ancient practice,
A bed once for Gwilym's song.
My lady, mistress of Môn,
Will give this time another.
I'll come to Cynwrig ap Dafydd,
There I'll go to daylight's dawn,
Easy to have with my welcome
Her fee, and Ithael's grandson's gold,
And a feast from Cynwrig's hand,
And wealth from the hands of Elin.

LAMENT FOR HIS SON

One boy was, Saint Dwyn, my bauble:
Woe's his father that he was born.
Woe's he that's left, from fondness,
To suffer now, lacking a son.
My two sides, dead is my die,
For Siôn y Glyn they're aching;
Everlastingly I groan
For a baron of boyhood.

A sweet apple and a bird
The lad loved, and white pebbles,
A bow of a thorntree branch,
A sword, wooden and brittle.
Scared of pipe, scared of scarecrow,
Begging his mother for a ball,
Singing to all his chanting,
Singing 'Oo-o' for a nut.
He would play sweet, and wheedle,
And then turn sulky with me,
And make peace for a wooden chip
And for dice he was fond of.

Ah that Siôn, pure and gentle,
Were a second Saint Lazarus.
Beuno once brought back to life
Seven who'd gone to heaven:
Woe once more, my faithful heart,
That Siôn's soul is not the eighth.
Oh Mary, woe's me that he lies there,
And woe's my side, closed his grave.
The death of Siôn stays with me,
Two stab wounds deep in my breast.
My boy, my twirling taper,
My bosom, my heart, my song,
My delight before my death,
My dream, my clever poet,
My trinket he was, my candle,
My fair soul, my single deceit,
My chick learning my singing,
My Iseult's chaplet, my kiss,
My strength, woe's me without him,
My lark, my weaver of spells,
My bow, my arrow, my love,
My little beggar, my boyhood.

Farewell the smile on my mouth,
Farewell to my lips' laughter,
Farewell now sweet entertainment,
And farewell to the plea for nuts,
And farewell now to the ball,
And farewell the high-pitched singing,

And farewell, my joyful darling,
Laid below while I live, Siôn my son.

DAFYDD NANMOR

THE PEACOCK

Radiant peacock with glowing gown,
Enamel gown's far-seen shimmer,
Greet, best of loves and gracious,
Green-winged are you, Gwen o'r Ddôl.
Stroll across the fords yonder
To Eiddig's manor, with no gain for him:
Shining cowl, see how things stand,
And cause hate between Gwen and her husband.

May's lovely mantle is yours,
Of birds' feathers and flowers.
Most closely, magician's nature,
You resemble barley ears.
Like a roof and hall of leaves
Are you, bird of fair bower.
There were placed on deposit
Golden nobles in your plumes,
In your hoop, small comely roof,
A thousand gilded wafers.
Of the same fine weave, new curtain,
Is your colour as leaves of yew.
Goldworthy angel's image,
You are wearing golden wings.
Speckled you are, like sound cloth,
A friar's embroidered vestment.
Gentle bird, you're ruddy-coloured,
Fair-branched bush, full of marigolds,
Semblance, you're no ill omen,
Of a multitude of moons.
Wings of gold like a bishop,
A noble has no finer hue;

Speckled outspreading pinions,
Gold buttons are on their tips.
You're fair, peacock, atop the court,
And the same hue as a rainbow.
A fine sight, like wreaths are you,
Green dragon of stained-glass windows.

Go to the spot, passion's choice,
And hurry, azure adder,
And come there like a fowler,
And fetch Gwen from her husband's house.

IN PRAISE OF RHYS AP MAREDUDD

Genau'r Glyn, Tywyn, multitudes have turned
    To Rhys' houses in hordes:
    May never a night of want
    Befall the halls forever.

Long life on his land like an oak to Rhys,
    The lifetime unending
    Till every star is numbered
    Or grain of soil or blossom.

Like blossoms in every form, like snowflakes,
    Like birds on a wheat-crop,
    Like the rainfall and dewfall
    Is my blessing for one man.

Dew's abundant blessing on each glen I've given
    To Rhys in Tywyn
    While the heavens are where they were
    Or stone or soil in hillside.

He buys the wine from the vast vineyards
    Across the southern sea,
    Eighteen cargoes and eight besides,
    Eighteen shiploads of winecasks.

Winecasks, weapons, there is need for them:
    Rhys ap Maredudd has,

Coming after him on roads,
Arms and men as many as trees.

As many as trees his gold coins for two thousand,
    For three thousand his silver,
And his payment to five thousand here,
And wine and mead for a hundred thousand.

A thousand or two have gone at his bidding,
And a thousand show his ample livery,
    And two thousand or one he has to make poems,
And a thousand to sing like bees' honey.

Like the number of the snowflakes over Rhydodyn,
Like the number of the leaves on ashtree twigs,
    Like seed sown till now every Mayday,
He's sowed money and dealt it to us.

A hundred mansions he has for the asking,
A hundred men in each vale, a hundred oaks on each hill,
    A hundred portions of the land he draws on,
And a hundred houses and a hundred small-holdings.

Ninescore horses in every year,
Ninescore breastplates he buys for defence,
    Ninescore slim spears he obtains for the land,
And ninescore regions follow him.

None from Italy or from Scotland,
Or at Calais, despite the enemy's strength,
    None from Wales, on a white wide-nostrilled steed,
Or from all England, will tremble less.

Eye has not seen beneath green holly,
Tongue has not told where men were summoned,
    No crowd has heard as far off as Llŷn
That any could outdo his food or his drink.

No white-shanked steed has been as swift,
Or stag from ford or roebuck from fern,
    Or silver salmon aswim on an ebb-tide,
As all those who resort to the houses in Tywyn.

Not stars or birds have circled as far,
Or sun or moon or ocean or lake,
   Or the bounds of the sky, since he came,
As his fame has gone from the shore of the Glyn.

LAMENT FOR GWEN

It means grief, trust in the world:
Earthly life's a brief illusion.
I loved a tall fair young girl,
And she died, the lovely maiden.
An evil fate, where's one blameless,
Was placing this face under ground.
If her cheeks have been buried,
Less the glow in many a cheek.
Woe's me, though six greater die,
If her like's in a grave hereafter.
Ah God, if she's been covered,
That I might be a shroud for her:
Woe's me, to have life, her silent,
Shovelled under while still I live.

Widowed of her on the hillsides
Are cuckoo and birches and woods,
And song of thrush, if she's buried,
Below the church, and nightingale.
If she's dead in Is-Conwy,
No more should May put forth leaves:
Withered the birches and branches,
And they will bear no leaves now.
Ah poor wretch, that I might have
Both of us dead the same day:
I'd not wish my life longer
Since she has no further life.
Ah, that I might lie one hour
Closed with the girl in the grave.
Unmanned am I, left without her,
A horned ox above my Gwen.
They have died, in my judgment,
The fair sun and the bountifulness.
I'm weak unless she rises
From the dead, sweetheart, to life.

No more, on pain of forfeit,
Will the sun's like be seen abroad.
There was not, when she was well,
Beneath dark brows one fairer.

Jesus once raised Lazarus
Alive from the grave, he was dead:
Let God deal with the tall bright girl
And raise for me the maiden.
Dark am I if Gwen is dead
As a leaf upon a yew-twig:
May she be the eighth pure spirit,
Slim girl, Beuno brings back to life.

NOBILITY

Rhys, you are summer's rose blossom,
Rhys' grandson, of no baser stock.
Nobility's been your groundwork:
You're Deheubarth's gift to God.
You're heritage and home to us,
The right foot of Tywyn's region.

You grow, as the ashtrees grow,
From a multitude of rulers:
Grain will grow, as with summer wheat,
No crest where roots are lacking;
Who grows from noble breeding,
He grows from his roots to his crest.
Good the summer, when stag's roaming,
For the wheat and for the vines:
Good for one of his sires' stock
His fashioning from chieftains.
There's no place that is not pure
In the book of Saint John's Gospel:
Fewer the stains, in its place,
Put in your book of lineage.
The stag sprouts larger antlers;
It's good blood that breeds a prince:
The noble, as an heir's cherished,
Will foster nobility.

Two streams within the valley
Cause a current in the lake:
Your father's estate is now yours,
And nobility makes you a chieftain.
Never has the ice lingered
On the wellspring in July:
No man, no peasants' rising,
Ever forced you to your knees.
On a bright day snow will not come
Where sun glows on the hillside:
No man goes but from fondness
Above you, the land's right arm.
Well does one swim a river
If his hair's kept above the waves:
You've come where they haven't gone,
You're on shore, through the current.
Slowly one goes to a hilltop
With a burden, against the grade:
Harder, when you were younger,
To bear adverse words from your mouth.

The salmon seeks fresh water,
The same wave his father took:
Your father's state is higher
Than anywhere in the Alps.
Of the deer running uphill
The strongest wins the hilltop:
Seek the slope, like a red roebuck,
To the gap Maredudd left.
The huntsman pursues the chase,
To the wind the hawk rises,
The stag's eager in summer,
And the lion, for the highest path:
Let tree know crest and blossoms,
Let eagle nest in oak's crest:
On the crest of nobility
Are you, Rhys, like sea on shore.
To you has come your high rank,
Will come your father's success.
To you, Rhys, that your beard grow grey,
May Moses' life's measure come.

RHYS GOCH ERYRI

THE FOX

Fox, white of tail, most wicked,
Fine slim dog, you crave fresh meat;
You crave a feast in the greenwood
At the dale's edge, hunter of lambs.
Hear my song, you'll dine on duck,
And on goose, it should suit you.
A fat bird you'll have, you're shrewd,
And you're a clever trickster,
Bold on slopes, white-bellied fellow,
And a plucky pilferer.

Have you some words of wisdom?
Give me them, fox, about this:
I love tender-hearted Gwen
Of the Dale, cheeks like Helen,
And another, bitter for me,
Fool from Eryri loves her.
Dafydd, an upright poet,
Nanmor is his famous name.
My plaint to you is pointed
At his peacock, dainty its gown,
Which, like a glowing greenwood,
Is love's herald to Gwen's home,
And that moon, Eigr of many,
He seeks to take with a trick.
If he nears her, seagull's colour,
With his many-hued magic cape,
He'll try to steal Gwen from her husband
For that fellow, beneath his cloak.

So, if the old goose you long for,
Daring wild dog, you'll have three,
Go to the Dale, a choice hen
And a lambkin you'll have there,
And walk amidst the bracken
Round the Dale, guard a fine girl,
And beware of loud noises,
Eiddig's gun, and his men and dogs.

If you spy the peacock, fine sentry,
Then go for him, shepherd fox:
Bold thief, try to herd him home,
Gwen of the Dale's enchanter.
To whatever spot, fur-padded
Small dog of thickets, he goes,
Watch the place where he's dwelling,
His flesh as fee, dog, is yours,
And revenge upon his jaws
His flight to hold Gwen spellbound.
I pray you, forestall his leap,
And rip the gold mantle's fringe,
Slay love's herald, Llawdden's brother,
And take his fine gown and his head.

As for Gwen, her fair brow's slender,
It's between me and the bard:
With song, if he'll be gracious,
We'll joust for the peacock's gown.

LLYWELYN AP GUTUN

THE DROWNING OF GUTO'R GLYN

Welshmen are stricken with sadness,
Town and country, for Guto'r Glyn:
He drowned on an ebbless sea-shore;
He's in heaven, since he didn't float.
Wasted for me that action
Had I no lament in mind:
Never will such, marble slabs,
Big hands steer through the ocean;
Because of his body's drowning
The strand's poetry will improve.
Woe's me, for his triple dip,
Would his purse had been in my clutches.
I saw him spin like a wheel
On his axe of a nose off Malltraeth:

Woe's me, the more my misfortune,
For the man's cloak and his cap.

Take, all of you, two fierce cheeks,
A fool to mock at Christmas.
In the sea, I would not spare him,
There's the bear-face of one I know;
There are mackerels in his rib-cage,
More than a shoal, on the mud;
There's a great lump of a fish,
A porpoise, in my friend's bosom;
One finds, if the river's empty,
Herrings coming from his boots,
And the cradle that held the cywydd
Is now a hollow for eels.

My warrior went by water,
And his song went with the wind.
See there, a cannon in size,
A chief bard's form full of dogfish.
The wave coming from the water
Would not leave the fords he strolled
But on the one side held him
Gripped fast, and gave him a shove.
It was strong, he's in motion,
The seashells stick to his hand;
Still on his horse he's driven
To and fro, a wicked shame.

There are jealous men joyful
To bury eulogies' hawk.
Who'll be the old bards' captain?
Who the great oak above bards?
Where's the kite's executor?
Who'll sing now? a pagan sea-god?
Who will prevent him, hag-cheeked,
Pinning the chair on his garb?
Who but the ghost of Gwido
Will halt him and hew him down?

One greater than the magician
Is now walking in his shape.
It's not a sail setting forth,

It's not the one-time Guto,
But is, calf's feet and figure,
A garment on Gwido's ghost.
A spectre, like a bullock,
Has stalked through the smoke of Môn;
Ferocious face, there he's driven
A swarm of priests scurrying:
Let them mercilessly send him
To God or the devil's hand.

GUTO'R GLYN

THE DRUNKEN DREAM OF LLYWELYN

A sad cry like Malltraeth's current
Is seven times worse than saints:
A poet is contemplating
My elegy, dead in the water.
Clever Llywelyn ap Gutun,
Does he foam less than that flood?

A harpist, inspired bard's brow,
He'll dunk poets on beaches.
True lyricist, ladies' man,
Splendid fellow, who's like him?
His lips were lively and faultless,
His nails even livelier.
Woe's me, only wise and witty
Until wine goes to his head:
Drinking would make his shrewd tongue
Turn ever on the water.

In his sleep he saw my image
In salt water off of Môn.
The man was in Llwydiarth:
And I was drowned? Was he drunk?
Cynfrig's wine, a potent gift,

And Huw's wine made him legless.
To Huw Lewis' court and its floor
Came high tide for a harpist,
And he dreamed, to damage poets,
That the flood rose to the roof.
Warfare of Llywelyn's sons,
They filled him with their liquor:
The deceitful Welshman was roaring
Between the fire and me, counting waves.
He's swearing, wherever I strand,
That I'm a wraith in Malltraeth,
That in me, grim existence,
Fish are coming into land;
A porpoise is in my bosom,
Or my ghost is in the net.
He kept watch on me, my guardian,
And fashioned my grave in the sea.
He wants me at rest in ocean:
He craves my cloak and my sword;
In cosy clay he'd plant me,
For my gold, above the ford;
He'd hang me, he'd not lament,
In Rhosyr for my clothing.
And it was a dream lacking omens
The fellow saw on Môn's soil:
I drowned yonder, he was saying;
Despite drowning, I was alive.

If the dream I'd see, Thursday night,
Saint Non's Day, will come to pass,
His wealth will go from Melwern
Washed to the heart of the Bog,
And him as well in his hall
Awash, the river will slay him,
The Efyrnwy over him,
And sea entering the Severn.
I intend, when he's extinguished,
To toss a lament in too.

Let's both swim, he was my comrade,
Heaven bless the dead, the seas:
If to hell we are sentenced,
Let him gain the land he's left;

If to heaven, the swim's simpler,
My soul there will turn to Môn.

LAMENT FOR LLYWELYN AB Y MOEL

There's a coffin in Ystrad Marchell
In the convent's graveyard and cell,
And it holds a hundred greetings
And the seven arts of love,
And a sword, byword of boldness,
And song, no laughter is left,
Where hand and spade worked to lay
Llywelyn, a place for weeping,
Y Moel's heir, Môn's not joyful,
Handmaids' book of courtly words,
Song's magician, no weakness there,
Love's goldsmith and its mirror.

Great is the wound to wordcraft,
Great, if song's nightingale's dead.
Sadder's the world for his loss,
Costly trespass there for Powys.
Great lamenting in Y Main,
And more above in Mechain,
Penwyn's stock, that a nightingale,
Second Sulien, wouldn't grow old.
They keen for the cywydd's bard,
The art's widowed, with him buried,
Land's widowed of fine cywyddau
Lacking Powys' bow of praise,
Widowed is the greenwood's music,
Widowed love-talk's alphabet.
No cuckoo or nightingale
Leaves Llwyn-onn for Llanwnnog;
No worthwhile love's still alive;
The blackbird's proud no longer.

Môn's daughters hear oak close
Around the love that praised Euron,
And inspiration's churn and song's
Honour tossed under green holly.
And Owain's thrush is silent,

A mute man in oak and stone,
And Meredudd's author's dead,
Marble in the choir hides him,
And the muse's guard-rail's broken,
Teacher of praise, and joy ebbs.
Llywelyn was a second Iolo,
Second Gruffudd or Dafydd for us:
He was master of cywyddau,
A bird from heaven for men.
He'd shape each inspired word
Like honey, or Mary's apples.
Whose now is the tongue's lovely praise,
Every bard's book's Roman Pontiff?
Where is one word with his ardour?
Where's due deference to the art?
Gone is bold wordcraft's husband
And the master to the house of oak.

Father Griffri, sad obligation,
You carried out Seth's service,
Who came with oil, a lord's share,
From three saplings to his father:
You also brought, gifts of man,
Such an oil to Llywelyn.
He has had in the abbey church
Adda Fras' status and honour,
The man who now lies under
The manor altar in his grave.

He too, a lord in our house,
Among lords has been buried.
His body's entered the order,
Mary's anchorite in the choir,
Into highest heaven the soul,
And heaven has a new cywydd.
My God has invited him
To the feast, and his gift is heaven.

COURTING GWLADUS HAEL
on behalf of Harri Ddu

To me, God's gift's a fine woman:
They say so much of Gwladus Hael,
The most loving girl there has been,
Well-formed were her auburn eyebrows.
A candle, she sings often
To win praise and inspire bards.
Much and lovely are myrrh and incense,
More the praise for Gwladus' words:
Her eulogy's sugar candy,
And a swarm's honey her praise.

Meurig's muse was, as a maiden,
Devoted to a sweet gold girl:
By Christ, paying court to her
Are two hundred of the gentry.
Hard at work is Ieuan Gethin
And gold is each word from his lips.
Harri has made her golden,
More persistent the praise than the rain:
The most faithful fellow courting
Is the dark man, from Caer to Gwent.
Gruffudd's strong son is an Ovid
For this girl, on a snow-white horse,
A Troilus for virtuous Gwladus,
Fighter, jouster, for the fair.
Oh gracious God, why won't she
Come to Harri beneath tall trees,
And Gwent, for a hundred gifts,
And Euas that invites her.

Consider, vow's second Luned,
He is a chieftain, that lad.
It was right to compose for him
And for the girl who'll love him.
Harri's been wondrously sulky
That I'd not sing for him and her:
Woe's me if he won't stop frowning,
Woe's one who gets part of his frown.
If the black prince be angry
She is able to make peace,

315

And to beg, for his love's sake,
He be not vexed, his father wasn't.

And I'll see to it that Ieuan,
Mottled hermit, is without his share,
And make Gwladus take to her heels
Cursing the master and teacher.
What sort of thing's grizzled Ieuan's
Non-stop sermon for Gwladus?
Though she's wooed, she isn't won:
Let the young girl love Harri.
Eager's the fair girl who sings
For Ieuan's loving cywydd:
Though she love an old man's muse
She'll not love play with the fellow.
And the good girl knows nothing
Of an old lord's lechery,
Enticing and weaving praise
And craving to commit a sin.
Ieuan's lips, refined language,
And his song are lecherous.

Though she love amusement, and song,
And a cywydd from you, Ieuan,
If she cares to come to Harri,
Our man will be playing all night.

A PRIEST'S LOVE

I know how, from love of a maid,
A suitor behaves, lust's labour,
And a fickle man's passions,
His love usury, long for spoils.
Courting one long-standing sweetheart,
Courting another, he's a cad,
Today one fine girl in mind,
Of another mind tomorrow.
If to one, he'd not wed her,
Cold nature, he fashioned song,
Tender lips, not unlikely
He'd sing to another, blithe judge.

Patcher of rhymes like a tollgate,
The whole pursuit's love of spoils.

I know a man, of good stock,
Who has loved in truer fashion,
Courteous saint, fluent speaker,
Sir Wiliam, second Abraham,
Fine author, Trahaearn's heir,
And bards' Dewi passing judgment.
The choir's Mordaf is my great lord,
Of Merthyr, where Mary works wonders.
Great is his longing to greet
One woman, the Virgin Mary:
She's his love, he'll do no wrong,
And Sir Wiliam loves no other.
He's no lover, faithful temple,
Of a frigid false-faced wench,
But loves the land of banquets,
In Tudful, mead-drinking man.
The man, God and Mary keep him,
Chaste maiden, is dying of love.
He is sending, as Môn knows,
God a host of love's heralds:
The host, no widowed muse,
Are prayers to learning's author.
He vows, fair jewel, to her
Lovely gems, she's so lovely,
Loud clear bells, the church put to rights,
Books and relics and crosses.
And it's she whom he greets daily
In his office, one with his love.

She'll turn away, God's wonder,
A much-praised man from afar,
Choosing one, the muse's prize,
From her parish, splendid scholar,
And no man, were it admitted,
Was worthy of her but him.
If there's a lord, strong opinion,
Whom she loves, behold the man.
If a man is a true squire,
He'll wish to join his parish:

If he owns, valiant Urien,
A house he loves, they both go.
God knows, if a holy man
Longs for her, he'll pursue her;
If he's wise, as we understand,
And generous, she'll love him.
He's our father, good house's ruler,
And our warden, far-famed lord,
Of her fair choir with noble love,
For Tudful, and her true poet.

He pledges himself to her
And fashions psalms to her beauty,
Odes of love, glad assertion,
And cywyddau of piety.
The cywydd from his mouth daily,
Well-ordered words, is the Mass.
For love of her, this good man
Knits a song out of syntax.
Well did, no fault could I find,
Tudful, for Sundays, choose him:
She will ever, for his grace,
Remain with him in Merthyr,
And he is her dear darling,
And in heaven they'll have a tryst.

WILIAM HERBART

Three warbands once went to Wales,
They thrust their way through Gwynedd:
Y Pil's forces, Sir Wiliam's,
The Viscount's, there was their goal.
Three ways, ancient Offa's Dyke,
Wiliam journeyed, Sarn Elen.
Lord Herbart, with your carts
And your warband, God guide you:
Before, the armies had rain;
Now, when you've come, fair weather.
I foretold that you'd gain Gwynedd,
And bring Môn to the man who'll rule.

The English, they'd give their eyes,
Should you attack Harlech, to take it.
Broad-based act of hostility,
Sharp-tipped for the foolish people:
Sharp-tipped act the course you took,
Broad-based ruler of Pembroke.
What better castle to hold
Once fair Pembroke's wall was broken?
You hurled, you shook till it tumbled,
Carreg Cennen's crest to the glen;
The whole dyke did not hold above
Harlech, more than a sheep-fold.
House stays you not, nor tower,
Nor hundred forts, nor conqueror.

Three hosts went from your three lands
Through Gwynedd like claps of thunder,
Three parties, their captains proud,
Of three thousand: nine thousand yeomen.
Your brothers, the mead's soldiers,
Your people, the South and Gwynedd,
All your folk, they are heroes,
They are dragons through the woods.
Your mounts, where sheep would not go,
Climbed through the heart of Snowdon;
Across rocks are your footprints,
You turned Eryri to tilth.
Your men split in three sections
Through moorland and wilderness.
If a while you kindled a fire
Through all-out war and slaughter,
It was insurrection's scourge,
Ripping and whipping Gwynedd.

If the land has been, brave Herbart,
Faithless, so once was Saint Paul:
Greed's to blame for what has been;
If that ends, it will be christened.
And you now, on your part, be not
Savage, loosing fire on men.
Slay not the hawks who feast us
In Gwynedd like Peter's bees.

Put no tax upon that land
That cannot be collected;
Crush not Gwynedd into fallow;
Surrender not Môn to greed;
Let not the weak complain of
Betrayal and theft from now on.

Bar Rowena's race from Gwynedd
And Horsa's offspring from ancient Flint:
Let no Saxon, my lord, hold a post
Or pardon a single burgess.
Judge rightly, lord of our language,
Burn the privileges they've had;
Welcome men of Wales this moment,
Constable from Barnstaple to Môn.
Lead Morgannwg and Gwynedd:
Make us one from Conwy to Nedd.
Should England and its dukes be angered,
Wales will turn to you at your need.

SHEEP-DEALING

Two things flow through every land,
Water and sun, and God gives them,
And the third, high lord of learning,
Our kinsman's purse, Corwen's priest.
The three-stringed purse has a way
With us like the tide flowing,
Ebbing when red gold's given
And filling to give the gold.
Free the sun giving fine weather,
More free is the wine-giving man,
No miserly lord, not spiteful,
Not mean, except about lambs.

My bargain with Sir Bened
Over lambs cost me his trust.
Through ice and snow they reached me,
Black, white, and branded alike.
And so I went sheep-dealing,
Worse and worse traffic in stock.
I had with me, as it chanced,

Men who were hired to drive them;
There were two men for herding,
And the third man was the bard.
To Y Rug and Cefn yr Ais
And then to Warwick I drove them,
And to England through each remote ford,
From pool to vale to far places.
No dog went without twenty,
No water left a lamb undrowned;
Missed a fair because of floods,
Night and the streams forbade it;
Every hedge hindered a third,
Every fence clung to their fleeces.
I tried, to no advantage,
Sixty towns to Coventry:
Some of them offered pennies,
Some three and a half for two.
I wasn't pleased with the trade,
Twenty lambs dead, worse bargain

We made for land further on,
York's roads, where fairs were better.
Spent in Lichfield my payment,
Twelve lambs, it was not enough.
Made for Stafford, wilderness,
Northwards, our language laughed at,
On and on through each foul bush,
The further off, the worse prices.
In selling the ones left us,
Some on credit, too late for me,
Some in hand, like interest,
Two white lambs for under a penny.

And he beneath the rock's edge,
With no reward, fair Sir Bened,
There's no return for failure,
He'll not believe how it was.
I'll be profitless when I reckon,
A vile sheep-dealer am I.
Losing the tithe has distressed me,
God knows Y Cwm's Dewi's expense.
More the wealth in Ardudwy
Than by this business is mine

Has Tudur, wild conduit's gush,
Penllyn, in herding wethers.

I had a sorry bargain,
Sorry, but I haven't lost all.
I've to hand, if it comes to that,
A long-horned lamb and earnest-money.
I'm promised twice as much
If I come on the same journey:
If sheep had double the value
In the March, I'd come no more.

LAMENT FOR SIÔN AP MADOG PILSTWN

My tears flow like a river,
I've wept blood upon Siôn's bed,
And thousands weep here in Maelor
Harder than a heavy rain.
Gold by Mary's smock and the cross
Beg life for Siôn ap Madog;
Wretched people there were wailing,
Many fasting for his sake.
God paid no heed to the grieving:
He would take no gold but him.
Right for all, face of sacrifice,
To fear One who'll take no payment.

Tonight there is uprooted
A great oak at Berwyn's base,
A hawk of wine-streams banished
Like a barren rootless dream.
He was peer of Bwrd and Otwel,
He had Hercules' good luck,
Wrexham's own Alexander
Judging between right and wrong,
Troilus, or a second Hector,
Of Trefor and both Maelors' span.
What role, while Siôn was living,
Had we bards and wandering men
Ever but hopes of one man?
What is the worth of man's hoping?

Let war come around the river,
Across the March, or strife in Môn,
I know not, with Pilstwn gone,
Who'll close the gap, who'll save us.

Who'd not bless himself for Siôn?
So fine, yesterday, in his mansion,
Today, underneath the shroud.
The church was sown with my torrents
Far and wide, I harrowed it,
A harrow's teeth in my rib-cage:
With sad cry I was tilling,
And below the cross is the ridge.
From God's wrath, from retribution,
Came the grave and mattock and spade.

Early the earth will level
The young as well as the old.
As if to a vineyard's press
The throng enters the churchyard.
Men who are youthful and brave
Go to heaven in the morning,
And some in their middle years,
The noonday of their lifetime.
A young man was Owain's kinsman
To be cast amidst oak and stone:
Dear God, why not leave one who gave
And take the life of a miser?

Rhiwabon's son's at the feast
Of saints, Siôn was an angel,
And sure as Pilstwn was born
There is an heir of his lineage.
There's a young deer in Maelor,
Hornless stag, who'll be a great man,
One under heaven who'll shine,
Descended from both good Hywels,
A brand from the great ember
That has been all Maelor's light.
Blazing is Môn's ashtree
From the roots of noble men's hearth:
I plead for his father's sake,

I beg of God two favours,
For Siôn, and fair Alswn, heaven,
And a blessing on the spark.

THE CITY LIFE

Young, I was one for hillsides;
Now, nearing man's proper span,
As old age will, it stays put,
My life's led in a city.
If someone desires physic
For a cold stomach, milk's bad:
Better for a decrepit bard
His pewter dish and his bottle.
I have the warmth of town dwellings;
I love the bread and beer and meat;
And houses of wood in the lowlands
Make me healthy like a green tree.
Therefore I make my dwelling
In the March, I've wine and mead:
It's a kind attractive city,
Most gifted city of all,
Curtain-walled is the castle,
The best town as far as Rome.

Croes Oswallt, friend of Jesus,
Was the conqueror's great fort.
The London of Owain's country,
Wine-filled houses and orchard-land,
It's a shining gracious school,
And it's the town of preachers,
With men skilled in grammar and verse
Touching God in a fair temple.
The best church, splendid chalice,
With its organ and its bells,
The best choir, with accomplished men,
Men and vestments, to Canterbury:
The best flock, with cheerful men,
Are the men of the white abbey.
The best for women's hairstyles
And their outfits is Oswallt town:

In it there's Cheapside's commerce,
And concord, and integrity.

A tall earl holds this lively place,
And he's the best earl in England.
Grace to the town and the men,
And may God leave it a guardian,
Its lords, a good place for one's health,
Its commons, and its fine yeomen.
With them am I abiding,
And ever their man am I.
My poetry could not part with
The town, more than water the strand.
A burgess am I, long marriage:
What should I pay, and to whom?
Let Oswallt's burgesses wait for
The payment until I grow hair.
If five pounds made one payment,
They themselves will pay them, each one.

Where noble men were, once a burgess
Was Owain Waed Da in our land.
The man for his kinfolk merely
Sang to purchase privileges.
The same gift I have from them,
In hand, and in place of Owain:
A cywydd when due's the payment,
A good song, it won't cause a feud.
Delight's of no less value
Than a gold noble in the box:
Longer last, the Welsh will sing them,
Name and word, longer than silver.
I'll compose song for my brothers,
The men let me be with them,
And I'll not, without permission,
Leave them to peddle a poem.

OLD AGE

Where are the old men? All dead?
Tonight I am the oldest.

I've been given more than a share
Of old age and bad temper.
I am a jabbering fellow:
I sound off about old men,
As Rhys, in summer, Bwtlwng
Keeps on, most eloquent lad.
It's asking for each good man
That causes me to babble.
It's vexing that, like young poets,
All old fools will not keep still;
More vexing, unless he's quiet,
Caring for the blind man all day.

The whole household will witness
That I'm calling from my bed:
I call a lord, and ask for him,
In my role, such is my nature;
Calling a saint on each feast-day,
I call for the Lord Dafydd.
Though disciplined folks dislike
My role, I'll not keep silent:
It's from much love and mead's warmth
I call upon my protector;
It's his bright wine and cheerfulness
Cause the noise and the babbling.

Foster-father he's ever been
To me here, Mary spare him.
Foster-mother in my life here
Is God's temple with his riches:
I go to his cellar, I stocked it,
I go on to his buttery;
To Dafydd, a Nudd, heedful,
I go to heaven, to Iâl's holy land.
Thousands, the more I'd praise him,
Receive, kind abbot, his food.
It's a good lord, bells in plenty,
Sustained splendid Glynegwestl.
The land's weak ones he cares for,
A dwelling he raised for Iâl:
A web of stones is his breastplate;
Glass and lead the mansion's hem.

A bard, winning gold and mead,
I roamed Môn once, Gwent, and Gwynedd;
Roamed nearer, I'll win gold,
Here in Iâl, since I'm sightless.
Though I am old and sickly,
I'll not whine of weakness and age:
If God leaves me a faithful abbot
And two Siôns, there is no lack.
Siôn Trefor, I'd count him a saint,
He's a seal on the two Powys;
Siôn Edwart I'll not exchange for
Two earls, to his manor I go;
Dafydd's court, blest is the journey,
Of Iâl, again a good place.
More and more, like the great river,
Be his honour and the two Siôns',
The three rulers, by thriving,
And the One who blesses them,
The one God, the true Father's favours,
Three and One, through providence.

MEDITATION

One high lord here is guardian,
Praising saints in Iâl's great house.
As a judge, he's Bernard's lamb,
And a teacher through his poems.
If Dafydd frames a fine cywydd
He'll make it Mary's today.
Woe is the greedy poet,
Woe's he that framed not such song.

I've sung praise the world over,
Babbling sweet nonsense the while,
And blaspheming since I was six:
He bade me give up the office.
'Be still,' he said, age's solution,
'Change like Saul, by praising saints.'
He begged me and he bade me
To glorify God before man,
And to sing, late is the time,
At once to the King of Heaven,

To share, before life shortens,
Too short is the longest life,
To share and to tithe wisely
From my ageing powers to God.

He shared his gift with us on high:
Let us give to him due payment,
To the Father, Son, and Spirit,
And all understood as God,
Heaven's God and Two of his kind,
God himself, undivided.
Good were six words freely given,
God's Son grown from Mary's womb.
God from virgin soil once fashioned
Two people, and gave them the world:
Land, wild, tame, field and forest,
Deep water, from the four elements.
God gave there from his sore bosom
Pierced with steel his blood for us:
Let us give hearts that are pure
Wholly to him hereafter.

Look on Christ, a pool of blood,
God's image full of gashes,
Who will come, Doomsday's judgment,
To gather us all in the flesh.
God the Father, I know sadness,
Raised in me three heavy thoughts,
Three swords that cleft me with wounds,
Heavy pain as I pondered.
I will die, as I am destined,
I know not at all what hour,
And I know not what I'll speak of,
Without hindrance, where I'll go.

My holy God, soul's healer,
So precious to me in my need,
Conquer my sin and my sickness,
Let me die a penitent.
I cry to the Creator,
I shed many tears at night
From great love of God and Jesus
And fear always, so just was he,

328

Fear of the cross on his breast,
And the judgment on the rainbow,
Fear of Heaven's Eagle with nine ranks of angels,
Fear of the pain that once slew him.
My ears ring with Doom's trumpet
That will summon me from my bed:
For what I've done, the payment
Will be bared in the long scroll.

By the Son and his many wonders
There's hope in the upraised host:
The Trinity there will listen
To me, in prayer, from above.
My sole Saviour, my mighty God,
Will be my support on Doomsday:
May my haven, my life's conclusion,
Be all heaven and his home.

DAFYDD AB EDMWND

A GIRL'S HAIR

Shall I have the girl I love?
Shall I have the grove of brightness,
Her silken crest like a star in
The sky, her head's golden rays?
Dragon flame lighting a doorway,
Three plaits like the Pleiades,
It ignites, a single bush,
From her hair's thatch, one bonfire.
A bush of broom or broad birch,
The yellow-haired maid of Maelor.
A legion like an angel host,
Many-linked is her mail-coat,
A pennon of peacock feathers,
Tall bush like the golden door,
Such spirited-looking hair,
Sun's essence, maidens' fetter.

All will know, if they're goldsmiths,
Whose is the fine shining hair.

There is round her head in summer
Something like the Golden Slope.
Crests of grain when they are closed,
Rush peelings like a marten's breast,
The lovely growth's the girl's gown,
A tent of sun, like harpstrings,
A peahen bearing always
Hair of broom, down to the ground.
Hard amber interwoven,
Golden grain like chains of twigs,
Her hair tall as trees is a wood,
A twig crown of new beeswax:
The bees' work has brought to ripeness
Shoots of sunshine from her flesh,
Saffron on sprigs of eye-bright,
Gold cherries like the stars of night.
Well has that crop been sprouting,
Fresh water-grass, gold water-hair.
Urine steeps it like pure herbs,
Bush of silk, the crown's linnet.
The gold crop binding her head
Is Mary Magdalen's broom-sheaf,
Her loose hair like red-gold reeds,
A dress of gold her tresses.
Her two breasts are entirely
Roofed with gold, twin miracles,
Head with lovely locks laden,
Flax upon a yellow bush.
Gold the bush when it's spread out:
Was ever bush so yellow?

To mark with the chrism of faith
Her head when she was christened,
And give a bush sun for a lifetime,
There's no such bush under the sun.

UNDER THE EAVES

I'm a man walking the night,
A snug house would be sweeter,
A dullard from late walking:
God send the good sense to sleep.

The cold night's black about me;
God save me, the night's so black.
Never small space next a wall
Held one whose face was colder.
Awake, sweetheart, and save me:
God, there's a wretch next your wall.
Give, you'll have threefold payment,
Your clothing, your alms to the weak,
Your hand to me, your lodging,
Your fair body, say it is mine.
Your courtesy's sweet language,
Your lip like a sip of mead,
Your form, your charm, your laughter,
Your slim brows have ruined me.
Your long hair like your bilberry brows,
Your eye dark as your eyebrow,
Your face like friars' habits,
Black and white, bewitches men,
Your flawless pale complexion,
Two brows black as Brabant cloth,
Your face like snow, night-fallen,
Your blush like a rose bouquet.

Loving you is what I've loved;
No Saxon would bear such hatred.
I bring song to you in anger
Under eaves, a song in vain.
Dark rain will wreak its vengeance,
Soak my hair, darken my face:
Hand your kind mother's kerchief
Through the window, to roof my head.
I'll sing to you in all lands;
I'll not despair of your payment.
I'm vexed with myself for loving:
You're of gentle birth, so am I.

You are surely well shut in;
You're a lovely girl, God shield you.

I bring your song in anger:
I've borne hatred, bring me a kiss;
Your counsel to curb anger,
Good to have it, your favour, dear.

LAMENT FOR SIÔN EOS

Wrong for one who remains after
To stay mum about a chance brawl,
The least wrong of wrongdoings
By the best of all in our tongue.

Oh men, were it not better,
If one's slain, not to slay two?
Avenging one enemy's blood
Has made the enmity double.
Sad was two good men's slaying
For naught but a petty cause:
Though he stabbed the man, no denial,
If he died, there was no intent.
The fault was with some of them
Striking back in a chance mingling.
Disputing family lines,
Some trouble came between them;
From that, the one man's slaying,
And avenging him, both men slain.

If body paid for body,
Better's recompense for the soul.
Afterwards there were pledges
Of his weight in gold for Siôn's life.
I was angered by Y Waun's
Surly law, it took Eos.
Y Waun, why not under seal
Apply Hywel's law to your Eos?
When these imposed upon him,
In its fullness, London's law,
They would not, for his life's sake,
Cut a cross or bare a relic.

The man who was music's father,
They'd judged that he should not live,
The twelve, they were united,
Dear God, on taking his life.

Music and its green mansion
And its wealth's forfeit, Siôn gone,
And a cry from heaven follows him,
And schoolless is his disciple.
Behold learning: gone to the grave;
Where it's lacked, fashion longing.
After Siôn there's no fine art
In song, nor man who knows it.
An arm broke Eos' tree-top tower:
Broken the beat of music's foot,
Broken was descant's schoolroom,
Broken learning, like breaking a string.
Is there from Euas to Môn
Sufficient learning for students?
Rheinallt himself doesn't know it;
Despite that, he plays a man's part.
His fellow has been struck dumb,
Shattered the harp of Teirtud.

You are silent, not a sound,
Golden harp of the harpists.
He'd hold a string under each nail,
Fingers for man's voice or solo,
A musing between finger and thumb,
Mean and sweet treble, three-fingered.
Is there one with fair Eos gone
His equal for a prelude,
Invention, or men's music,
And twined tune before a lord?
Who now in sweet harmony,
Without him, could do what he did?
There's not a man or angel
Would not weep when he played the harp.
Ah do not play it tonight
After the master's judgment.

The musician won't bear their judgment,
Y Waun's men, at heaven's gate.

Who judges, he will have judgment
From this world to long-lasting life,
And the same mercy he shows
God as a judge will show him.
If on him just was the judgment,
Be the judgment on them the same.
He will still possess his life,
Just changing worlds, by their judgment:
Life for my man in the night,
Life in God for Siôn Eos.

IEUAN BRYDYDD HIR

SAINT WINEFRIDE'S WELL

Virgin of the border region,
Who sent the stone across the sea,
From you a sick man and poet
Would have grace and a free soul.
In the breast, like manna on high,
The muse seethes for Gwenfrewy.
There's a mansion like sunshine for her,
Heaven's stronghold for our lady,
And at the town are wonders,
Rough water, and blood on the rock.
The best of wine, I'd sing truly,
Is this water to quell disease.

Caradog 'Lawog with his sword,
He did wrong, naked impulse,
When he cut off, why not respect it,
The moon's head, caused pain and wrath.
Beuno, law's head, restored it:
She came to life once again.
Fifteen full years in prayer
She spent, she was none the worse:
She kept, without breaking faith,
Christianity's credo.

334

None in France had her beauty;
None has had a life like hers.

Let our destiny go to her
As folks go by the thousands:
If one comes lacking a sense
He'll find it, just lighting a candle,
And speak, if he has been dumb;
A deaf man, he'll hear clearly;
One unable to walk starts running;
A blind man starts seeing well.
No less generous than Dwynwen,
Not concealed, Gwen's miracles.
She's kind as Saint John's Day's sun;
She'll quell a sufferer's anguish.
Great the water, like sea on fire,
Like treacle in the wretched's belly,
It will ebb no more than Troy-town,
Won't fall silent in doing good.

There is, place of faith, in her wellspring
Life, like the baptismal font;
And there, it belongs to Gwen,
Is Jordan for both Gwynedds.
I'd come to her, Gwen, beneath the roof,
And her wine-pipes, with all assembled:
There I'd have, one sick and lonely,
A little, like John's holy life,
To drink, she was well instructed,
With the maid whose ways were like his.
I will have sips of her wonders:
I'll be sound because of her feast.

OLD AGE

Woe's he that sets, fool's thought,
His heart on the world, base traitor.
Whoever is wise and wealthy
And healthy, free, and fine for now,
Let us all dare confess it,
He'll not stay that way very long.

While I was in the great tumults,
A boisterous mad young lad,
Sudden folly, free and easy,
Strong and healthy, then I played,
And today I'm ill and decayed,
Bedridden, full of confusion.
I'm vexed by youth thereafter,
Heigh-ho, but a day, it's gone by.
I'm like the gift of a sermon
To the world, a worthless thing,
Like a foe, public memento,
To my soul that is within:
They won't believe, I'm failing,
Free and healthy, one like me.
From disease I'm the same image,
And downcast by anxiety,
As one of the three monarchs
Who grew black upon the earth.
God's allotted misery:
My body knows grief and affliction;
See, I am joyful the more:
The mark will make my soul healthy.
For this I suffer penance,
For the world's pride and vanity.

Legs, they are in splinters
Like two sticks fashioned of beech,
Shape of the shoulders deformed,
Body colourless and fleshless;
My backbone has been spread out
Like pebbles or a drift-net's corks;
Strange my ribs when they're numbered,
Like a frame where the roof's come off;
Like flails, withered the muscles,
Are my arms on both my sides,
And my hands, before leafy May,
The image of a cook's skewers;
The cheek is sad and wrinkled,
Like glass its transparency,
And my eyes, sunk in the depths
Of my head, won't let me slumber.
A man colder than Snowdon
Or Berwyn am I, I swear;

No shelter or clothing or fire
Will take away my coldness:
I'm shivering in my skin;
I'm an aspen leaf's shiver.

Mary, praiseworthy queen
Of sea and land and sunshine,
You're a healer, Jesus' mother,
For your poet, the greatest hope:
If from you I have salvation,
I desire it for my soul.
Jesus, as the choice is mine,
You'll grant my request, I ask for
Fitting, before I'm buried,
Atonement for all my wrongs.
For your pain in crucifixion,
And the blood from the feet, Triune God,
My Dear One, for the moment
Of pain for me here in the world,
Bring, Lord, to a blameless place
My spirit free in my need,
To your heavenly shore, to your light,
To your land, God, to behold you.

GWERFUL MECHAIN

THE HARP

Gwerful I, of the bankside,
Of Ferry, where silver's loved.
Keeping the Ferry's custom,
A faultless tavern, am I,
Pouring boldly, not mirthful,
In a house, needing a harp.

When I thought, gracious present,
Where I'd gain a horsehair harp,
I sent a plea, ready donor,

To Ifan ap Dafydd's home,
A baron bestowing bread,
Barons his two good grandsires.
I was by blood related
To the best men of Y Rhos;
He's not unkind to kindred,
His cousin, I seek a gift.

A fine gift he'll gladly make,
If kind, complete with horsehair,
With pegs along its full length,
From one end to the other,
The tuner next its corner
With it wherever it goes,
And its neck like those of geese,
And its back full and hollowed.

Here for a cywydd I'll have
A gift, it's Ifan gives it.
And I will give to Ifan
A roast and mead if he'll come,
And welcome when cuckoos sing,
And dinner for two pennies.
A white gown gives sweet welcome
To the men who come with coin.
I'd wish, by men's agreement,
To be faultless to my guests,
To sing sweetly for pleasure
In their midst while pouring mead.

VIVAT VAGINA

Every poet, trystless day,
Drunken fool, clumsy tactics,
Bare praise, I can't approve it,
I am royal beyond measure,
For poems to the world's women
They'll compose unfruitful faith,
Incompletely, rejected gift,
All day, by God the Father,
Praising hair, passion's mantle,
And what goes with a living girl,

And on down, praising frownless
The brows up above the eyes,
Praising too, pleasing outcrop,
The smoothness of soft young breasts,
And white arms, transparent vesture,
Owed respect, and the darling's hands.
There with his best sorcery
Before nightfall he has sung,
God on high will confess it,
Fruitless eulogy with his tongue,
Leaving the centre praiseless
And the place where children are bred,
And the snug quiff, fine eminence,
Soft, plump, cleft glowing circlet,
Whereas I'd woo, sound craft-work,
The quiff underneath the clout.
You're a piece with unfailing power,
The feathered crutch's flawless court.
Here's my credo: the quiff is lovely,
Circlet of broad-edged lips,
Dingle deeper than hand or ladle,
Trench to hold a two-handed prick,
Cunt there next the full-cheeked rump,
Songbook with red facing pages.
And the bright saints, churchly men,
Refrain not, height of favour,
Offered the chance, flawless blessing,
By Beuno, from copping a feel.
For this reason, fitting rebuke,
You stiff poets nowadays,
Let, without fail, for reward,
Songs of the quiff spread freely.
Ode's sultan, it is silken,
Little seam, fair cunt's fine veil,
Folds in a place of welcome,
The sour grove, it's full of love,
Noble forest, flawless gift,
Soft frieze, fur for fair bollocks,
Girl's thick grove, precious welcome's round,
Splendid bush, may God preserve it.

TUDUR PENLLYN

THE OUTLAW

Bright night be yours, warm your bower,
Tall Kai of the green trees and leaves:
You are in midsummer, Dafydd,
A bold woodsman all day long.
The strength and grasp of Siancyn,
Strong court, the valley's rock,
Your castle is now the copse,
The dale's oaks are your towers.
The blessing of Nanconwy's stags,
Song that lasts, longer honour's yours.
Most sweet is your skill, Dafydd,
In minstrelsy, exiled stag;
Outstanding gem, you're handsome,
Every gallant's butterfly.

Your wealth is your rank and fame,
Dafydd, Dafydd's grandson, Ifor.
A daredevil in warfare
You've been judged, and you're no less;
No finer feat did Roland
Perform than you've done with steel:
When there's song of valiant deeds,
You're raised above all heroes;
In every great hall's exploits
Once more you are raised on high.

Are you not Llŷr Llwyd's soldier,
Peacock, for Pembroke, of war?
You're nephew, Dafydd, bright-red gem,
To Master Owain's uncle;
Nobility's yours by birth,
One of Harri's tall kinsmen.
Honour to you, lasting long,
Was given by Lord Richmond.
From the best of forebears you come,
From Rhys Gethin, you're Elffin;
Absalon in Meirionnydd,
And sheriff of cuckoo and copse;

Meirig's grandchild, no mistake,
And your grandmother was Cynfyn.

You are the stags' companion,
The Earl's kin, a conqueror;
And you, the sword of the lords,
Are ruler in our region.
Gwynedd is yours, and peaceful,
And support throughout the South.
Beware the towns, wise progress,
And the towers of the other side.
Good is the day's safe-conduct,
Better, Cadell's grandson, the trees;
Good are walled town and border,
Best is the glen and grey rock;
Good the burgess' day's pardon,
And a shaft against Saxons no worse.

Love the castle of the copse,
Love the soldiers who love you;
Guard the camp, the woods, the pass,
Guard the right to Coed-y-Betws;
Eight score kinsmen around you,
Eight hundred who love you are near,
Eight hosts, by Saint Peter, are yours,
Eight woodlands, and God preserve you.

GUTUN OWAIN

THE HOUNDS
Petition to Hywel ap Rhys on behalf of his nephew, Dafydd ab Ieuan

I hunt game on the holding,
My hunting-ground mountainous Mael.
I'd love to hunt this dawning
A stag over hills with hounds,
Hunt the hinds of the region,
Had I the hounds and the land.

From one who's been no miser
Are there hounds for me to have?
Two hounds of his, sweet-sounding
From Edeirnion's princely hawk.
Hugh of Gwynedd, fine province,
Hywel's the lord of Rhys' line.
I'll have from Dafydd's grandson
Stag's pursuers on a slope:
The fair hawk's my kind uncle,
And as his nephew I ask.
A baron is he, who buys mead,
Kingly, sustainer of Gwynedd.
He it is who for thriving
Is the best man in Y Rug,
The same heart, the same bounty,
Same fame as Nudd has our lord.

Three things the baron's fond of,
Falconer, hunt master, hounds.
And I have set my heart on
One of these, and the gift is hounds.
Two with voices like songbirds,
Two yoke-fellows in two chains,
They give cry to the master
When they get wind of the stag.
They proclaim by their fierceness
The sure scent of the fair hind.
Lads keeping their heads down low,
Where they go, men will follow.

A conversation with Annwn
The hounds hold in wooded ground,
Shaping song in cuckoo's copses,
And shaping death for the fox.
Well they time, on the glen's floor,
Their tune in trailing reynard;
They ken the canon's measures,
They make music chasing a hind,
Chasing the fawn, a carol,
A cywydd chasing the stag,
Bards of heavenly concord,
Bells of Durham pealing back.

My aim is to have the hounds
From Hywel, another Beli.
Let him give Mael's land he owns
Two of the organs of Gwynedd.
Dafydd, open hand in giving,
I'm his nephew, Ieuan's son.
Goal of praise, I'm a trader,
Let him trade, his nephew am I:
His kinsman's song for the baron;
For his kinsman, two of his hounds.

LOVE'S LANGUAGE

Girl of saintly disposition,
Oh God, bewitching are you.
You have, a good spirit's yours,
Yes, the Scythian's language,
Prudent enchanting image,
Jewel that will fool the just.

Your eye, mocking and merry,
Glossy black, would slay a lad.
I've taken note of signals
You made to me, one or two,
Taken note of a stray glance,
Noted sly signs of the forehead,
Read the slim eyebrow, my dear,
And watched it Sunday and feast-day,
Delightful golden writing,
Girl's hint to encourage a lad.
I see that you are speaking
As though both of us were dumb.
Fools will not perceive this year
Significance in our signals.

Speak sweet words to me with your face
From your heart, none will hear you.
You know how, you are gentle,
To speak in a soft gesture;
It knows what, this heart of mine,
Your mind is from your manner.
The eyes speak to one who's wise

Sense where fools will not seek it,
A mirror's slanting turnings,
Thieves finding a place to look.

I'm the one can catch sight of
Every such turn of the eye.
I look at, though I'll deny it,
You slyly when someone is there:
A sinner's single glimpse of
Heaven before he's in pain;
Dafydd ap Gwilym's sidelong
Look at Dyddgu, lively girl;
A lad's look at a secret tryst;
A hawk's look at a woodcock;
A thief's look under his brow,
That's the way, at shops' jewels;
A loving prisoner's look
Through the door's bars at daylight.

My girl, though not once do we have
One word of conversation,
We can through the branches' tips
Give a glance at each other.
A gesture will speak sweet words
Knowing no fear of slander.
Is there one beneath the sky,
No, except me, who'll know it?
One deceit and one mockery
Are we, by God and Mary,
One shrewdness, one cunning speech,
One fondness needing no language.
The One and Three of our prayers,
May they make the two of us one.

A WINTER HAVEN
in praise of Dafydd ab Ieuan, Abbot of Valle Crucis

Dafydd, to his open court I'll go, to complain
    Against the winter's cold:
    Gold and wine each hour I'll have,
    Warmest acre beneath the Cross.

Red wine's warmth like Gruffudd Gryg
And white wine and mead and nurture,
If God send, after fine weather,
The merciless frost and snow.

Merciful the Crucifixion on the great wooden Cross
    That ransomed the five ages:
We beg, we pray, two ages, the Hand
That gave it to better the weather.

    None but who gave it will break the weather:
    Our houses and our fire wouldn't thaw it.
    I would like the earth to be set free
    And it's God on high who will do it.

The Bernician's peacemaker lord won't do it,
    Or king, or emperor:
White snow, a hundred men with wild fire
Wouldn't clear it, without One Man's work.

    From the earth we'll petition
    The Man who is Three and One,
    The omnipotent Lord God,
    Father, Son, and Spirit, and Man:
    His judgment, pure Virgin's burden,
    Will thaw the frigid days' snow.

God our King sends the frigid East Wind
    As far as the South:
If the moon is cause of cold weather,
The weather will warm with the sun.

If God's given cold weather that hinders earth's folk
For me there is comfort here in my land.
To the valleys' fresh woods, leaving the hillsides,
Go the hinds when it turns freezing cold,
And I will come down from mountain to choir,
To Ifor's three feasts, to lord Dafydd.

Abbot famous as Dyfnwal, made of four elements,
With his boldness, leader the length of Meilienydd,
Did paradise ever, I'll enter his walls,
And choir more delight with sacred song?

High Mass, the organ's angelical
Fresh stream, and divine words from Dafydd's lips.

His house and his wine will foster a poet,
Lord who honoured me, fame of Merwydd's feasts,
And he is our earl there, source of rejoicing,
And pope of a paradise to cherish poets,
And he'd have every day a hundred tunes
And Dafydd would grace all sorts of guests.

He'll provide drink from flourishing orchards
And from wheat malt and splendid grapevines.
What the bees carry from the meadow corners
Will make liquors in his enclosures.
The best of fruits, like Gweirydd the Strong,
That grow from the earth, Dafydd bestows.

I'm a second Myrddin, on a short bright day,
Who led the valiant to Arderydd's field,
One possessed of true song, his sister Gwenddydd,
Who would often feast him within her courts.
Living there every day free of care,
He was as devoted as I to Dafydd.

On Hyrddin's manna an hour seems a summer day:
Let eighteen hours pass, we'd visit his new house.
It's a downhill path for me to his courts,
And uphill to leave them: are there finer drinks?
It's a fostered boy's grief fills the breast
If delayed in coming, or on leaving Dafydd.

Rhys Sais' descendant is the best in our age
Of abbots for me in all of Christendom.
Sixty ages, Jesus, prospering still,
May he be in Llangwestl, never begrudging.
If an oak's been old, or the stag of Glyn Dyfrdwy,
May Dafydd's life in his two courts be twice as long.

HUW CAE LLWYD

THE CROSS

The One who stretched out on the cross
His arms for the world's five ages,
Good is the place he was given
Above us, his arms outspread
Above the green land, splendid church,
Of Hodni, heaven-honoured,
Where above the crest of the rock
God's cross bears Christ in beauty,
And his name was truly inscribed,
Jesus, there in Ystrywaid.
It was like this, says the world,
Friday, after Shrove Tuesday,
His wounds glistening brightly,
Heaven's God, the gash in his breast.

Three nails were used to martyr
Holy God's two hands and feet:
Both his feet were pinned by one,
A stripe of blood across them;
He bore, was it not of his goodness,
Sharp steel hammered through his hands.
Through ribs and robe a blind man
Ripped him open with a spear;
Down through his hair were driven
Three thorn-spikes to deepen his pain.

I sought to observe each wound
Upon the God of heaven:
No single spot did I find
Unbloody and unbroken.
Who else would act so bravely,
Under heaven, for mankind's sake?
His heart and his five wounds were
His pledge to heaven for us:
Let us then pledge hearts made pure
To him, and let them do homage.
Our sin, if we refuse it
Submission, he will forgive.

Let us go, if we're guilty,
For God's grace, this Feast of the Cross,
Where he has done, with them wailing,
Many wonders for their aid:
He restored full strength for some;
He made the dead live for others.
I breathe a sigh for the spark
Of the real wonder that feeds me.
No fool am I for sending
This prayer to gracious God:
That my soul may be enlightened,
Holy Son, sanctify me;
The Blessed Son's body is strong,
Let me be saved, Doomsday's Saviour;
From all cruel wickedness
And pain, defend me ever;
And let my soul not be parted
From your land and your blessed hosts.

The day that brought Jesus from death
To life, it was a fine morning:
For all the crippled and blind
Whom he's healed, it was splendid.
May the blood which from his feet
Flowed for us give me refuge;
From his pierced side I have longed
To have the sweat of Jesus.
But two drops from the passion,
His tears, have saved me from plague.
God the Father, above all,
Hear me for my innocence:
I will make, divine its praise,
The Son a cywydd, invite me;
I'll go gladly to the fair feast,
Perfect, unceasing, unending.

TUDUR ALED

LOVE'S FRUSTRATION

My passion for Iseult's twin
Goes worse than a wild arrow.
Loving a maiden's portrait
Is as hard as toting stone.

Non and Edith's sister in faith,
You'd be sister to the Virgins;
Your name is adding one more
To the eleven thousand.
Heed one who's weak, cheeks wasting,
From your hue, my gold-browed dear:
Because gold grows on your crown
Your blushing is so lovely.
Your complexion makes you proud,
You like to look in the mirror;
Mark your image there in the glass:
God is the one devised it.

So slim is your cinctured waist
You could spin in my handspan.
God, there's no church, noble girl,
Not empty if you're absent:
Yes, God, the church would be crowded
If your face alone were there.

Why must I picture the face,
Because of your folly, to see you?
No delight, under the stars,
The same as you, fair maiden.
No girl drives me to suffer
In wind and water but you,
Coming from the far corners
Over land, and how hard it was,
You would not, at journey's end,
Step once across the threshold.

God, how gently you gestured,
A gentleness filled with stone.

It's my life, my anguish speaks,
In two places of darkness,
Your bright eyes, blue-grey in hue,
You struck, dear, with your unkindness.

May your arms, at last, above me,
Be the angels of my bed.
Precious they are, your kisses:
But two could bring a man health.
You'd not give one, for life's need:
Sell some, by the One that made you.

Auburn your brows, white your hand,
White is your cheek, and wine-flushed.
Fair one, the pain you cause me
Eight-plated steel could not bear.
Into the grave should enter
One with half my sleeplessness.
I lie on one side, sleepless,
A bird's sleep, tonight, is mine,
The sleep of fish in the sea
Reclining in rough water.
More in one night I tremble
Than the aspen does in eight.
Your hue held in mind, in sleep,
Turns me away from slumber.
The world finds me a byword,
And never a pang have you.

To have you, at the grave's edge,
I'm no man, merely wastage,
This is my only longing,
Though improper, my pure soul.
The scarcer you make your speeches,
The stronger my long weakness grows.

I'm no better, frustrated,
For this, than a sanctum's thief,
Waiting near you seven eves
With seven excuses to see you.
Unwise, one who won't be silent,
And wise are you, keeping still.
I could have, girl, no happy life,

Nor fail one night to greet you.
No more of words too distant,
In mercy, give better words:
I beg of you, my seagull,
Sentence me to live or die.

THE STALLION
Petition to the Abbot of Aberconwy on behalf of Lewis ap Madog

With one who safeguards Gwynedd
I would feast on Conwy's bank:
He's abbot over eight districts,
Aberconwy, field of vines,
A lord giving feasts gladly,
Twice the custom, at an abbot's board,
Spices in the one man's dish,
An orange for some others.
Thrice a prince's kitchen's strain,
His cook works hard at turning.

Conwy, in a warm valley,
Fair stream where I'd have fresh wine,
Wine-rich mansion, honey's temple,
Passage and pantry below:
For his wines at any time
Here was the head of all nations,
Glyn Grwst and Austin's fine fort,
Green glen of wine in gallons.
Where would I seek the saints' session?
With him and his fellow monks,
Men reckoned like the Romans,
White and red the robes they wear.
If his breastcloth and cope were white,
So dressed he'd pass for a bishop;
In fine miniver he'd pass for,
If he tried, the Pope of Rome.

Folly, and a troublesome task,
Contending for someone's favour:
For the place that this man gained,
Aberconwy, he was leader.
They'd take a thousand small rents:

351

He'd obtain the rent of Maenan.
The man on Meirionydd's ground
Has a band like woodland blossoms,
Soldiers between Maelor and Rhos,
Tegeingl, his close relations.

Lewis ap Madog's sure hope is,
Requesting and given a horse,
And choosing it before May,
A fair girl and steed to bear her.
A stag's look he seeks for a cywydd,
Dimple-nosed, loose in his skin,
Nose responsive to a bridle,
Wide muzzle like a French gun,
Bear's muzzle, jaw in motion,
Bridle's loop holding his nose.
Lively eyes that are leaping
Like two peeled pears in his head;
Two slender and twitching ears,
They're sage leaves on his forehead.
A glazier's tended his crupper
As though polishing a gem,
His skin like silk newly woven,
And his hair like gossamer,
Silk in a skylark's doublet,
Camlet clothing a young stag.

Like the deer, his eye frenzied,
His feet weaving through wild fire,
He was spinning without hands,
Or weaving silk, moved closer.
Pursuing the thunder's course
And trotting when he pleases,
He'd toss a leap to the heavens,
Confident that he could fly.
Sturdy colt chewing up a highway,
Fair's warning bell, flee from his path.
Stars come from the road, or lightning,
Whenever his fetlocks lift.
Frisky on thirty-two nails,
A spark is every nailhead:
Spinning up on a hillside,
He holds nailheads to the sun;

The sparks were coming from them,
Each hoof's sewn with eight stitches.
His vigour I'd compare to
A red hind fleeing from hounds.
In his mind he was floating:
A most lively beast he was.
If driven to the hayfield,
His hoof will not break eight stalks.

He was a river-leaper,
The roebuck's leap from the snake.
He'd face whatever he pleased:
If rafter, he'll try to clear it.
Never need, to make him leap,
For steel against his belly,
With a keen rider, no clod,
He would know his intention.
If he's sent across a wall,
He will run, the lord's stallion,
Bold jumper where thorns grow thick,
All-out thrust in Llaneurgain.
Best ever, when set running,
Fine horse to bear a fair girl:
Here there awaits me a maiden,
Fair girl, if there were a horse.

For a hind's form what payment
Betters praise of the slim foal?

A PLEA FOR PEACE
to reconcile Hwmffre ap Hywel and his kinsmen

The great stags, our source of mead,
Are from one shire in Gwynedd.
Old Ynyr's seed, my sworn lord,
My guide, may land be Hwmffre's,
Hywel's heir, he ruled a world,
Siencyn's son, our short-lived pillar.
A knight, with blood as noble
As ten earls, and duke are you:
Forfeit this not hereafter
Through false counsel, broad-branched oak.

From slander to you and your uncles
Empty is the hindmost yoke.
Your cousins, I know these men,
Form a chain, trees of Ynyr:
These are, of the ancient bloodline,
Eight of them, men of your blood:
Morgan, honoured sprig of Einion,
Steadfast Wiliam, spear in his hand,
Two bodies for Siencyn's one,
Two of Derwas' gold roses;
Tudur Fychan, the land's shield,
Derwas' bull, his feet gilded;
Seven cousins I'd not take,
Siôn's son Siencyn, before him;
Hywel, offspring were his,
Fychan, dragon of Mechain,
Siôn, noble man of his stock,
And Wmffre, jewelled his bridle;
Brave Gruffudd, stag of keen steel,
Of Iefan's blood and Dafydd's;
Morgan Siôn, so full of welcome,
Of Penllyn, spear swift and sharp.

Strong your kind, like rooted oaks,
And the whole grove's uprooted.
And where have there been such trees
If all would trust one another?
Simpler, like Brutus, to wreck a house
Than raise it, famous building.
Ynyr of Nannau's offspring,
Woe to us if you grow weak.

Dear God, why should men be vexed
Because of a slanderer's malice?
Blood feuds, from a feeble cause,
Led to conflict at Camlan.
Three futile frays through hatred,
Ancient folly, with many slain:
Battle begun by a pup;
Sad deed, Arderydd's battle;
More wicked, Mordred's treason,
How he provoked, for two nuts,

Strife once more by two shepherds
Because of a skylark's chicks.

Men hate one another like this
Today, because of positions:
Before, ousting men was hateful;
Today, woe for men who make peace.
I can find here no friendship,
Nor a man to plead for good;
Trusted, truly, is no one
Except the one who's two-faced;
The wicked today's in the right,
To the good none will listen.

Our leaders had no need of
Their resorting to the lords:
Though you give them gold today
You'll not end it in your lifetime.
If there's wrath between Rhos' blossoms,
Look whether the cause was good:
No stranger's able to do it;
This you can do for yourselves.
Harm and hatred, from losses,
Arbiters, once, could dissolve:
This generation has nothing,
Through anger, but squandered wealth.
No good comes of the expense,
But devilish wrongdoing.

Wales is worse for this stripping,
England better from our shame.
A hundred bills heaped on us there;
Jesus' cross, shield us from sessions.
One kinsman blames another,
Easily this hand blames that.
Let someone strip, sift, untruthful,
His fellow's fault, he's believed:
Word of wrongdoing remains,
Many times staining the bloodline.
One kinsman's shamed, not another:
Truth told, it's the other's fault.
Better to keep back the black

Hurtful word than to deny it:
Stop an arrow, it's absurd,
Once it has left the bowstring.

No joy for us, unseemly it was,
And you so many, to chide you:
Wisdom should come, splendid clan,
From folly, and a bard's frankness.
The scroll I hold shows a wheel,
A face pictured at its centre.
See there, around the wheel's rim,
Four true words, without stopping:
Peace, the world's pulse of power,
It is this that breeds wealth as well;
Proud wealth, I know the wheel's work,
If it is strong, breeds warfare;
Warfare breeds a misery,
Want, with anger and anguish;
Want, for unhappy wretches,
If it's widely spread, breeds peace.
These words are on the wheel's edge,
Could one but acknowledge them:
Man's rise, he'll not stay below,
And fall is written round it.
If it turn once to mischance,
God, may it turn to good fortune.

Here were two noble houses:
For a quarrel, Hwmffre's vexed.
Making peace today on high
Atop the wheel would keep you:
Let its rim rise, God will guard you;
Allow all of your blood to rise.
Trees should bear leaves together:
Safeguard the trees at your side;
The grove, would all were pleasant,
Is a grim grove without love.
Men higher than a gold seal
And sharing a noble bloodline,
Though there's a frown, they will spare;
Because of a frown, they'll deal gently.
None have lived without weakness,
However pure are their hearts:

Be there peace, and reconcilers,
If five thousand men were slain.

An alms it were, no one slain,
Unstained to plead for union.
If your long grudge has chilled us,
Grace will kindle warmth at once:
Well-bred blood that was frozen,
Melt those of your blood towards you;
Draw the ice to the fire now,
Dissolve your wrath, noble stag;
Today let there be water,
Beneath the ice, it's thin and cold.
Draw poison from your true blood;
The sweet blood's scent is treacle.
Have sense, heart-rending your strife,
And set good sense above you.
Take no note of injuries,
And offer amends and denial:
If you're kind, like your father,
Amends and denial you'll make.

Among you, bring your kinsmen,
By all grace, the saints' miracles.
By the lance and holy Jesus,
By his pain over Lazarus,
May the Trinity bring union
By fair Mary's tears for her Son.

NOTES

After the title of each poem, I have listed first the text on which the translation is based. Other texts are listed when I have adopted some of their readings or am indebted to their annotation. I have provided such clarifying information as seemed essential, and occasional critical comments, but in general I have not attempted to discuss variant readings, to defend my interpretations, or to offer solutions to ambiguous or difficult phrases and passages.

Names of persons and places and some unfamiliar words are to be found in the Glossary, but when a poem required much genealogical information I have supplied it in the Notes.

Very little is known in most cases of the poets' lives, and I have supplied biographical information only when it seemed useful. The dates when they were active are given, but these are frequently only approximations.

I. THE EARLY POETS (*c*.575–*c*.1100)

The following abbreviations are used for texts frequently cited:

CLlH   Ifor Williams ed., *Canu Llywarch Hen* (Cardiff, 1953).
EWSP   Jenny Rowland, *Early Welsh Saga Poetry: A Study and Edition of the Englynion* (Cambridge, 1990).
LlDC   A.O.H. Jarman ed., *Llyfr Du Caerfyrddin* (Cardiff, 1982).
PLlH   Patrick Ford ed., *The Poetry of Llywarch Hen* (London, 1974).

TALIESIN

He lived in the latter half of the sixth century. Sir Ifor Williams conjectured that he had been a court poet in Powys, then settled further north at the court of Urien of Rheged, and travelled occasionally to other British kingdoms such as Elmet (in the region of modern Leeds). In later Welsh tradition he became the subject of saga, and his own poetry was mixed with both saga-poems and prophetic verse in the thirteenth-century manuscript known as *The Book of Taliesin*. In a late prose romance Taliesin is presented as a magician as well as poet, with a mysterious birth, strange transformations into animal forms, and the power to rescue his ruler, Elphin, from his enemies by poetic spells. The sequence of the translations is based on a possible rather than a proven chronology: I have placed poems dealing primarily with inter-Celtic warfare before those dealing with a battle against the Anglo-Saxons and with the death of Urien's son.

The Battle of Gwen Ystrad. Ifor Williams & J.E. Caerwyn Williams eds., *The Poems of Taliesin* (Dublin, 1968), II. Since Catraeth in this poem is under Urien's rule, the poem is clearly earlier than Aneirin's *Gododdin*. The enemy may have been Picts; they were not Anglo-Saxons, who did not fight on horseback.

Idon's lavish wine: the river was red with blood.

In Praise of Urien. Williams, III. Urien is praised in this poem both as a defender of the Britons against the English ('Lloegr-men') and as a kind of high king, powerful enough to control the neighbouring British rulers, presumably of Gododdin, Strathclyde, and Elmet. Urien and three other rulers, Rhydderch, Gwallawg, and Morgant, joined forces for a time against the English, but Urien was killed by Morgant when the leaders quarrelled. Ifor Williams suggested that Urien was arrogant, more the warrior than the diplomat, and found it not surprising that his allies should have turned against him.

The Court of Urien. Williams, IV.

The War-Band's Return. Williams, V. Ifor Williams suggested that the poem is best read as a dramatic monologue in which the poet's fears for his ruler's life are interrupted by Urien's safe return. The catttle-raid was against a neighbouring British region, Manaw Gododdin, north of Rheged.

not one sneeze or two: the idea that a sneeze purported good or ill fortune was common in the early Middle Ages.

The Battle of Argoed Llwyfain. Williams, VI. The battle was with Angles from Bernicia and Deira, led by 'Fflamddwyn', whose name ('flame-bearing') may refer to his burning of British settlements or may be a translation of his Anglo-Saxon name. Owain is one of Urien's sons, presumably the eldest; he is called 'bane of the East' because the Anglo-Saxons were 'easterners' in their continental origins and their occupation of British territory.

Petition for Reconciliation. Williams, IX. The cause of Urien's displeasure is not known, though the poem refers at one point to mocking Urien's age. Ifor Williams suggested that he may have been offended by Taliesin's visits to other courts and praise of other rulers, e.g., two extant eulogies of Gwallawg, ruler of Elmet, which I translated for Thomas Owen Clancy's *The Triumph Tree* (Edinburgh, 1998).

Lament for Owain ab Urien. Williams, X. It would seem from this poem that Owain outlived his father Urien, for whom no elegy survives. For the reference to Fflamddwyn, see Taliesin's earlier poem on the battle of Argoed Llwyfain.

ANEIRIN (*c.*590?)

Hwn yw e gododin. aneirin ae cant. 'This is *The Gododdin*: Aneirin sang it', i.e., composed it. The apparently simple statement at the beginning of the thirteenth-century manuscript known as *The Book of Aneirin* precedes two separate texts, each by a different scribe, each copying a different earlier text. Both texts are obviously incomplete, each contains material not in the other, and there are often considerable differences between the stanzas common to both. Whether *The Gododdin* should be considered as a single work or a group of elegies has been a matter of frequent contention among modern commentators, and points to the uniqueness of the poem. Despite the incomplete survival of the work and the serious textual problems with some portions of it, and though some material was probably added later, *The Gododdin* has its own kind of unity, and in either text has a powerful cumulative effect that is absent if one reads only excerpts.

While a ninth-century text names Aneirin along with Taliesin as one of five outstanding poets of the sixth century, nothing is certain about him beyond what *The Gododdin* itself makes clear: that he was a younger contemporary of Taliesin, a court poet at Din Eidyn (now Edinburgh), and a survivor of the military venture that is the subject of his poem.

The basic facts about that venture are taken for granted by the poem itself. Mynyddawg Mwynfawr, ruler of Gododdin, assembled warriors from his own and other British realms at Din Eidyn, and after about a year of training and feasting the three hundred or so rode south against the crossroads encampment of the English at Catraeth (present-day Catterick), an expedition that ended in the deaths of all but a few men. Whatever may have been the actual importance of this battle at the time, it became symbolic of the heroic attempt to halt the English conquest, not least because of Aneirin's poem.

For this translation stanzas have been numbered according to the sequence in each text, with asterisks indicating stanzas excluded for reasons stated and bracketed dots for omissions where the text is so corrupt that it seemed pointless to venture a translation.

The Gododdin *(Text A)*. Ifor Williams ed., *Canu Aneirin* (Cardiff 1938, 1970); A.O.H. Jarman ed., *Aneirin: Y Gododdin* (Llandysul, 1988); John T. Koch ed., *The Gododdin of Aneirin* (Cardiff, 1997).

Stanzas 1–36 correspond to those under Roman numerals in Williams. For the subsequent stanzas the numbers in Williams have been noted, e.g., CA LXVI. Where stanzas in the A-text correspond in any way to the B-text, these have been noted with reference to the translation in this volume, e.g., B 18.

4. There is a play on the hero's name Gwefrfawr, 'rich in amber'. The stanza, like some others, is incomplete. Ysgyrran's son may be Mynyddawg.

9. The hero of this stanza is named elsewhere as Llifiau (A 22) and Llif (B 13), referred to in the latter as coming from 'beyond Bannog' and therefore a Pict.

10. In this stanzas as in others the hero is not named, presumably because some lines of the original poem were lost in transmission.

16. The stanza plays on the hero's name, Blaen, meaning 'foremost', 'first'.

20. B 12.

21. This stanza probably belonged to the chain of stanzas 8–11, though it is possible that the opening line of those stanzas was later repeated. The three men are presumably those named in stanza 18.

22. B 13.

23. B 11.

25. It was customary for the ruler to distribute gifts on New Year's Day.

26. B 18.

34. The hero's name in the last line may be 'Wid', which may be Pictish.

36. The second line of this stanza is apparently missing, since the following line begins 'than Cynon'.

37. CA XXXVIII, B 30.

38. CA XXXIX, B 31.

39. CA XLII, B 30.

40. CA XLIII, B 5.

41. CA XLIV, B 6.

42. CA XLV, B 25, 35.

43. CA XLVI.

Stanza 44 in the A-text (CA XLVII) is an interpolated verse from the later Llywarch Hen cycle and has not been translated for this anthology.

45. CA XLVIII. This stanza and the following, with their references to the poet's having been imprisoned and rescued, may be later interpolations from a saga about Aneirin. In any case, the line 'I, not I, Aneirin' (*mi na vi aneirin*) is puzzling. If the stanza is from a saga, then the later poet may be noting his use of dramatic monologue; if it is in the original poem, Aneirin may be distinguishing between his ordinary warrior self and his role as poet. Since the verb 'sang' (*ceint*) here as elsewhere can refer either to composing or reciting the poem, it is also possible that the line was interpolated by a later reciter.

46. CA XLIX.

47. CA L.

48. CA LI, B 3, 24.

49. CA LII.

50. CA LIII. This stanza may be an interpolation from another poem, since it would seem from the final lines to be unrelated to the material of *The Gododdin*. These lines are interpreted in Williams as referring to the Deirans being driven into hiding; the present translation follows Jarman as well as Kenneth Jackson's translation in *The Gododdin: The Oldest Scottish Poem* (Edinburgh, 1969).

51. CA LIV, B 7.

Stanza 52 in the A-text is a reciter's prologue. Stanza 53 in the A-text (CA XXXIX B) repeats stanza 38, except that the first line is replaced by a variation of the opening lines of 54–56: 'Ready warriors rose for combat,/ To Catraeth, swift spirited war-host.' Since this appears to be a scribal error, I have excluded 53 from this translation.

54. CA LVI.

55. CA LVII.

56. CA LVIII.

57. CA XXXVII. This stanza is conspicuously out of place in the A-text. Ifor Williams shifted it in his edition to conclude the chain that begins with stanza 34.

58. CA LIX.

59. CA LX.

60. CA LXI, B 20.

61. CA LXII.

62. CA LXIII, B 14, 15, 16, 36.

63. CA LXIV, B 40.

64. CA LXV.

65. CA LXVI, B 37.

66. CA LXVII, B 40.

67. CA LXVIII. Williams, Jackson, and Jarman accept *merch eudaf hir* as the reading, and speculate on whether this could refer to Mynyddog's wife. The present translation is based on the conjecture that *merch* was a scribal error for *meirch*, which admittedly does not do much to clarify what seems to be only part of an original stanza. The wearing of purple may suggest Roman imperial lineage.

68. CA LXIX, B 27.

69. CA LXX, B 31.

70. CA LXXI, B 30.

71. CA LXXII.

72. CA LXXIII.

73. CA LXXIV.

74. CA LXXV, B 35.

75. CA LXXVI.

76. CA LXXVII.

77. CA LXXVIII.

Stanza 78 in the A-text concerns a battle that took place at Strathcarron, some years later than the one at Catraeth.

79. CA LXXX.

80. CA LXXXI.

81. CA LXXXII.

82. CA LXXXIII.

83. CA LXXXIV.

84. CA LXXXV.

85. CA LXXXVI.

86. CA LXXXVII, B 2.

Stanza 87 in the A-text is a mother's song to a small boy, and is translated among the miscellaneous poems in the present collection.

88. CA LXXXIX. The A-text scribe ended his copying of the poem with this stanza, leaving the remainder of the page and the following page blank, an indication that he was aware his text was incomplete. The later B-text scribe began copying a different and earlier text of the poem at the end of the A-text.

The Gododdin *(Text B)*. Williams; Jarman; Koch. The number of each stanza in Williams has been noted, e.g., CA LXIII D. Where stanzas in the B-text correspond in any way to the A-text, these have been noted with reference to the translation in the present volume, e.g., A 59.

The opening two stanzas in the B-text are clearly additions to the original poem and have therefore been excluded from the translation. The first deals with a later battle at Strathcarron; the second is a reciter's prologue.

3. CA LI C, A 48. See also B 24 and the note.

4. CA LXXXVII B, A 86.

5. CA XLIII B, A 40.

6. CA XLIV B, A 41.

7. CA LIV B, A 51.

8. CA XC.

9. CA XCI.

10. CA XCII.

11. CA XXIII B, A 23.

12. CA XX B, A 20.

13. CA XXII B, A 22. See also A 9 for another stanza on this hero.

14. CA LXIII D, A 62.

15. CA LXIII B, A 62. This stanza seems to be a truncated version of B 14 except for the final line naming a different warrior, rather than one stanza in a chain using the same opening lines. See also B 36.

16. CA LXIII C, A 62. The first two lines of this stanza have been excluded as a probable interpolation, since the original presumably repeated the opening line of stanzas 14 and 15. Jackson translates the omitted lines as: 'The bright flood, the grey wolf, the terrible following water'.

17. CA XCIII.

18. CA XXVI B, A 26.

19. CA XCIV.

20. CA LXI B, A 60.

21. CA XCV.

22. CA XCVI.

23. CA XCVII.

24. CA LI B, A 48. This appears to be another version of B 3 rather than a different stanza repeating the opening and closing lines. In both cases the text is extremely corrupt.

25. CA XLV B, A 42.

26. CA XCVIII.

27. CA XCIX.

28. CA C.

29. CA LXIX B, A 68. The final line is missing but has been presumed from A 68.

30. CA XL, A 39.

31. CA XLI.

32. CA LXXI B, A 70.

33. CA LXX B, A 69.

34. CA CI.

35. CA XLV C, A 42. See B 25, with which this stanza presumably once formed a chain, if it is not another version of it.

36. CA LXIII E, A 62. See B 14 and 15

37. CA LXXV B, A 74.

38. CA CII. The stanza contains the earliest reference to Arthur as a British hero, although it has been argued that the line referring to him is a later interpolation.

39. CA LXVI B, A 65.

40. CA LXIV B, A 63.

41. CA CIII. Third Fearsome One: there is a traditional triad concerning *Tri Engiriol*, the 'Three Fearsome [or Violent, or Terrible] Ones of Britain'. See Rachel Bromwich, *Trioedd Ynys Prydein* (Cardiff, 1961), p. 196.

42. CA LXVII B, A 66. The B-text breaks off in the middle of the last word of the second line of this stanza. Three vellum folios, i. e., six pages, were cut out at the end of the manuscript, so that it is uncertain how much is therefore missing from the B-text.

THE FALL OF RHEGED (8th-10th century) *EWSP*, pp. 419–428; *CLIH*, III; *PLIH*, st. 102–160. The identity of the speaker or speakers of the Urien poems is uncertain, though prior to Rowland it was usually considered to be Llywarch Hen, since these poems occur in the manuscript between two poems dealing with him. Rowland also questions whether, in the poems dealing with Urien's head and corpse, the speaker fought on his side or in opposition. What is supported by historical tradition is that Urien fell in battle against other British rulers, Unhwch, Dunawd, and Morgant.

2. The head was apparently cut off during a hurried retreat, presumably to preserve it from desecration by the enemy; Urien's corpse, as the following poem shows, was later recovered for burial. The poem plays with the meanings of the word *pen*, both physical head and 'chief', the 'head' of a kingdom, and of *porthi*, meaning both to nurture and to carry.

8. In the manuscript Dunawd is named again to start the second stanza. I have followed Rowland's suggestion that this was a scribal error and that Unhwch should be named here instead.

11. In the manuscript the last line of the third stanza is missing. The line in the translation is conjectural, based on consistency with the picture of warriors petitioning the leader for gifts in the preceding stanza.

POEMS FROM THE LLYWARCH HEN SAGA

Any historical events that may have been the source of the saga would have taken place in the late 6th century. The poems were composed two or more centuries later, and by various hands. The sequence here has been devised as the clearest for a general reader and should not be taken as a suggestion of the original sequence (if that ever existed). I have noted Rowland's dating of each poem; the source texts are those cited for 'The Fall of Rheged'.

Ifor Williams, on the assumption that Llywarch was also the speaker in the group of poems dealing with his first cousin, Urien of Rheged, suggested that there was an original saga in prose, lost or never recorded, with verse used for dialogue and monologue, and that this told of the fall of Rheged, Llywarch's subsequent wandering herding cattle in poverty, and his settling in Powys, where he and his sons guarded the border against English invaders. Whether such a saga ever existed, the heart of the surviving poems is a situation in which Llywarch as an old man urges son after son to fight heroically, as he once did, and mourns when each is killed.

Invitation to Llanfawr. *EWSP*, p. 414; *CLIH*, p. 21; *PLIH*, st. 218–27. Rowland dates the poem mid to late ninth century. I have omitted the last two stanzas as probable additions from other poems in the saga; the poem itself seems to have been added to earlier Llywarch poems as a link to poems on the fall of Rheged.

Lament for Pyll. *EWSP*, p. 408; *CLIH*, p. 5; *PLIH*, st. 82–92. Rowland dates the poem mid to late ninth century. She states that st. 37 is an interpolation, and I have therefore omitted it.

Exhortation to Maenwyn. *EWSP*, p. 410; *CLIH*, p. 20; *PLIH*, st. 161–168. Rowland dates the poem tenth century. She considers st. 7 a probable interpolation, and I have therefore omitted it. The reference to Maelgwn, presumably Maelgwn Gwynedd, suggests that in one version of the saga Maenwyn had been serving that ruler; historically this would have been impossible, since Maelgwn died in the earlier sixth century.

whetting Maenwyn: a play on words. 'Maen' means stone: to sharpen a stone is impossible, but the warrior can be made eager for battle.

Llywarch and Gwên. *EWSP*, p. 404; *CLIH*, p.1; *PLIH*, st. 54–66. Rowland dates this and the following poem late 8th to mid 9th century.

Lament for Gwên. *EWSP*, p. 406; *CLIH*, p. 3; *PLIH*, st. 67–81.

On the basis of Rowland's comments I have transposed her stanzas 17 and 18 and omitted her stanza 23 as an interpolation.

Complaint in Old Age. *EWSP*, p. 415; *CLIH*, p. 8; *PLIH*, st. 33–53. Rowland dates the poem mid to late 9th century. I have followed her suggestion in transposing stanzas 9 and 10.

POEMS FROM THE HELEDD SAGA

Rowland dates the poems mid to late 9th century, two centuries later than the defeat of Cynddylan, ruler of Powys, by English invaders. She notes that 'available evidence ... strongly suggests that the picture presented ... of Cynddylan's fall has no historical basis, or rather, the picture of the cataclysmic defeat attributed to his reign has its historical basis in another time and place.'

The poems are spoken by Heledd, Cynddylan's sister, after her brothers have been killed in battle near Pengwern, modern Shrewsbury. It is not clear from the surviving poems how Heledd alone survived or why she blames herself for the fate of her family: Rowland notes that the latter must have been central to the story, since it would account for the exceptional use of a woman as the dramatic speaker.

As with the Llywarch Hen poems, I have arranged the poems in a sequence I thought would be helpful for a general reader, and this should not be taken as a suggestion of the original sequence if any. The source texts are two of those used for the preceding sagas.

Lament for Cynddylan. *EWSP*, p. 429; *CLIH*, p. 33. Rowland prints the first stanza separately as a 'prologue' to the whole body of poems. Following her suggestion, I have transposed her stanzas 8 and 9 and omitted stanza 17.

Culhwch warrior: presumably a warrior like Arthur's cousin Culhwch ap Cilydd, whose story was told in the eleventh-century prose tale of 'Culhwch and Olwen' and is included in *The Mabinogion.*

The Eagle of Pengwern. *EWSP*, p. 434; *CLlH*, p. 38. I have followed Rowland's suggestion and transposed her stanzas 40 and 41.

Baschurch. *EWSP*, p. 435; *CLlH*, p. 39.

The Hall of Cynddylan. *EWSP*, p. 431; *CLlH*, p. 35.

Sisters. *EWSP*, p. 444; *CLlH*, p. 43.

Brothers. *EWSP*, p. 440; *CLlH*, p. 44.

Ffreuer. *EWSP*, p. 436; *CLlH*, p. 40.

The White Town. *EWSP*, p. 436; *CLlH*, p. 39.

Heledd Wanderer. *EWSP*, pp. 437–440; *CLlH*, pp. 41–43. In the case of this one poem, I have combined stanzas printed under separate headings by Rowland and Williams, while omitting others on the pages noted. The fragments suggest a single original poem in which Heledd roams the countryside, impoverished, and contrasts her present condition with her past life. Gorwynion is very likely one of Llywarch Hen's sons; if these stanzas were part of the original poem, then Heledd looks back to an earlier time when Llywarch's sons defended Powys. Gyrthmwl and Ercal are place-names; Morial may be a warrior mentioned in *The Gododdin.*

A MISCELLANY OF POEMS

None of the poems have known authors; while most are presumably by professional bards, some may be by monks. I have arranged them in a loosely chronological order (the dates of most are very uncertain), and grouped them to show, in certain cases, similarities in theme and technique.

Song for a Small Boy (*c.* 650?). The source texts are those for *The Gododdin:* Williams, *CA*, LXXXVIII; Jarman, *A*, 103. The poem is the penultimate stanza in the A-text, to which it clearly does not belong. The presumption has been that the scribe found it in the margin of his manuscript and copied it unthinkingly. The use of past tense gives the poem an elegiac tone one would not expect in a 'cradle song', so that its incorporation with other elegies is perhaps not as surprising as has been thought.

Lament for Cynddylan. *EWSP*, p. 174; R. Geraint Gruffydd, 'Marwnad Cynddylan', in Gruffydd ed., *Bardos* (Cardiff, 1982), pp. 10–28. The poem, presumably composed shortly after Cynddylan's death (*c.* 655), pre-dates the Heledd saga that deals with the same tragedy. One or more lines appear to be missing at the beginning: these might have explained the unclear opening stanzas which seem to praise the ruler of Gwynedd. From the place references in the poem, it appears that Cynddylan distinguished himself as king of Powys in cattle-raids to the south as well as in either fighting against or joining forces with the Anglo-Saxons of

Mercia. I have omitted the final two lines (69–70), which Rowland states are perhaps interpolated or corrupt: in translation, they say 'And though God bring me not to doomsday's mount,/ None committed a sin equal to mine', which may have been a later attempt to supply an ending if the original one had been lost.

In Praise of Tenby (9th century). Rachel Bromwich ed., *The Beginnings of Welsh Poetry: Studies by Sir Ifor Williams* (Cardiff, 1980), pp 155–72. I have omitted the final section in Williams' text as apparently unrelated to the poem.

The poem appears to be a *dadolwch*, a plea for reconciliation, but it differs from others of its kind because the lord from whom the poet was estranged, Bleiddudd ab Erbin, has died, and the plea is addressed to his son. The occasion may have been a New Year's feast, since this is frequently mentioned. The reference to a 'cell' the poet often visited indicates that there was a small library in the fortress, or at least a manuscript in Welsh or Latin.

to the Picts: contrasting the contented landsmen with sea-rovers raiding the coast of South Wales; these may have been Norse and Irish as well as Pictish.

Better Dyfed's serf: Deudraeth is in Merioneth; the line praises Tenby in the South by jeering at life in the North.

in each pairing: the warriors were seated two by two.

The Leper of Aber Cuawg (9th century). *EWSP*, p. 448; *CLlH*, p. 23; *PLlH*, st. 1–32.

I have not followed Rowland, who treats this as a 'penitential' poem, in her transposing of the last two stanzas. It strongly resembles some of the Llywarch Hen poems in its dramatization of the unidentified speaker and its use of natural setting and gnomic sayings, and some lines suggest a background story of betrayal and of lost comrades. What is clear is that the speaker is a nobleman suffering from an incurable disease, forced to live in solitude, unable to join his fellows at feasts and in battle.

a house of oak: perhaps an oratory. The meaning of this and the following line is unclear; it may refer to prayers said for lepers, or to the leper's own attempt at devotions.

Winter and Warfare (9th-10th century). *EWSP*, p. 454; *LlDC*, #30; *PLlH*, st. 169–205. Rowland notes (p. 240) that this work 'appears to be more composite and corrupt than most *englynion* poems. At least three poems can be distinguished: the monologue of the warrior, [st.] 1–21; the dialogue of Pelis and the warrior, [st.] 22–29; and the *marwnad* [elegy] of Mechydd, [st.] 31, 32, 34, 36. There is good reason to suppose the first two poems to be related; the relation of the *marwnad* to the others is uncertain. Despite its intrusive material, the poem is very successful on an artistic level'. On the basis of Rowland's observations, I have omitted stanzas 16–19, 30, 33, and 35, and indicated a tripartite division with asterisks to clarify somewhat the poem or poems. The references to Owain of Rheged and Llywarch Hen indicate that it is related to other saga material.

Geraint ab Erbin. *LlDC*, #21, st. 1–9; *EWSP*, p. 457. Rowland dates the poem mid to late 9th century. I have based the translation on Jarman in preference to

Rowland's composite text, but taken her comments on the lack of obvious connection between st. 1–9 and what follows as suggesting a later addition and therefore omitted the subsequent stanzas in Jarman.

The poem may originally have belonged to a saga about Geraint or Arthur. Geraint is presented without the touches of romance he acquires in later tales, but he is linked with Arthur's battles against the Saxons in the southwest of Britain, since Longborth is probably the name of a harbour in Devon.

In Memoriam (10th–11th century). *EWSP*, p. 462; *LlDC*, #34, ll. 43–63. The allusions are all to sixth-century northern British heroes.

Mourning in Maytime (10th–11th century). Marged Haycock ed., *Blodeugerdd Barddas o Ganu Crefyddol Cynnar* (Llandybie, 1994), #16; *EWSP*, p. 203; *LlDC*, #8.

On the basis of the fourth stanza, Rowland considers this a poem about going on pilgrimage to the Holy Land.

Prelude to a Pilgrimage. (10th–11th century) Haycock, #26; *EWSP*, p. 452; *LlDC*, #26. A single sneeze was considered an evil omen, especially in setting out on a journey.

Mountain Snow. (10th–11th century) Kenneth Jackson ed., *Early Welsh Gnomic Poems* (Cardiff, 1935), III.

Riddle. J.G. Evans ed., *The Book of Taliesin* (Llanbedrog, 1910). Answer: the wind. Possibly from the tenth century, this is the sole example of a medieval riddle poem in Welsh. A number of such poems survive in Anglo-Saxon, and like these the Welsh poem may be influenced by continental Latin poetry. I have concluded the poem where it seemed most natural, omitting four garbled lines before the final four.

the five epochs: in medieval thought, these are (1) from the Creation to the Flood, (2) from the Flood to Abraham, (3) from Abraham to David, (4) from David to Israel's captivity, (5) from the captivity to Christ. The sixth and final epoch is from Christ to Doomsday.

The Prophecy of Britain (*c*.930). Ifor Williams ed., *Armes Prydain* (English Version by Rachel Bromwich, Dublin, 1972). For all the prophetic element, the poem is chiefly a protest against the heavy taxes imposed on the Welsh by the English stewards of Cirencester (Caer Geri), located in the Anglo-Saxon kingdom of Wessex.

they: Cynan and Cadwaladr, mentioned by name later, an evocation of two heroes of past struggles with the English. Which Cynan is meant is uncertain, but Cadwaladr is the son of Cadwallon of Gwynedd, who had allied himself with the king of Mercia to defeat Edwin of Northumbria in 633 and had briefly occupied that kingdom for the Welsh. Cadwaladr's death in 681 was seen by the Welsh as the end of British rule outside Wales.

Dublin's men: distinguished from the Irish because of the Norse settlement there. The poet apparently considers them 'Celts', but because of intermarriage, Celts of their own kind.

Clydesmen: the inhabitants of Strathclyde, in southwestern Scotland, which had remained an independent Celtic realm until the early ninth century.

Northmen: the North Britons of earlier centuries.

Myrddin foretells: a reference to other prophetc poems in which Myrddin is the speaker.

Aber Peryddon: its location is uncertain, but from the context it must have been a river-town on the southeastern Welsh border.

Gwrtheyrn of Gwynedd's scavengers: a scornful reference to Welshmen who collaborated with the English. Gwrtheyrn (Vortigern) was a fifth-century Welsh ruler who welcomed the Saxons.

When they purchased Thanet: a reference to the first settlement of Anglo-Saxons in Britain, accusing their leaders Hengist and Horsa of a fraudulent treaty when they gained the island of Thanet in Kent by agreeing to aid the Britons against the Picts and the Irish in the early fifth century.

After secret slaying: probably an allusion to an incident in which Britons, meeting with Anglo-Saxons for a peace talk, were slain with concealed knives.

CaerWynt: Winchester, the capital of Wessex.

Dyfed and Glywysing: southwestern and southeastern kingdoms in Wales, which had co-operated with the English during Alfred's reign and after.

Garmon's kin: Garmon is an Irish saint, and the reference is to the men of Leinster. St Patrick went from Britain to Ireland c404 and brought the Irish Christianity: now the Irish can repay the favour by aiding the Britons.

From Manaw to Llydaw: from Edinburgh to Brittany.

From Dyfed to Thanet: from the southwest coast of Wales to the southeast coast of England.

From Gwawl to Gweryd: from the Roman wall (near Carlisle) in the west to the Firth of Forth in the east. The poet is invoking the memory of ancient British rule over the north, stressing it by the allusion to Yrechwydd.

God's princes: the line seems to refer to bitter conflicts between the Celtic and English churches.

Cynan will make peace: an allusion to a lost story of a quarrel between the two heroes.

Sandwich: a port in Kent where Anglo-Saxons landed and were victorious in the fifth century.

Benediction. Haycock, #5; *LIDC*, #9.

The world's three well-springs: perhaps the sun, the moon, and the ocean.

II. THE POETS OF THE PRINCES (*c.* 1100–*c.* 1285)

MEILYR BRYDYDD (fl. 1100–1140)

Meilyr the Poet, the earliest known bard to use the techniques of the *Gogynfeirdd*, became chief poet at the court of Gruffudd ap Cynan (1081–1137), and an elegy for Gruffudd is one of his three surviving poems. Gruffudd, of Norse as well as Welsh ancestry, succeeded after several failures in returning from exile in Ireland, conquering the kingdom of Gwynedd, and establishing that kingdom as the dominant one in Wales for the following centuries. Meilyr's son and grandsons were also court bards of Gwynedd: a line of poets and warriors thus served, for a century, a line of rulers. As noted in the Introduction, there is a traditional belief in Irish influence on Welsh poetry as a result of Gruffudd's exile and return, and it may be through Meilyr that techniques learned from the Irish were used in developing the 'new style' of the court bards in the twelfth century.

Poem on his Death-Bed. J.E. Caerwyn Williams ed., *Gwaith Meilyr Brydydd a'i Ddisgynyddion* (Cardiff, 1994), #4; Catherine A. McKenna ed., *The Medieval Welsh Religious Lyric: Poems of the Gogynfeirdd, 1137–1282* (Belmont, MA, 1991), #1.

May I be in that dwelling: a petition to be buried on Bardsey Island (Enlli).

GWALCHMAI AP MEILYR (fl. 1130–1180)

Meilyr's son was court bard to Owain Gwynedd (*c.* 1100–70), son of Gruffudd ap Cynan and ruler of Gwynedd. Owain was, to say the least, strong-willed in building his own power and that of his kingdom: he drove his brother Cadwaladr into exile in England while gaining temporary control of western mid-Wales, and held his brother-in-law, Madog ap Maredudd of Powys, in check; he joined his nephew, Rhys ap Gruffudd, ruler of South Wales, in organizing Welsh opposition to the Anglo-Norman king, Henry II. Gwalchmai may have become estranged from Owain during their final years; he wrote a eulogy and an elegy for Madog ap Maredudd, who fought against Owain, and there is no evidence that he wrote an elegy for Owain.

Exultation. Williams, *GMB*, #9. Lacunae in the manuscripts make translation of some passages impossible; these omissions are indicated by asterisks.

The poem is called 'Gorhoffedd', 'Boast', in the manuscript, and Thomas Parry concluded from this and several similar poems that 'there was in this period a kind of poetry called "Boasting" or "Vaunting", which contained, among other things, amatory verse – probably a kind of playful miscellany'. But no other long poem in this period centres in quite this way on the poet's eulogizing not of others but himself and his experiences of nature, war, and women. The poem contains references to Owain Gwynedd's battles in the south as well as the north, possibly allusions to events between the death of Henry I in 1135 and the accession of Henry II in 1154, years in which Owain and other Welsh rulers rose against the Anglo-Norman lordships that the first Henry had established and succeeded in restoring the kingdom of Deheubarth and regaining northern territory as far as Chester.

bane of Edwin and Angles: probably a symbolic allusion to Edwin, king of Northumbria, who conquered the Chester plain and occupied Anglesey in the early seventh century.

Pledges are his: presumably treaties between Owain and lords in southwestern Scotland.

The Battle of Tâl Moelfre. Williams, *GMB*, #8, p. 176. It is debatable whether this and the following poem are sections of a single long poem, which is the way they are presented in Williams' edition.

Henry II launched a campaign against Owain Gwynedd in 1157, combining a land attack aided by Owain's exiled brother Cadwaladr and Madog of Powys with a naval assault by ships that sailed from Pembrokeshire to North Wales. Tâl Moelfre is a headland on the north coast of Anglesey; the poem celebrates a victory over raiding parties from the ships. Despite this triumphal poem, Owain eventually paid homage to Henry and remained fairly quiet until resuming hostilities in 1165.

Plea for Reconciliation. Williams, *GMB*, #8, p. 177.

Gwalchmai's Dream. Williams, *GMB*, #12.
The poem seems much more 'private' than other devotional poems of the period. Whatever the dream or vision may have been, the poet laments three deaths – of Madog, ruler of Powys, of the poet's son Goronwy who was one of Owain Gwynedd's household guard, and of Genilles, referred to earlier in 'Exultation' and presumably the poet's wife – before turning to acknowledge what is required of him as a Christian.

OWAIN CYFEILIOG (c. 1130–97)

Owain, prince of Cyfeiliog, the western region of Powys, was the son-in-law of Owain Gwynedd and the nephew of Madog ap Maredudd. He founded the Cistercian monastery of Ystrad Marchell and retired there in 1195.

The Drinking-Horn. Gruffydd Aled Williams ed., 'Canu Owain Cyfeiliog', in *Gwaith Llywelyn Fardd I ac Eraill* (Cardiff, 1994), #14. I have ventured to place ll.13–14 and 16 in this edition after l.8 in the translation, since they seem introductory to the passing around of the horn, and to omit l.15, which despite editorial attempts to amend and explain it, seems to have strayed in from a love poem. The line by itself makes most sense as 'full of yearning for my beautiful maiden of the hue of the ninth wave', but it is hard to see how this would fit into the surrounding lines.

Williams believes the poem was actually composed by Cynddelw, though he concedes there may have been collaboration between poet and prince, and he elsewhere describes the horn in detail, stating that the work 'was composed in honour of members of Owain's war-band following their return from a successful expedition to Maelor in north-east Wales in 1156 to free Owain's brother, Meurig ap Gruffudd, from prison ... The poem's conception is unique in the context of the Welsh poetry of its day: it consists of a dramatic representation of a feast held at Owain's court at Welshpool, in which Owain greets a servant commanding him to offer the *Hirlas* drinking horn to each hero in turn.' ('The Feasting Aspects of *Hirlas Owain*', in *Ildánach Ildirech: A Festschrift for Proinsias Mac Cana*, edited by John Carey, John T. Koch, and Pierre-Yves Lambert [Andover & Aberystwyth, 1999], pp. 290–1.

If the poem frequently reminds one of Aneirin, it is by intention. Owain sees himself and his warriors in terms of the earlier culture, and deliberately echoes and alludes to *The Gododdin*. The last section of the poem strikes me as curiously rambling, and I cannot help thinking that it sounds very much like a man who has drunk a bit too much. Such dramatic realism would be untypical for a poem at this period, but so, as Williams has commented, is the 'element of bantering humour … reminiscent surely of festive activity', and if he is right and the poem was in fact composed as a dramatic monologue by Cynddelw (or even if Owain himself composed it), then why not this final touch?

HYWEL AB OWAIN GWYNEDD (*c.* 1140–1170)

The illegitimate son of Owain Gwynedd and an Irishwoman named Pyfog, he took a leading role in his father's struggles with other Welsh rulers and with the Anglo-Normans. Though an exact chronology cannot be established, it may be Hywel who was chiefly responsible for the beginnings of Welsh love poetry.

In Summer. Kathleen Anne Bramley ed., 'Gwaith Hywel ab Owen Gwynedd', in *Gwaith Llywelyn Fardd I ac Eraill* (Cardiff, 1994), #7.

The Chosen One. *GLLF,* #8.

Complaint. *GLLF,* #9.

Desire. *GLLF,* #10.

Rejection. *GLLF,* #11.

The Battle of Tâl Moelfre. *GLLF,* #12. See the note on Gwalchmai's poem. Hywel fought beside his father in the battle, and is surely the beardless warrior of the final line.

Exultation. *GLLF,* #6. This and the following poem have usually been treated by editors as a single long poem, but I agree with J. Lloyd-Jones in *The Court Poets of the Welsh Princes* (London, 1948) that 'we have in the two portions a fusion of two distinct and independent poems, one in praise of country and the other a forthright love poem' (p. 22).
  Despite the similarities between this and Gwalchmai's 'Exultation', the poems seem to me very different: Hywel has, as Gwalchmai does not, a central focus, love of the poet's homeland of Gwynedd. The geographical references suggest that the speaker is in southern Scotland, possibly on the mission to Dumbarton mentioned by Gwalchmai, and has arrived there in haste from the battlefields of Powys.

In Praise of Fair Women. The opening lines seem to be Hywel's salute to his father and king, Owain Gwynedd, as he begins his impudent song at the court.
  From Caer's portals: from the northeast to the southern coast of Wales.

PERYF AP CEDIFOR (fl. 1170)

Lament for Hywel. Morfydd E. Owen ed., 'Gwaith Peryf ap Cedifor', in *GLLF,* #19. Hywel was killed at Pentraeth in Anglesey by his half-brothers Dafydd and Rhodri. The latter's mother was Owain Gwynedd's second wife Cristin: Peryf puns bitterly on her name, and refers to her sixth-century ancestor, Brochfael of Powys, with a jeering twist of sound and sense that English cannot do justice to:'Brochfaeliaid brychfoelion'. Peryf and his brothers defended Hywel, and at least three of them were killed with him.

CYNDDELW BRYDYDD MAWR (fl. 1155–1200).

Cynddelw was called 'the Great Poet' originally, it seems, for his size, but it became a term of praise with which, judging by the tone of certain works, he was in full agreement. He apparently began his career as court poet to Madog ap Maredudd, king of Powys, but after Madog's death he composed eulogies for most of the notable Welsh lords of the later twelfth century.

To a Girl. Nerys Ann Jones and Ann Parry Owen eds., *Gwaith Cynddelw Brydydd Mawr* (Cardiff, 1991), I, #4. The final line is the first recorded use of 'Eiddig', meaning 'The Jealous One', for the husband of a woman loved by the poet.

In Praise of Madawg ap Maredudd. *GCBM*, I, #1. Madog was the last of his line to rule the whole of Powys, succeeding his father in 1132. He was married to Owain Gwynedd's sister, and was the father-in-law of Rhys ap Gruffudd, prince of Deheubarth. Madog, whose lands bordered England, opposed Owain Gwynedd's attempts to gain control of North Wales, and he joined Henry II in his campaign against Gwynedd, probably guided by the determination to retain Powys' independence, which ended soon after his death in 1160.

   nine-metred verse: the metre is based on a nine-syllable line.

   Cadfan's heir: see the Glossary. This may be an oblique suggestion that Madog, not Owain, deserved to rule Gwynedd

   And I, bards, within: an assertion of Cynddelw's rank as chief bard, with the pride characteristic of much of his work.

A Love Poem for Efa. *GCBM*, I, #5. I have ventured to translate by assuming a scribal error in l. 129: *pell*, 'distant', rather than *pall*, 'tent, mantle'. The change gives a reading consistent with the rest of the line and the rhetorical pattern of the following lines, and a more plausible reading than editorial attempts to explain the text as it stands.

   Efa was the daughter of Madog; the Llywelyn referred to in the final stanza was Madog's son. The poem refers at one point to danger faced by Madog and his sons, and possibly to the death of one of Efa's brothers, perhaps in battle against Owain Gwynedd. Cynddelw evokes by allusion the poetry of Taliesin, referring to Cynfarch, father of Urien of Rheged, and Owain, Urien's son. Though Hywel ab Owain Gwynedd in one poem also addresses his horse, this poem makes the first recorded use in Welsh poetry of a *llatai*, a love messenger, a common device in later love lyrics which dwell far more than Cynddelw does on the qualities of the messenger itself.

Lament for Madawg ap Maredudd. *GCBM*, I, #7.

The Fall of Powys. *GCBM*, I, #8. After Madog died and his heir Llywelyn was slain in battle, Powys was divided among Madog's surviving sons and nephews. The poem recalls earlier victorious battles before lamenting Llywelyn's defeat and death.

In Praise of Owain Gwynedd. *GCBM*, II, #1. The key points of Owain's reign were noted in the comments on Gwalchmai's poems. This eulogy refers to triumphs in both North and South Wales, probably in battles against Henry II after 1164. The poem seems to assert Owain's right to rule all Wales, especially in its omission of the role played by Rhys ap Gruffudd in the south.

dragon of the east: Henry II of England.

Brynaich's men: an evocation of the sixth-century battles against the Bernicians recorded in Taliesin's and Aneirin's poems.

As at Baddon: an allusion to the great victory of the British against the Anglo-Saxons at Mount Badon c519, traditionally associated with Arthur.

Lament for his Son. *GCBM*, I, #30.

Petition for Reconciliation. *GCBM*, II, #10. Rhys ap Gruffudd participated with his brothers in the revolt of South Wales against the Anglo-Normans and eventually became the leader of the resistance. He made peace with Henry II in 1158, accepting the title of 'the Lord Rhys' instead of 'Prince of Deheubarth', but he continued the attempt to regain his power. In 1164 Rhys again led Deheubarth against its Anglo-Norman overlords, and was joined not only by his uncle, Owain Gwynedd, but also by the rulers of Powys, Madog ap Maradudd's sons and his nephew Owain Cyfeiliog. Although the alliance was soon ended by mutual distrust, Henry's invasion of 1165 was forced to turn back, and Rhys consolidated his control of South Wales. After Owain Gwynedd's death in 1170, Rhys dominated relations with England: he made peace again with Henry, led a group of Welsh lords to confer with Henry as their overlord at Oxford in 1177, and remained loyal until Henry's death in 1189, after which he resumed warfare against the border lords until his own death in 1197.

Poem on his Death Bed. *GCBM*, II, #18; McKenna, *Medieval Welsh Religious Lyric*, #3.

GRUFFUDD AP GWRGENAU (fl. 1200).

Lament for Gruffudd ap Cynan. Morfydd E. Owen ed., 'Gwaith Gruffudd ap Gwrgenau', in *Gwaith Llywelyn Fardd I ac Eraill* (Cardiff, 1994), #31. Gruffudd ap Cynan, a grandson of Owain Gwynedd, entered the abbey of Aberconwy some time before his death there in 1200, and this perhaps explains why the elegy, unusually for the period, begins with a lengthy homily.

Lament for his Comrades. *GLLF*, #32. The only one of the companions who can be identified is Gwilym Rhyfel, a fellow-poet.

LLYWARCH AP LLYWELYN (Prydydd y Moch) (fl. 1173–1220).
Why Llywarch acquired the nickname meaning 'Poet of the Pigs' is not known. Younger than Cynddelw, he was the court poet of Gwynedd from the time of Owain Gwynedd's death through the rise of Llywelyn ab Iorwerth..

A Love Poem for Gwenlliant. Elin M. Jones ed., *Gwaith Llywarch ap Llywelyn* (Cardiff, 1991), #14. As in Cynddelw's poem to Efa, the poet uses a horse as love-messenger, and the mixture of elements in the poem suggests the influence of Gwalchmai's 'Exultation'. Gwenlliant was probably the daughter of Hywel ab Iorwerth, who governed Caerleon during the late twelfth century. The poem outlines a journey southwards, and may refer to the death of Owain Cyfeiliog.

Ordeal by Hot Iron. *GLl*, #15. Elin Jones describes the ordeal as follows: 'The accused, after fasting three days, would pick up a piece of hot iron in his hand, take three steps, and put it down. Then his hand was bandaged and left for three days before being examined. If the wound was clean and healing, he was judged not guilty; if it was festering, he was guilty.' The iron was blessed by a priest before the ordeal. It is not known whether Llywarch's own experience was the basis of the poem.

Admonition. *GLl*, #2. Dafydd, one of the sons of Owain Gwynedd, played a leading part in the revolt against Henry II in 1165, and in the struggles with his brothers that weakened Gwynedd after his father's death. He died in 1203. Because Dafydd held as his inheritance the region that included Aberffraw Llywarch sees him as the rightful ruler of Wales. Whatever Llywarch may have done that offended Dafydd, he states in very strong terms what he sees as the proper relationship between prince and chief poet.

In Praise of Llywelyn ab Iorwerth. *GLl*, #20. Owain Gwynedd's grandson, known as Llywelyn the Great, brought leadership to Wales after the bitter internal struggles in both north and south at the end of the twelfth century. By 1199 Llywelyn had defeated his uncles and ruled all of Gwynedd; in 1216; after reconciling the heirs of the Lord Rhys and winning back much of South Wales from Anglo-Norman lords, he was recognized by other Welsh rulers as overlord of independent Wales until his death in 1240. He married King John of England's natural daughter, Joan, in 1205, and joined John in an expedition against Scotland in 1209, but was in conflict with him after 1210. Llywelyn endeavoured to pass on his realm undivided to his eldest son Dafydd, but Dafydd was unable to control the other Welsh rulers and the unity of Wales was destroyed once more by 1247.

Pledge to England he spurns: Llywelyn had in fact submitted to John early in his reign, but he joined the English barons after their revolt against John's rule that culminated in Magna Carta.

EINION AP GWALCHMAI (fl. 1203–23).
Son of Gwalchmai, grandson of Meilyr Brydydd, he was for a time court poet in Gwynedd, but turned to composing devotional poems and may have become a monk.

Lament for Nest. Williams, *Gwaith Meilyr Brydydd*, #26. Nest was the daughter of Hywel of Tywyn, in Merioneth.

like Elifri: he is mentioned as Arthur's head groom in the medieval tale of Geraint, but the allusion is not clear.

Prayer. Williams, *GMB*, #27

MADOG AP GWALLTER (fl. 1250).

Not a court poet, though he uses the same techniques, but a Franciscan friar. Andrew Breeze has noted that his nativity poem 'echoes other thirteenth-century poems associated with the friars' in the 'tenderness' of its treatment and the emphasis on the humbleness of Christ's birth *(Medieval Welsh Literature*, p. 58).

The Nativity. Rhian M. Andrews ed., 'Gwaith Madog ap Gwallter', in *Gwaith Bleddyn Fardd ac Eraill* (Cardiff, 1996), #32.

BLEDDYN FARDD (fl. 1257–85).

Lament for Llywelyn ap Gruffudd. Rhian M. Andrews ed., *Gwaith Bleddyn Fardd ac Eraill* (Cardiff, 1996), #50. Llywelyn was the grandson of Llywelyn the Great and shared his ideal of a united Wales. He dispossessed his two brothers and became sole ruler of Gwynedd in 1255, and he regained the territory in the north and south that had been lost after his grandfather's death. At a council of Welsh rulers in 1258 Llywelyn was recognized as 'Prince of Wales', a new title that was accepted by the English king, Henry III, in 1267. During the following decade the enmity of Llywelyn's brother Dafydd and of Welsh rulers who did not wish to accept Llywelyn as their overlord, the strong determination of Edward I, who became king of England in 1272, and Llywelyn's attempts to expand his domain and refusal to do homage to Edward led to the English invasion of 1277, in which Llywelyn was defeated and the unity he had striven for was again broken. Dafydd had aided Edward against his brother, but was dissatisfied with his territorial rewards and was joined by Llywelyn in revolt in 1282. After considerable losses in central Wales but successful resistance in the north, Llywelyn journeyed to lead the armies of mid-Wales: he was killed on a scouting expedition during a battle at Builth, 11 December 1282. Although Llywelyn is called 'our last prince' by the Welsh and for most historians his death marks the Conquest of Wales, his brother Dafydd continued the struggle until he was captured by hostile Welshmen and given up for English trial and execution at Shrewsbury in June of 1283. In 1301 Edward's eldest son, who became Edward II, was given the title 'Prince of Wales'.

Bleddyn Fardd's elegy stresses Llywelyn's dominion over all Wales. Present also are parallels between Llywelyn and Jesus Christ.

like Priam: the significance of the comparison lies in the medieval belief that Priam's fallen kingdom of Troy was renewed after many years by one of his descendants, Brutus, who founded the kingdom of Britain.

Lament for Gruffudd's Three Sons. *GBF*, #54. Unlike the previous poem, this elegy expresses a sense of guilt for the constant warfare that had marked the era, and of a Wales completely fallen now that the three princes of Gwynedd are dead. Owain Goch ap Gruffudd was the eldest son; after Llywelyn had defeated him in 1255, he imprisoned him until 1277.

GRUFFUDD AB YR YNAD COCH (fl. 1282).

Lament for Llywelyn ap Gruffudd. Rhian M. Andrews and Catherine McKenna eds. 'Gwaith Llywelyn ap Gruffudd', in *GBF*, #36; Gwyn Thomas ed., *Llywelyn 1282* (Gregynog, 1982). This elegy, so unrestrained in its sense of loss, its vision of the end of the world now that Llywelyn has fallen, must have expressed at least as much as Bleddyn Fardd's quieter, more resigned poem the feelings of many Welshmen at the time. As Glyn Roberts writes, 'in the long story of Wales, the fall of Llywelyn ap Gruffudd in 1282 is one of those historical turning points at which history really turned' (*Wales through the Ages*, p. 129). In the last part of the elegy, the poet plays bitterly with the two meanings of *pen*, 'head' and 'leader': Llywelyn's head was cut off and exhibited by King Edward's orders in London.

till the eighteen were slain: the men killed when Llywelyn's scouting party was overtaken by English raiders.

till he left Emrais: a reference to Llywelyn's fatal journey from Snowdonia to mid-Wales.

Meditation. *GBF*, #42. The poem has usually been attributed to Elidir Sais (c. 1195–1246), but the present edition makes a convincing case for Gruffudd ab yr Ynad Coch. If it is indeed his, and it is Llywelyn ap Gruffudd who is referred to in the poem, this makes a somber sequel to the preceding elegy.

III. THE POETS OF THE GENTRY (c. 1285–c. 1525)

The following abbreviations are used for texts frequently cited:

BBB   *Blodeugerdd Barddas o'r Bedwaredd Ganrif ar Ddeg*, edited by Dafydd Johnston (Swansea, 1989).

BYU   *Barddoniaeth Yr Uchelwyr*, edited by D.J. Bowen (Cardiff, 1959).

DGA   *Dafydd ap Gwilym Apocrypha*, edited by Helen Fulton (Llandysul, 1996).

DGG   *Cywyddau Dafydd ap Gwilym a'i Gyfoeswyr*, edited by Thomas Roberts and Ifor Williams (Cardiff, 1935).

IGE   *Cywyddau Iolo Goch ac Eraill*, edited by Henry Lewis, Thomas Roberts, and Ifor Williams (Cardiff, 1937).

OBWV   *The Oxford Book of Welsh Verse*, edited by Thomas Parry (Oxford, 1962).

IORWERTH FYCHAN (fl. 1290)

A Love Poem for Gweirfyl. Christine James ed., 'Gwaith Iorwerth Fychan', in *Gwaith Bleddyn Fardd ac Eraill* (Cardiff, 1996), #29.

GRUFFUDD AP DAFYDD AP TUDUR (fl. 1300)

The Silent Girl. Dafydd Johnston ed., *Gwaith Gruffudd ap Dafydd ap Tudur ac Eraill* (Aberystwyth, 1995), #4.

IORWERTH BELI (fl. 1315)

Complaint against the Bishop of Bangor. R. Iestyn Daniel ed., 'Gwaith Iorwerth Beli', in *GGDT*, #15; *BBB*, #2. The bishop of Bangor from 1309 to 1327 was Anian Sais, i.e., Anian the Englishman, perhaps referring to his mixed parentage or his fluency in the language, and it is likely that he was the subject of this complaint for patronizing musicians at the expense of the traditional poets. (Iorwerth cites Llywach ap Llywelyn, Cynddelw, Gwilym Rhyfel, and Dafydd Benfras as distinguished predecessors). The poem makes plain the situation of the highest class of poets after 1282, dependent now on the patronage of the higher clergy and the gentry. Tudur Wion, also called Tutcyn derisively, is not otherwise known, but was clearly regarded by the poet as an inept Welsh-speaking bard, appointed because he knew English to be the leader of the musicians.

GRONW GYRIOG (fl. 1320)

Lament for Gwenhwyfar. W. Dyfed Rowlands and Ann Parry Owen eds., *Gwaith Gronw Gyriog ac Eraill* (Aberystwyth, 1997), #2.

The burial in the Franciscan priory at Llan-faes, near Beaumaris on Anglesey, was not unusual at this period for a woman who has been identified as probably the daughter and the wife of powerful noblemen of Powys.

DAFYDD AP GWILYM (fl. 1340–70)

A member of one of the most important families in South Wales, he was probably born at Brogynin in the parish of Llanbadarn Fawr, near modern Aberystwyth, and buried at the monastery of Strata Florida. His uncle, Llywelyn ap Gwilym, was Sub-Constable of Newcastle Emlyn in 1343. Little is known of his life, though the poems have caused much biographical speculation: they show, at least, that he travelled widely through Wales and had a considerable acquaintance with noblemen and lords, as well as women, in many regions. No chronological ordering of the poems is possible, and therefore the sequence of my selection is arbitrary except for taking literally the references to old age in the final group. (It should be remembered that old age at the time could mean over fifty years old.)

The Girls of Llanbadarn. Thomas Parry ed., *Gwaith Dafydd ap Gwilym* (Cardiff, 1952), #48; Rachel Bromwich ed., *Selected Poems of Dafydd ap Gwilym* (London, 1985), #38; Alan Llwyd ed., *50 o Gywyddau Dafydd ap Gwilym* (Swansea, 1980), p. 25.

A Celebration of Summer. Parry, #27; Bromwich, #4.

The Rattle Bag. Parry, #125; Llwyd, p.84.
The bag, made of hide, filled with stones, and carried on a pole, was used to frighten wild animals away from the sheep.

In a Tavern. Parry, #124; Bromwich, #40; Llwyd, p. 78.

Reproach to his Penis. Dafydd Johnston ed., *Canu Maswedd yr Oesoedd Canol* (Cardiff, 1991), #1.

The Skylark. Parry, #114; Bromwich, #23.

The Mass of the Grove. Parry, #122; Bromwich, #24; Llwyd, p. 55.

Morfudd's Embrace. Parry, #53; Llwyd, p. 70.

A Simile for Morfudd. Parry, #42; Bromwich, #8; Llwyd, p. 22.

Morfudd and Dyddgu. Parry, #79; Bromwich, #14; Llwyd, p. 103.
Dyddgu, a nobleman's daughter, is praised in nine of Dafydd's poems, in one of which he also speaks of wooing two other women as well as Morfudd..

The Wind. Parry, #117; Bromwich, #29; Llwyd, p. 155.
   the Hunchback: Morfudd's husband, called by Dafydd *Bwa Bach*, 'the little hunchback'.

The Magpie. Parry, #63; Bromwich, #25; Llwyd, p.52, p. 84. Rachel Bromwich notes that 'the Magpie's flaunted domesticity is a symbol of all the conventional social values on which Dafydd claims to have turned his back ... magpies pair for life and the male does in fact assist in building the nest.'

Morfudd Grown Old. Parry, #139; Bromwich, #17; Llwyd, p.89, p. 111.

Love's Journey. Parry, #83; Bromwich, #35.
In *Mawl a'i Gyfeillion* (Swansea, 2000), Professor R. M. Jones argues convincingly that the poem is by implication a kind of elegy for Morfudd, and quotes Professor R. Geraint Gruffudd in support: 'The image evoked is that of Dafydd searching relentlessly throughout Wales (although most desperately on his home ground) for some remembrance of Morfudd, haunted all the while by recollections of expulsion from Eden, and by intimation of final condemnation' (p. 135). The place-names that have been identified are in mid-Wales, near Dafydd's birthplace and presumably Morfudd's home.

The Ruin. Parry, #144; Bromwich, #49; Llwyd, p. 118.

GRUFFUDD AB ADDA (fl. 1340–70)
The Maypole. *BBB*, #45; *DGG*, lxv.

The Thief of Love. *DGG*, lxvi.

GRUFFUDD GRYG (fl. 1355–1380)
The April Moon. Johnston, *BBB*, #39; *DGG*, lxxiv.
The poet's voyage to the shrine of St. James at Compostella in Spain, at some time during the reign of King Henry of Castile (1369–79), is interrupted by bad weather.

Lament for Rhys ap Tudur. *BBB*, #41; *DGG*, lxxx. A fictitious elegy, a form sometimes used for eulogy, since Rhys, whose family was loyal to Richard II, was executed for his part in Owain Glyndŵr's rising in 1411, and Gruffudd Gryg had died several decades earlier. Rhys held the office of Forester of Snowdon by royal appointment.

Dafydd's Wounds. Parry, *Gwaith Dafydd ap Gwilym*, #147.
This is the first poem in a bardic contention between the two poets.

The Fickle Girl. *DGG*, lxxxiii; *DGA*, #15.
    the course that the man: a proverbial example of how not to catch a cow. The girl has been foolish to break with him before she is sure of happiness with her new lover.

The Yew Tree. *BBB*, #42; *DGG*, lxxxii.

Christ the King. *BYU*, #2; *DGA*, #51.

MADOG BENFRAS (fl. 1340–1360)
The Saltman. *BBB*, #43; *DGG*, lxx.

IORWERTH AB Y CYRIOG (fl. 1350–1370)
The Brooch. Rowlands and Owen, 'Gwaith Iorwerth ab y Cyriog', in *Gwaith Gronw Geiriog*, #5; *BBB*, #47.
    Precious stones were believed to have protective and curative powers.
    Myddfai: the Physicians of Myddfai, in Carmarthenshire, were a famous thirteenth-century family of doctors whose manuscripts contain instructions for the diagnosis and treatment of various ailments.

LLYWELYN GOCH AP MEURIG HEN (fl. 1350–90)
The Coal-Tit. Dafydd Johnston ed., *Gwaith Llywelyn Goch ap Meurig Hen* (Aberystwyth, 1998), #9; *OBWV*, #50.

Lament for Lleucu Llwyd. Johnston, *GLIG*, #12; *BBB*, #61. A striking use for elegy of the conventional situation in which a lover outside addresses his beloved within the house.

The Snow. Johnston, *GLIG*, #8; *BBB*, #60. A eulogy of the poet's nephews Hywel and Meurig, sons of Meurig Fychan. Their houses were at Cae Gwrgenau in Merionethshire.

Confession. Johnston, *GLIG*, #7. The first stanza ends with a vision of the Last Judgment; the three hosts are the saved, the damned, and the sinners who must suffer in Purgatory before they may enter heaven.

IOLO GOCH (fl. 1345–98)
Bard and Beard. Dafydd Johnston ed., *Iolo Goch: Poems* (Llandysul, 1993), #25; D. R. Johnston ed., *Gwaith Iolo Goch* (Cardiff, 1988), xxv; *IGE*, ii.

The Ploughman. Johnston, *IGP*, #28; *GIG*, xxviii; *IGE*, xxvii. Johnston comments that 'the deeply conservative social philosophy expressed in this poem is probably a response to the disturbances of the Peasants' Revolt of 1381.' Chaucer gave a similarly idealized eulogy in the prologue to *The Canterbury Tales*.

Portrait of a Maiden. Johnston, *IGP*, #24; *GIG*, xxiv; *IGE*, i.

Lament for Dafydd ap Gwilym. Johnston, *IGP*, #21; *GIG*, xxi; *IGE*, xiv. Perhaps a fictitious elegy.

The Ship. Johnston, *IGP*, #33; *GIG*, xxxiii; *IGE*, xxv. The poem is addressed to Rhys ap Robert of y Cilmael, near Abergele, who was a relative of Iolo, sheriff of Flintshire in the 1350s, and died in 1377.

The Horse. Johnston, *IGP*, #13; *GIG*, xiii; *IGE*, xviii. Ithel ap Robert of Coedymynydd, near Carwys in North Wales, was Iolo's third cousin and Archdeacon of St Asaph. The places named are on the road from Denbigh to Iolo's home in Llechryd.

A Pilgrimage to Saint David's. Johnston, *IGP*, #29; *GIG*, xxix. Two pilgrimages to St David's were usually considered equal to one to Rome and three equal to one to Jerusalem. Iolo uses legendary material from both an earlier life of David and oral traditions.

 the black Lenten fast: the early Christian requirement to abstain from both meat and fish during Lent was modified in later centuries to allow fish to be eaten.

Sir Hywel of the Axe. Johnston, *IGP*, #2; *GIG*, ii; *IGE*, ix. Hywel ap Gruffudd was knighted and appointed constable of Cricieth castle for his exploits with a battle-axe at the battle of Poitiers in 1536, and died in 1381. The poem draws on the earlier medieval tale, *The Dream of Macsen Wledig,* in which a Roman emperor dreams of the court at Caernarfon.

Lament for Ithael ap Robert. Johnston, *IGP*, #15; *GIG*, xv; *IGE*, viii. The opening lines refer to an earthquake in 1382 and employ metaphorically the symptoms of pneumonic plague, possibly the cause of Ithel's death.

Sycharth. Johnston, *IGP*, #10; *GIG*, x; *IGE*, xiii. Owain Glyndŵr (*c*.1354–*c*.1416) was a direct descendant of the rulers of Powys and Deheubarth and less directly related to the former royal line of Gwynedd, the basis on which he was proclaimed Prince of Wales after his rising in 1400. The poem was composed some years earlier, after Owain had attended the Inns of Court in London and served in Richard II's invasion of Scotland in 1385. The great wooden manor-house in Powys, compared by Iolo to St Patrick's Cathedral in Dublin and a new cloister at Westminster Abbey for being in the latest architectural style, and called by Johnston 'a resonant symbol of the ideal social order', was burned down during Owain's war with Henry IV.

Lament for Llywelyn Goch ap Meurig Hen. Johnston, *IGP*, #22; *GIG*, xxii; *IGE*, xv. On the basis of Iolo's elegy, Llywelyn may well have equalled Dafydd ap

Gwilym as a love poet, but only the two poems to Lleucu Llwyd translated in this book survive.

DAFYDD BACH AP MADOG WLADAIDD (fl. 1380–1390)

Christmas Revels. R. Iestyn Daniel ed., *Gwaith Dafydd Bach ap Madog Wladaidd 'Sypyn Cyfeiliog' a Llywelyn ab y Moel* (Aberystwyth, 1998), #1; Johnston, *BBB*, #63.

The poem is a eulogy of Dafydd ap Cadwaladr, whose principal court was at Bachelldre in Montgomeryshire.

three stag lifetmes: the stag was thought to be a very long-lived animal.

GRUFFUDD AP MAREDUDD (fl. 1350–90)

Although he was a contemporary of Dafydd ap Gwilym and Iolo Goch, it would seem from his surviving poems that Gruffudd used exclusively the verse-forms and style inherited from the *Gogynfeirdd*.

Lament for Gwenhwyfar. *BBB*, #67. Because of the length and nature of the poem, I have thought it helpful to divide and number its four basic 'movements'. Even more than some poems of the *Gogynfeirdd*, the elegy is best read as though it were a musical composition in its statement and variation of a few basic themes. D. Myrddin Lloyd has remarked that 'no translation or comment can begin to convey the surpassing quality of the diction, the smoothness and simplicity attained by expert control of intricate metrical patterns, suffused by intense feeling. Seldom has the horror of early death been expressed with such skill and anguish combined, and this poem ranks high among the finest achievements of Welsh verse' (*Guide II*, p. 38).

GRUFFUDD LLWYD (fl. 1380–1420)

In Defense of Praise. Johnston, *BBB*, #80. Gruffudd exemplifies his defense by eulogizing the brothers Hywel and Meurig, sons of Meurig Fychan, praised in Llywelyn Goch's 'The Snow'.

Sending the Sun to Morgannwg. *BBB*, #82; *DGA*, #42.

Owain Glyndŵr. *BBB*, #78; *IGE*, xlii. The poem was obviously composed some time before Owain's rising in 1400, but expresses some of the discontent in Wales that led to it. Owain's father-in-law, Sir Dafydd Hamner, a judge in Richard II's courts, and Sir Grigor Sais, a notable soldier from Flintshire, were the only Welsh knights at the time. For Sir Hywel of the Axe, who died in 1381, see Iolo Goch's earlier eulogy. Caw was a legendary hero of northern Britain; Brân, Constantine, and Arthur were all treated as conquerors of the Romans in Geoffrey of Monmouth's twelfth-century history of the kings of Britain.

POEMS OF UNKNOWN OR UNCERTAIN AUTHORSHIP

A number of these poems from the later fourteenth and the fifteenth century were once attributed to Dafydd ap Gwilym but excluded by Sir Thomas Parry from his edition. The first three are now generally accepted as probably Dafydd's. 'The Skull' was usually attributed to Llywelyn Goch but has been excluded from Dafydd Johnston's edition. 'The Virgin Mary' was at one time attributed to Iolo Goch; 'A Visit to Flint' has been claimed for both Lewys Glyn Cothi and Tudur Penllyn; 'Lent' is often assigned to the fifteenth-century poet Bedo Aeddrem.

The Snow. *BYU*, #24; *DGA*, #41.

The Bower of Broom. *BYU*, #25; *DGA, #24. On Dyfed*: in 'Manawydan Son of Llyr', one of the tales in the collection known as *The Mabinogion*, a fall of mist comes over the region rendering everything invisible.

The Stars. *DGG*, xl; Parry, *OBWV*, #64; Fulton, *DGA*, #40.
Bright scales: in the tale of 'Lludd and Llefelys' contained in *The Mabinogion*, Lludd traps fighting dragons in a silk covering and hides them in a stone coffer somewhere in Snowdonia.

The Skull. *DGG*, lxxxvii.

The Swan. *BYU*, #28; *DGA*, #31.
her name: Dwyn.

Love's Architect. *BYU*, #29; *DGA*, #13.

The Virgin Mary. *IGE*, xxxi.
Ave: a frequent medieval comment, that 'Ave' (Latin 'Hail') reversed the letters of Eva, as a sign that Mary undid the harm done by Eve.
    The incident with the fruit tree is a popular legend found also in the English 'Cherry Tree Carol.'

The Salmon. *DGG*, xxix; *DGA*, #37.

The Nun. *BYU*, #30; *DGA*, #19.

A Visit to Flint. *BYU*, #23; Thomas Roberts ed., *Gwaith Tudur Penllyn ac Ieuan ap Tudur Penllyn* (Cardiff, 1958), #30.

Lent. P. J. Donovan ed., *Cywyddau Serch y Tri Bedo* (Cardiff, 1982), xxxv.

SIÔN CENT (fl. 1400–1430)
The Bards. *IGE,* lx.
The poem is from a bardic contention with Rhys Goch Eryri, the 'old man' referred to in the opening lines.
    Thomas Lombard: the identity of the books referred to in these lines is uncertain.

Repentance. *BYU*, #4.

The Purse. *IGE*, lxxxvi.
The attribution of this poem to Siôn Cent has been questioned, but the use of a refrain, rare in the poetry of the period, is found in some of his other poems.

The Vanity of the World. *OBWV*, #58; *IGE*, xcvi.

LLYWELYN AB Y MOEL (fl. 1410–1440)
The Battle of Waun Gaseg. Daniel, *Gwaith Dafydd Bach*, #9. This and the following poem probably refer to Llywelyn's experiences during the later years of Owain Glyndŵr's rising.

The Wood of the Grey Rock. Daniel, *GDB*, #10.

LEWYS GLYN COTHI (fl. 1445–90)
He supported the Lancastrians in the Wars of the Roses, and was outlawed because of this. E.D. Jones calls him 'a classic example of the fifteenth-century *pencerdd* [the highest class of poet]', saying that he 'stands out amongst his contemporaries as the only one whose poems are textually securely attested' (*Guide II*, p. 223), since he himself recorded most of them.

After a Pilgrimage. Dafydd Johnston ed., *Gwaith Lewys Glyn Cothi* (Cardiff, 1995), #90. Lewys' patron, on whose behalf he made the pilgrimage to Rome, was Wiliam Fychan, of the Vaughan family of Tretower in South Wales, captain of Aberystwyth castle. Growing his beard was apparently a penitential gesture: the poet compares himself both to the hermit St Anthony of Egypt and an early saint of Northumbria, John of Beverley.

The Coverlet. Johnston, *GLGC*, # 227; Bleddyn Owen Huws ed., *Detholiad o Gywyddau Gofyn a Diolch* (Swansea, 1998), #3.
Lewys Glyn Cothi was noted for his attention to genealogy, as can be seen in this poem. Elin was the daughter of Llywelyn ab Hwlcyn of Llwydiarth in Anglesey. Cynwrig ap Dafydd was her third husband, Prysaeddfed their estate in Anglesey. Mahallt, daughter of Hywel Selau, was an ancestress of Elin. Cynddelw was either another ancestor or the great twelfth-century poet, or both.

Lament for his Son. Johnston, *GLGC*, #237. Lewys' son was five years old when he died.
    twirling taper: a flaming stick that was whirled in a circle to amuse a child.

DAFYDD NANMOR (fl. 1445–1480)
He was said to have been exiled from his native Gwynedd because of his love for the married woman he addressed as Gwen o'r Ddôl. He settled in South Wales, where his patrons were the family of Rhys ap Maredudd of Tywyn.

The Peacock. Thomas Roberts ed., *The Poetical Works of Dafydd Nanmor* (Cardiff, 1923), xxvi.

In Praise of Rhys ap Maredudd. *BYU*, #11.

Lament for Gwen. *BYU*, #40.
    A horned ox: an allusion to Hugh the Strong's oxen, one of which died of grief for its mate.

Nobility. *BYU*, #12. The poem is addressed to Rhys, the son of Rhydderch of Tywyn and grandson of Rhys ap Maredudd. Saunders Lewis noted that the poem, composed 'to cheer and encourage the young man to raise his head, make good, and emulate his father and forefathers', draws on the medieval concept of divine order known as the Great Chain of Being. 'Every line of the poem, every comparison is drawn from the doctrine of the Chain ... Dafydd Nanmor summons the entire world-view of the Ages of Faith to sustain his young pupil. The examples he offers are not lucky or pretty similes. They are not fortuitous. They are the detailed and pertinent elaboration of a doctrine of correspondences that run through all creation ... It is an appeal to the implicit faith in God and God's purpose in creation.' (*Presenting Saunders Lewis*, pp. 157–8)

RHYS GOCH ERYRI (fl. 1385–1448)

As the dates indicate, this selection should be placed earlier in the anthology, but I thought it more effective to place it after Dafydd Nanmor's poem to the peacock. Because of the dates, Rhys' authorship has been questioned.

The Fox. *IGE*, cix.

LLYWELYN AP GUTUN (fl. 1450–1470)

The Drowning of Guto'r Glyn. *BYU*, #21. This poem, and Guto's response that follows, have as their setting the Christmas festivities in a noble household.

 Pinning the chair: the symbol of the chief bard.

GUTO'R GLYN (fl. 1435–1490)

He was a supporter of the Yorkist cause during the Wars of the Roses, especially of the Herbart family, and died, old and blind, at the monastery of Valle Crucis.

The Drunken Dream of Llywelyn. *BYU*, #22.

 His nails: in playing the harp.

 Llywelyn's sons: a reference to Llywelyn ap Hwlcyn of Anglesey, father of Huw Lewis and father-in-law of Cynfrig ap Dafydd.

 the land he's left: his own estate at Melwern.

Lament for Llywelyn ab y Moel. *OBWV*, #72; Ifor Williams and John Llywelyn Williams eds, *Gwaith Guto'r Glyn* (Cardiff, 1939), v. Guto refers in the elegy to Euron, for whom Llywelyn composed love songs, to Owain, presumably Owain Glyndŵr, to Meredudd, an ancestor, praises Llywelyn as the poetic successor of Iolo Goch, Gruffudd Gryg, and Dafydd ap Gwilym, and compares his burial in Strata Marcella Abbey to that of another poet, Adda Fras, at Maenan Abbey in Aberconwy.

 Seth's service: an allusion to a popular medieval legend, that Seth sought oil from the tree of mercy in Eden as a curative for his dying father Adam.

Courting Gwladus Hael. *GGG*, lxxvii. Harri ap Gruffudd of Euas in southeast Wales, nicknamed Harri Ddu (Black Harri), was a soldier with the Yorkist forces. Ieuan Gethin, Harri's rival for the love of Gwladus Hael (Generous Gwladus), was a nobleman of Glamorgan.

A Priest's Love. *OBWV,* #73; *GGG,* xciii.

Wiliam Herbart. *OBWV,* #70; *GGG,* xlviii.
Wiliam Herbart (d. 1469) supported the Yorkist cause in the Wars of the Roses, and most notably captured the Lancastrian strongholds of Pembroke and Harlech. Though Wiliam was fighting on behalf of Edward IV, Guto praises him as a Welsh hero able to right the wrongs done under English rule and to unite Wales.

Sheep-Dealing. *GGG,* xxxi.
   Losing the tithe: the sheep, which were the parson's tithe.
   Y Cwm's Dewi: a compliment to the priest as 'the St David of Y Cwm'.

Lament for Siôn ap Madog Pilstwn. *BYU,* #18.
   Owain's kinsman: his grandmother was Owain Glyndwr's sister.
   both good Hywels: Siôn's wife Alswn was the daughter of Hywel ab Ifan, whose ancestor was the son-in-law of the tenth-century ruler Hywel Dda (Hywel the Good).

The City Life. *GGG,* lxix. The town is Oswestry, in Welsh *Croesoswallt*, meaning 'Oswald's Cross', because the Northumbrian king St Oswald was killed near there in 642, fighting against the Mercian king Penda. Its lordship was held by the Earl of Arundel. Guto was granted a citizen's privileges for his poetry, as with an earlier poet, Owain Waed Da, who had relatives in the town.
   the conqueror: Owain Glyndŵr.

Old Age. *BYU,* #9. The poem praises Dafydd ab Ieuan, abbot of the Cistercian monastery of Valle Crucis, near Llangollen, and also two local patrons, Siôn Trefor and Siôn Edwart.

Meditation. *BYU,* #8. The references to the Crucifixion and the Last Judgment are apparently based on depictions of these at the monastery.

DAFYDD AB EDMWND (fl. 1450–1495)
Noted chiefly for love poems in the tradition of Dafydd ap Gwilym, he reformed Welsh prosody at the Carmarthen eisteddfod *c.*1451), increasing the technical difficulties a bard needed to master, as a means of safeguarding the privileges of qualified bards, and was the bardic teacher of Gutun Owain and Tudur Aled.

A Girl's Hair. W. J. Gruffydd ed., *Y Flodeugerdd Newydd* (Cardiff, 1909), p. 111.

Under the Eaves. *BYU,* #39.

Lament for Siôn Eos. *OBWV,* #75; Grufydd, *YFN,* p. 108. Siôn Eos (the Nightingale) was a noted harpist found guilty of murder by a jury in Chirk under English law and hanged. Welsh law, referred to as the law of Hywel the Good, would not have exacted capital punishment.
   cut a cross: Gruffydd noted that uncovering a relic and cutting a cross was 'the ceremonial of ancient trials'.

IEUAN BRYDYDD HIR (fl. 1450–1485)

Saint Winefride's Well. M. Paul Bryant-Quinn ed., *Gwaith Ieuan Brydydd Hir* (Aberystwyth, 2000), #29. Holywell, in Flintshire, is still a site of pilgrimage. Winefride, Gwenfrewy or Gwenffrewi in Welsh, was a seventh-century saint, niece of St Beuno, who restored her to life after she was raped and beheaded by a prince, Caradog. The healing waters issued from the spot where her blood was shed.

Old Age. Bryant-Quinn, *GIBH*, #13.

   the three monarchs: a popular homiletic tale told of three proud kings encountering the blackened forms of three emperors on the ground, who said: 'Such as we are, such you shall be'.

GWERFUL MECHAIN (fl. 1460–1500)

The only woman poet of note in this period.

The Harp. Leslie Harries ed., *Barddoniaeth Huw Cae Lllwyd, Ieuan ap Huw Cae Llwyd, Ieuan Dyfi, a Gwerful Mechain* (M.A. thesis, National Library of Wales, 1933) lxvii.

Vivat Vagina. Johnston, *Canu Maswedd*, #5.

TUDUR PENLLYN (fl. 1465–1485)

A supporter of the Lancastrian side in the Wars of the Roses.

The Outlaw. *OBWV*, #89; Roberts, *Gwaith Tudur Penllyn*, i. The poem is addressed to Dafydd ap Siancyn of Nanconwy, a poet and Lancastrian supporter who lived as an outlaw during Edward IV's reign.

GUTUN OWAIN (fl. 1460–1500)

The Hounds. Huws, *Detholiad o Gywyddau Gofyn*, #11; *OBWV*, #84.
Bleddyn Huws has commented that 'in the earliest examples of the genre the poets request gifts for themselves, but from the mid-fifteenth century onwards there is a marked increase in the poems composed on behalf of patrons, reflecting the custom whereby the nobility exchanged gifts, either with their own relatives or with close friends, and commissioned poets to mark the event'. ('"Praise lasts longer than a horse": Poems of Request and Thanks for Horses', in *The Horse in Celtic Culture: Medieval Welsh Perspectives* edited by Sioned Davies and Nerys Ann Jones [Cardiff, 1997], p. 141.)

Love's Language. *OBWV*, #85.

A Winter Haven. E. Bachellery ed., *L'Oeuvre Poetique de Gutun Owain* (Paris, 1950), xxvi. The poem praises the same abbot as did Guto'r Glyn's poems in old age.

HUW CAE LLWYD (fl. 1455–1505)

The Cross. *BYU*, #3. A number of bards composed poems like this, praising and contemplating a cross erected in a public place.

the spark: the Holy Eucharist.

TUDUR ALED (fl. 1480–1525)

Love's Frustration. T. Gwynn Jones ed., *Gwaith Tudur Aled* (Cardiff, 1926), cxxix.

the Virgins: who went, according to the *Brut*, to be wives in Brittany.

the eleven thousand: the virgins martyred with St Ursula.

The Stallion. *OBWV*, #90; Huws, *Detholiad*, #17.

See the note on Gutun Owain's 'The Hounds'.

A Plea for Peace. *OBWV*, #93. Unlike earlier works that petition for reconciliation between a poet and his patron, Tudur Aled's poem attempts to reconcile feuds within a family. Professor R.M. Jones says that the quarrel was begun about a will, when Hwmffre's father, Hywel, forced his own father, Siencyn, to leave his property exclusively to himself and his wife, Mari, thereby following English rather than Welsh custom, and in the subsequent quarreling, Hwmffre relied on English law, while his uncles and cousins appealed to Welsh law. The rather daunting roll-call of relatives at the beginning of the poem emphasizes its central theme, the need for family harmony as part of the divine order: as Professor Jones notes, the poem rises beyond the immediate occasion to not only a wider concern with Welsh divisions caused by English law but to a 'general, almost cosmic level'. (*Mawl*, p. 148)

the hindmost yoke: the place of greatest importance before the plough, requiring the best oxen.

Three futile frays: in *Trioedd Ynys Prydein: The Welsh Triads*, edited and translated by Rachel Bromwich (Cardiff, 1961), the three are the Battle of Goddeu, 'brought about by the cause of the bitch, together with the roebuck and the plover', the Action of Arderyyd, 'brought about by the cause of the lark's nest', and Camlan, 'brought about because of a quarrel between Gwenhwyfar and Gwenhwyfach' (p. 206). As Bromwich notes, Tudur has apparently confused the causes of the second and third battles.

GLOSSARY

I have glossed the names of persons and places when this was needed to clarify a poem or seemed of special interest. Some allusions in the poems are unglossed because they are unknown or I was unable to find the necessary information.

ABERFFRAW The royal seat, in Anglesey, of the rulers of Gwynedd.

ABER LLEU Perhaps opposite Lindisfarne, since traditionally it was while beseiging Lindisfarne that Urien was slain by his fellow British rulers.

ABERTEIFI Cardigan.

AENEAS The hero of Vergil's Roman epic, *The Aeneid*, and according to legend the great-grandfather of Brutus, who after banishment from Italy led a group of Trojans to found a new Troy in the island named after him, Britain (*Prydain*).

AERON A region in northern Britain; the exact location is unknown, but it may have been part of Rheged.

AMLYN and AMIG Two close friends, heroes of a very popular medieval tale, in which Amlyn sacrifices his children to cure Amig of leprosy.

ANGHARAD A beautiful and generous woman of the twelfth century, daughter of Owain ab Edwin, a chieftain of eastern Gwynedd.

ANNWN The underworld or otherworld in Welsh mythology.

ARFON The region of northwestern Wales facing Anglesey.

ARGOED A region in Powys; there was also a northern region of the same name in sixth-century Britain.

ARWYSTLI A section of southwestern Powys.

AUSTIN Augustine. There were two St Augustines, the famous Latin father (354–430), and the missionary who brought Christianity to the Anglo-Saxons in 596.

BANNAWG The barrier of high land where the Bannock Burn rises, probably the sixth-century boundary of Pictland in western Scotland.

BELI A sixth-century ruler of North Wales.

BELYN A seventh-century ruler of southern Gwynedd.

BENLLI A legendary giant.

BEUNO A Welsh saint of the seventh century.

BODFAEAW A district on the coast of Gwynedd.

BRABANT CLOTH Fabric made in Brabant, a province of Belgium.

BRAGGET A malt liquor, containing beer and honey.

BRÂN AP LLYR LLEDIAITH Legendary gigantic ruler of Britain.

BRÂN FAB YMELLYRN A sixth-century ruler in northern Britain.

BREFI The site in South Wales of a famous synod of bishops, abbots, and priests. When St David preached there, the ground is said to have risen beneath his feet, and he was proclaimed archbishop.

BREIDDYN A mountain south of the Severn.

BRENNYCH   The Anglo-Saxon kingdom of Bernicia, forming the northern portion of Northumbria.

BRUT   The Welsh translation (three different ones were made) of Geoffrey of Monmouth's Latin *History of the Kings of Britain* (1136).

BRYCHAN   The fifth-century prince, of Irish descent, who gave his name to the kingdom of Brycheiniog in southeastern Wales, modern Breconshire.

CADELL   The reputed founder of the royal line of Powys in the fifth century. *Cadelling*, 'descended from Cadell', became a standard epithet in the eulogies.

CADFAN   There is an early Welsh saint of this name, hence the allusion to the church consecrated to him in Einion ap Gwalchmai's elegy for Nest. Elsewhere, the Cadfan alluded to is the king of Gwynedd who died *c.*625, and whose court at Aberffraw appears to have justified the memorial inscription 'most learned and most renowned of all kings'.

CADWALADR   Son of Cadwallawn, grandson of Cadfan, who was evoked in verses prophesying a British conquest of the English. Henry VII claimed him as an ancestor.

CADWALLAWN   Son of Cadfan and seventh-century king of Gwynedd, who joined with Penda, the Anglo-Saxon king of Mercia, to overthrow Edwin of Northumbria.

CAEO   A district in South Wales.

CAER   Chester.

CAERFYRDDIN   Carmarthen.

CAER FFILI   Caerphilly.

CAERGYBI   Holyhead.

CAER LLION   Caerleon.

CAER LLIWELYDD   Carlisle.

CAER WEIR   Durham.

CAERWYS   A district in norheastern Wales.

CAER WYSG   Usk.

CAMLAN   The legendary site of Arthur's last battle.

CARREG CENNAN   A castle in Carmarthenshire.

CELLIWIG   The Cornish site of Arthur's court in the native Welsh romances.

CEMAIS   A region in Powys.

CERI   A district in Powys, on the English border.

CHEAP   Cheapside, the famous London market.

COEL HEN GODEBAWG   A northern British king of the early fifth century.

CRWTH   A traditional stringed instrument, played with a bow.

CYBI   A saint, Cornish in origin, who is said to have been allowed by Maelgwn Gwynedd to live as a hermit at Caergybi, Holyhead, in the sixth century.

CYGREAWDY FYNYDD   Great Orme's Head, on the north coast of Wales.

CYNAN GARWY   A ruler of Powys in the second half of the sixth century.

CYNFARCH   Early sixth-century ruler and father of Urien of Rheged.

CYRCHELL   A river in Anglesey.

DEHEUBARTH   South Wales.

DEIFR   The Anglo-Saxon kingdom of Deira, forming the southern portion of Northumbria.

DERFEL   Derfel the Strong, patron saint of Llandderfel.

DERWENNYDD FALLS   Lodore Force, which flows into Derwentwater in Cumbria.

DEWI   David, the patron saint of Wales, who lived in the latter half of the sixth century.

DIN ALCLUD   Dumbarton, in southwestern Scotland.

DINBYCH   Denbigh.

DISYNNI   A river in Merioneth.

DOGFEILING   An early Welsh kingdom, founded by Dogfael ap Cunedda in the early fifth century and later absorbed into Powys.

DÔN   A Celtic goddess, one of whose sons was the magician Gwydion in *The Mabinogion*.

DUNAWD FAB PABO   A ruler in northern Britain who died *c.*595.

DWYN, DWYNWEN   A saint of the fifth century, patroness of lovers.

DYFED   Southwestern Wales.

DYFI   A river in mid-Wales.

DYFR   A maiden of Arthur's court noted for beauty.

EDEIRNIAWN   An early Welsh kingdom, founded in the fifth century by Edern ap Cunedda and later absorbed by Powys.

EDITH   St Edith of Wilton (961–84), King Edgar's illegitimate daughter who became a nun in spite of her father's opposition.

EFRAWG CAER   York.

EFRDDYL   Urien of Rheged's sister.

EFYRNWY   A river in northeastern Wales, flowing into the Severn.

EIDYN   Din Eidyn, Edinburgh, the main fortress of the Gododdin.

EIDDIG   'The Jealous One', the name given by the bards to their ladies' husbands.

EIGR   The wife of Uthr Pendragon and mother of Arthur, renowned for her beauty.

ELFED   Elmet, the region east of the Pennines, including Leeds.

ELFOD   A bishop (d. 809) famous for his adoption of the Roman dating of Easter in 768, a much-disputed matter which the Welsh church had rejected in 602. He is sometimes associated with the monastery of Cybi at Holyhead.

ELIFRI   Arthur's head groom in the medieval tale of Geraint.

ELMO HEN   A sixth-century ruler or warrior in northern Britain.

ELPHIN, ELFFIN   One of the sons of Urien of Rheged. In later saga and romance he is treated as Taliesin's patron.

ELUCIDARIUM   A twelfth-century religious treatise, translated into Welsh *c.*1200.

EMLYN   A region in South Wales.

EMRAIS, EMRYS   Ambrosius, fifth-century Romano-Celtic ruler particularly associated with Snowdonia.

ENLLI   Bardsey Island, off the tip of the Llŷn peninsula, site of an abbey from the sixth to the sixteenth century, and traditionally the burial place of 20,000 saints.

ERBIN   Father of the Arthurian hero Geraint.

ERYRI   Snowdonia.

GARWY HIR   A legendary warrior and lover.

GLYN DYFRDWY   The home region of Owain Glyndŵr.

GLYN EGWESTL   The site of the monastery of Valle Crucis, in northeastern Wales.

GLYN NEDD   The Vale of Neath.

GLYN RHOSYN   The Vale of Roses, St David's in Menevia, where St Patrick supposedly settled before he was called to evangelize Ireland *c*.432.

GODODDIN   The name of both a region and its inhabitants in southeastern Scotland.

GORWYDD FPYNT   A mountain in northern Breconshire.

GWALLAWG   Sixth-century king of a region in northern Britain, possibly in southern Scotland.

GWENDDYDD   A woman associated with Myrddin (Merlin), either as sister or lover.

GWENHIDWY   A mermaid, with long hair.

GWENT   Southeastern Wales.

GWGAN AP MEURIG   Ninth-century ruler of Ceredigion.

GWIDO   According to stories popular after his death in 1324, his ghost walked as punishment for not having done enough penance in life, and created a disturbance in his widow's house to ensure that she suffered sufficiently before his death.

GWYNEDD   Northwestern Wales.

HAFREN   The river Severn.

HIRIELL   A hero traditionally associated with Gwynedd.

HODNI   Brecon.

HORSA   One of the leaders of the Anglo-Saxon invasion of Britain in the fifth century.

HUGH THE STRONG   Emperor of Constantinople in a twelfth-century romance about Charlemagne.

HYRDDIN   A wood near the monastery of Valle Crucis.

IÂL   A region in northeastern Wales.

IFOR HAEL   'Ifor the Generous': Ifor ap Llywelyn of Basaleg in South Wales.

INDEG   A beautiful woman in early Welsh romance, one of Arthur's loves.

IS CONWY   A region in North Wales.

ISEULT   Tristan's beloved in medieval romance.

KAI   One of Arthur's knights, who could grow as tall as the tallest tree.

LEGO   Possibly Waterford in Ireland.

LIONHEART   King Richard I of England.

LORD RICHMOND   Henry Tudor, Earl of Richmond, who defeated Richard III and became King Henry VII in 1485. His uncle was Jasper Tudor, Earl of Pembroke.

LUNED   A beautiful maiden in Welsh romance.

LUCIDARUS   Iolo Goch mistakenly assumes this is the name of the author of the *Elucidarium*, a twelfth-century religious work by Honorius of Augustodunum.

LLANDDWYN   The church of St Dwyn in Anglesey.

LLANGWESTL   The site of Valle Crucis monastery.

LLAWDDEN   A fifteenth-century bard.

LLEISIAWN   A traditional hero of Powys.

LLEON   Caerleon, in South Wales.

LLEUDDINIAWN   The region of Lothian in southeastern Scotland.

LLIW   A river, possibly the Dee in North Wales.

LLOEGR   England, as still in modern Welsh. The word's origin and etymology are uncertain.

LLOFAN LLAW DDIFRO   A nickname meaning something like 'little hand exile-hand', possibly the speaker in 'The Fall of Rheged' who cut off Urien's head.

LLWYFENYDD   A region in the sixth-century kingdom of Rheged, perhaps its heartland.

LLYDAW   Brittany, which was colonized by Celts from Britain after the Anglo-Saxon invasion.

LLŶR   God of the sea, and legendary ruler of Britain.

MAELGWN GWYNEDD   King of Gwynedd in the early sixth century.

MAELIENYDD   A district in southeastern Powys.

MAELOR   When Powys was divided after the death of Madog ap Maredudd in 1160, 'Welsh Maelor' was ruled separately from 'English Maelor'.

MAIG   A sixth-century ruler of Powys.

MALLTRAETH   A region in Anglesey.

MANAW   A region or kingdom in central Scotland.

MANGNEL   A type of catapult with a wooden arm which when old lost its spring.

MARCH   The borderland between Wales and England.

MEIRIONYDD   The southern portion of Gwynedd, modern Merioneth.

MELWERN   The home of Llywelyn ap Gutun in northeastern Wales.

MENAI   The strait separating the island of Anglesey from the mainland of North Wales.

MENW   A legendary sorcerer.

MERWYDD   A legendary giver of feasts in Anglesey.

MEURIG   A fourteenth-century lord of the royal line of Powys.

MÔN   Anglesey.

MORDDAF HAEL   A sixth-century ruler of northern Britain whose generosity became legendary.

MORGANNWG   Glamorgan.

MORGANT   A sixth-century ruler in northern Britain.

MYNYW   Menevia, the diocese of St David's in Pembrokeshire.

MYRDDIN   The earliest reference to him, in *The Gododdin*, is as a bard. Later references indicate that he fought on the side of one British king, Gwenddolau, against another, Rhydderch Hen, in a losing battle at Arfderydd (modern Arthuret, near Carlisle) *c.*575, and that he went mad as a result. Legends developed of his fleeing to the woods and acquiring the gift of prophecy. The extant poems containing prophecies as well as fragments of the experience of madness and isolation in the wilderness were composed centuries later. He became

Merlin in later Arthurian romance, but no connection is made in early Welsh literature between Myrddin and Arthur.

NEDD   Neath.

NEST   A notoriously beautiful woman of the early twelfth century, daughter of Rhys ap Tewdwr, mistress of Henry I, and wife of Gerald of Windsor, who was abducted by Owain ap Cadwgan, a prince of Powys She is not the woman named in Einion ap Gwalchmai's elegy, but may be alluded to metaphorically in Llywarch ap Llywelyn's love poem to Gwenlliant.

NON   A sixth-century saint, mother of St David. Her feast-day is 3 March.

NUDD HAEL   A sixth-century ruler in northern Britain whose generosity was proverbial.

OFFA'S DYKE   Offa (757–796) was king of Mercia in central England. The dyke, or earthwork, constructed after a Welsh attack in 784, runs along the border from near Prestatyn in the north to the mouth of the Wye in the south. It has been for the Welsh a symbol of the division between Wales and England.

OTIEL   One of Charlemagne's warriors.

PASGENT   One of Urien of Rheged's sons.

PENARDD   A region in mid-Wales.

PENFRO   Pembroke.

PENTRAETH   A district in Anglesey.

PORTH WYGYR   On the northern coast of Anglesey.

PORTH YSGEWIN   On the southern coast of Wales.

POWYS   Northeastern Wales.

PRYDERI   The son of Pwyll in *The Mabinogion*. His name means 'care' or 'thought'.

PYD   Father of Penda, Anglo-Saxon ruler of Mercia in the seventh century.

PYWER LEW   One of the legendary ancestors of the princes of Powys.

RHEGED   The kingdom ruled by Urien in the sixth century, centering on modern Cumbria.

RHIANNON   In *The Mabinogion*, she bore a son who vanished the night after his birth and was accused of killing him. The Birds of Rhiannon are said to sing so that they wake the dead and put the living to sleep.

RHEINALLT   Possibly Hywel ap Rheinallt, a North Wales bard of the late fifteenth century.

RHODRI   Rhodri the Great, king of Gwynedd from 844 to 878.

RHUDDLAN   Fortress in northeastern Wales.

RHUFAWN BEFR   An early ruler in northern Britain.

RHYDDERCH HAEL   A sixth-century ruler in northern Britain of legendary generosity.

RHYS BWTLWNG   Possibly a singer who won the prize at the Carmarthen eisteddfod *c.*1450.

ROWENA   The daughter of Hengist, one of the leaders of the fifth-century Anglo-Saxon invasion of Britain.

SANTIAGO The shrine of St James at Compostella in Spain, a popular goal for pilgrims.

SARN ELEN In the medieval Welsh tale, 'The Dream of Macsen Wledig', Elen, a princess of North Wales, marries the Roman emperor Macsen and causes roads to be built linking all the strongholds in Britain. She is called 'Elen of the Hosts' because the British would not have assembled in great numbers for anyone else.

SAUL St Paul.

SIR FULKE Fulke Fitz Warine, a hero in French romance.

SULIEN An eleventh-century bishop of St David's, famed for his learning.

TAF A river in southeastern Wales.

TALGARTH A parish in Arwystli.

TEGEINGL A district in the northeastern corner of Wales.

TEIFI A river in central Wales.

TEIRTUD A magical harp in the tale of 'Culhwch and Olwen', that could play of itself.

TIBOETH The name of St Beuno's book in the church of Clynnog, which had a black stone on its cover.

TWRCH TRWYD The great boar that must be hunted as one of the tasks in 'Culhwch and Olwen', in *The Mabinogion*.

TYSILIO A northern Welsh saint of the later sixth century.

UNHWCH A sixth-century warrior associated with Urien of Rheged.

UWCH AERON A region of central Wales.

YNYR The thirteenth-century ancestor of a powerful noble family at Nannau in Merioneth.

YRECHWYDD A region governed by Urien of Rheged in the sixth century. The exact location is not known.

YSTRAD TYWY The region around the river Towy, in southwestern Wales.

Y WAUN Chirk.